UNMASKING
SHAME

Compassion and Connection
at Every Stage of Life

LIV LARSSON

friare
LIV
www.friareliv.com

Title in original: *Ut ur skamvrån, Vägen till medkänsla från barn till vuxen*

Unmasking shame - Compassion and Connection at Every Stage of Life
ISBN 978-91-89435-13-1

Author: Liv Larsson
Editing: Hans van Veen
Proofreading: Belinda Poropudas
Translation: Neo Rung and Liv Larsson
Inlay and cover: Linda Michelin

Published by:
Friare Liv AB
Mjösjölidvägen 477,
946 40 Svensbyn
Sweden

info@friareliv.se
www.friareliv.com

CONTENT

PREFACE

"Why didn't you warn me?!" my son hissed at me.

He had just tripped over a step, spilling his juice, and was watching his cinnamon bun roll away in front of several others at the café we were visiting. I held back commenting, reminding myself that he sounded the way he did because he was probably ashamed. Then I realized that I was also felt some nuance of shame. I didn't enjoy the way he talked to me. With a deep breath, I reminded myself that I could wait a moment in order to have my need for dignity and care met. Instead of hissing back at him, I leaned forward and whispered:

"I guess that was really embarrassing. Let me see if I can find us something to wipe up with and get you a new drink."

Soon we were sitting at a table, ready for our sweets. After confirming that I understood the embarrassment of the situation, and after acknowledging his need for dignity, our connection was reestablished. Then I was able to tell him about the discomfort I had felt in the situation, when he had "scolded me" in front of others and that I wanted to experience more dignity than I had done.

Furthermore, I expressed appreciation to him for helping me meet my need for dignity by talking about the situation. And I also noted to myself how pleased I was in how being able to hold my impulse in the situation also really met my need for dignity.

We had a nice time together and you can imagine how differently it would have ended if I had yelled back at him at that moment of shame. I am happy to talk about this situation as I am proud that I was able to hold back my impulse to immediately throw that shame back at him, something I don't take for granted or that I manage every time I get frustrated.

The feeling of shame is present in both children and adults, but in later life we may have, at best, developed a certain capacity for self-reflection that helps us make choices that also include the needs of others. In the café situation, instead of suppressing my desire, I was able to contain my wish to be treated respectfully, and to wait to act on it until there was better timing.

I was able to hold back the impulse to respond immediately, something that was more challenging for my son, with his young immature nervous system, and who still needed some work on impulse control. The way I waited to express how I wanted to be treated was not about giving up on myself. It was about wanting to maximize the odds of being truly listened to, and therefore I decided to bring it up later. Since I trusted that I would find an opportunity to do so later, I was able to respond to him in a way that connected us. I found it in me to show understanding for how embarrassing he found the situation, without commenting on how he handled it in relation to me.

The adage that children don't do as we say, but do as we do, is often true when it comes to dealing with feelings of shame. And it is not easy to be a role model if your nervous system is buzzing with stress. As a role model, I also want to remind myself to calibrate my expectations as if I have a five-year-old, not an 18-year-old in front of me.

When I run training sessions on shame, I invite participants to explore past situations that were embarrassing, shameful or humiliating. Even though they are grown-ups, participating voluntarily, and are curious about shame; and even though many of the situations happened long ago, most of them try to avoid the feelings of shame arising in the exploration. With support, most people can slow down enough to accept and learn to relate to the experience of shame in new ways. Some of the exercises that I do with participants in my training, who have developed the ability to create distance even with uncomfortable memories, I would not do with children, as this would cause unnecessary stress. During a training session, we examine how shame is constructed, and what we can use it for. We explore human needs that are linked to shame so that we can take more responsibility in order to influence a situation that is important to us.

Through twenty years of coaching and teaching on the topics of shame, guilt, and vulnerability, I know that we can make friends with shame. We can use it to our advantage, rather than letting it diminish us. It is a relief knowing we don't have to get rid of it, harden ourselves, or become controlled and self-sufficient, rather, we can use it to become more human. And on top of that, we can even use it to become more compassionate. I see shame as a survival advantage, an emotion that, with support, develops into sensitivity to the needs of others, and ultimately into compassion. Vulnerability is a great asset in developing empathy, at least if it is balanced with a certain self-distance.

This book draws on my experience as a mediator, facilitator, and trainer. It is based on over three decades of working with shame and communication around the world, and on my studies in neuropsychology and human development. In 2011, my book, *Anger, Guilt and Shame, Reclaiming Power and Choice*, was published.[1] The book contained the first description of the tool The Compass of Needs, and has been published in more than ten languages. Maybe you are reading this book because you have already read my previous one and liked it but realized, like me, that there is more to explore. Or maybe you missed something and are curious if I have captured it in this book.

One motivation for updating my views on shame is that although the book *Anger, Guilt and Shame*, has been very important for many, in my view my coverage of the causes of shame were too limited. Fifteen years ago, while working on that book, I was influenced by social theorist Riane Eisler and her book *The Chalice and the Blade*.[2] Her world view revolved around cultural evolution and the possibility of a more just and cooperative society. Inspired by Eisler, but also by the man behind Nonviolent Communication, Marshall Rosenberg, I described two basic social configurations: the dominance model and the partnership model to clarify that there are different value systems that influence how we think and act as individuals. I realize that the simplicity of two different systems is easily perceived as one leading to feelings of shame and the other not, which I have discovered rarely is a correct assumption. Our emotions are indeed influenced by our thinking, but they are affected by more than that. Emotions are based on who we are as individuals, our biology, our psychology. On top of that all the individual parts of emotions are influenced by the collective we grow up in, with different values, language, culture and beliefs.

Dividing our outlook on life into the two different systems is valuable if it prevents us from placing all responsibility on the individual. However, by describing only two systems, we risk oversimplifying something that is much more complex than that. A dualist approach might get us stuck in simplistic categories such as good/bad, either/or, and to miss important nuances in people's development.

There are many challenging situations for a child that adults may think they should be able to shake off or handle easily. We fail to understand where they are in the socialization process. Furthermore, we may not realize that their nervous systems and brains need time to grow and mature. Maybe we think the child shouldn't care so much, should speak up, and we fail to take into account that the child is going through a process where acceptance from peers is crucial for them.

"Where are my keys?" my dad asked, narrowing his eyes at one of us siblings.

"Where you put them," my oldest sister replied.

We giggled, but my dad didn't laugh and kept his eyes on her.

"Someone must have taken them. Or moved them."

Mom sighed.

"Why can you never learn to keep track of them? None of us have taken them. What would we do with them?"

Mom was right. The set of keys that Dad was once again looking for were for the locks on the doors at his workplace. None of us in the family were in the least bit interested in his keys. Many decades later, long after I had started studying shame, I realized that Dad was ashamed. Probably words like "I'm hopeless," rang through his head as well, accompanied by "I will never learn to keep track of things." Shame gnawed at his self-image as "a responsible man." What would happen if someone discovered this, exposing him, an educated person, unable to keep track of his own things?

He wanted others to perceive him as someone who had things under control, and every time he lost something, it tarnished his self-image. Blaming us was a way to create some relief as it shifted the focus away from his own shortcomings.

Now, understanding that our self-image is directly linked to shame, which has the power to define who we are, I can more easily comprehend his anger and frustration. Anger shifts the focus from a mildly (or strongly) humiliating situation to something else, and can really hurt important relationships.

When my father had calmed down, and by then my mother had usually found the keys, he apologized and admitted that he had been careless. But the apology didn't seem to help him learn from the shame. It took him many years until he became able to pause in the moment, acknowledge his sense of powerlessness and ask for help instead of getting angry and accusatory.

Reflecting on my relationship with my father during my teenage years, I've come to see my son's embarrassment of me as a natural part of his own maturation process, rather than a reflection of my own shortcoming. A teenager's rebellion is not a rejection, but an important desire to stand on their own two feet.

Another incident from my life, that has stayed with me as I pondered what it was like to be a teenager, happened to me at sixteen in an elevator that got stuck between two floors. As I reached to press the alarm button, one of the other teenagers moved in front of me, to stop me from pressing it.

"We have to ask for help. Nobody knows we are stuck in here."

"No way!" exclaimed the three guys, who like me were trapped in the elevator, with a unanimous voice.

After waiting a while and a lot of discussion, one of them finally said, "Okay, but you are the one to push the button." Decades later, when I started exploring how shame affects us and our communication, I realized that my friends probably did not want to appear weak or helpless. They were so ashamed, that they were willing to sit passively and hope that the elevator would start working again and they could get out unnoticed. Perhaps because they were male and wanted to appear strong and capable and the alarm button was a threat to their self-image. Shame is rarely truly logical, the fact that the elevator didn't work had nothing to do with their strength. As a teen-age girl, I didn't have to be strong or cool all the time, I could call for help.

Inability to cope with shame can be found in simple everyday events like asking for directions, but also behind addictions of various kinds - alcohol, work, drugs, sex - and is a driving force in perfectionism and workaholism. The person who tries to be perfect at all times needs to be in complete control and to never leave anything in the open to be exposed to shame. But it is possible to learn to use shame to repair relationships and develop compassion. Accepting the humanity of shame strengthens our ability to empathize.

As adults, we resort to shame avoidance strategies depending on a variety of aspects such as our level of maturity, emotional support, culture, etc. For example, according to various surveys, Swedes are more likely to feel ashamed if we have visitors and an unclean home, while this is less important in other cultures.[3] However, what we feel shame for within a culture varies as well, and someone of the same nationality or culture will not feel ashamed of the same thing.

When I heard Marshall Rosenberg talk about shame, my attitude turned from:

"shame is a problem to be avoided at all costs" to:

"shame is there as an opportunity for deeper compassion and a way to integrate needs for belonging, acceptance and dignity." Rosenberg's advice was to "never do anything to avoid shame." Although at first, I didn't grasp what he meant, over the years I have realized what an opportunity each moment of shame can be.

My hope with this book is to show how an increased knowledge of shame, not only helps us as adults to develop in many areas of our own life, but also how we become role models for the next generation. Spending time as a child with adults who know how to process their shame in a connective way is a gift whose value should not be underestimated. One of my motivations is that you will become more comfortable with feelings of shame, and therefore, will be able to more easily connect with what you need.

Writing this has been a long, challenging and meaningful process. I dove into topics such as loneliness, vulnerability, emotion research, prediction, intimacy, self-image, lying, bullying, brain development and methods such as adult development, integral theory and Spiral Dynamics. Studying researchers such as Lisa Feldman Barrett and Terri O'Fallon have had a huge impact on my creative process.

There are claims in this book that I cannot back up with research, but after three decades of studying and most of all working with shame. I can only partially "prove" why tools like NVC or the Compass of Needs are so helpful. But I know their value after 25 years of working with them in groups and with individuals all over the world.

Emma, Tom, their parents, and others in the examples in the book are a compilation of various people I have met during my more than thirty years as a trainer, mediator and coach. Facts have been changed to protect people's privacy, but all events are based on real people's experiences of shame and development.

Reading the Book

The suggestion for how to read this book is to start with the first two chapters. After that, you might want to jump into the chapters where the ages of the children in your environment are. Please do so, but also notice that with this approach you might miss out on picking up some pieces of information that a later chapter builds on. To explore how shame affects us through different life stages, chapters 3-5 and 8 focus on different levels of development linked to age.

SHAME – A BRIDGE BETWEEN INNER AND OUTER LIFE

"Stop it!"

Emma, 13, frowns when seeing her mother, Mari, taking a few dance steps in the grocery store.

"But you love this song," Mari replies, holding out her hand to the thirteen-year-old. You love to dance. Dance with me."

"You are so ridiculous. Stop it."

The girl turns her back on her mother and walks away with firm steps. Mari looks disappointedly after her daughter and wonders what happened to the little girl who always loved to dance, wherever they were.

Mari hasn't kept up with Emma's development. What used to be fun and a usual occurance is now shameful. When Emma was younger, she identified - like most children - with her family. The family's behavior was to be copied to ensure her place in it. If they danced, she danced too. If they did not dance, she did not dance. Sometimes she would try to influence one of her family members to get up on a dance floor with her, but if no one around her joined in, she also refrained.

Sometimes as a parent it is a challenge to let go of things that were abundant when your children were young; like feeling free to dance in the mall or sing on a walk through town. But as people around us evolve, young and old, it is valuable to keep up with the times. There is more to life than getting caught up in analyzing how someone "is" or "should be." Why not enjoy the fact that children learn new things, grow different preferences and develop? What about surfing the wave and growing with them?

The advice children hear from caregivers on how to relate to their inner selves affect them, but children are even more impacted by seeing how adults deal with challenging situations. It is one thing to hear what someone says and another to witness adults who seem to be able to deal with uncomfortable emotions like shame without taking their discomfort out on anyone else.

Adults who can admit to shortcomings and apologize when they cross someone else's boundaries, show that they are willing to take responsibility for their actions. They also show that this restoration of their dignity can be done without pushing someone else down. This gives us different tools than from adults who never admit to making a mistake or who withdraw instead of repairing connection. How Mari, in the example above, expresses her disappointment when Emma walks away, affects them both. For example, she may blame her daughter.

"You always used to be so much fun to be with, don't be so boring."

Emma slows down and looks around, and Mari sees her chance to convince her daughter that she shouldn't be embarrassed about dancing in the grocery store.

"You have nothing to be ashamed of, you are different from your friends, braver than them. Come on now."

Mari's way of communicating gets in the way of their connection, which she doesn't realize at this moment. If she had instead supported Emma to make her own choices, it would affect their relationship differently. But Mari wants to keep her lively little girl and finds it difficult to fully accept that her daughter is moving into a new context, creating new relationships beyond the safety of the family's smaller world. She misses the connection they used to have, when they spontaneously danced even if no one else did. Mari wants to encourage boldness and independence, but fails to realize that this is not the most important thing in her daughter's life at this point.

Her daughter's teenage life is currently about fitting in and being accepted by her peers. Instead of being inspired by her mother, Emma avoids embarrassment and shame by cutting herself off from her. Instead of staying with the uncomfortable feeling of shame about her embarrassing mother, Emma gets angry and leaves. Creating distance between herself and her mother moves her energy and helps her feel more autonomous. At the same time, distancing can damage the connection, especially if Mari does not understand what is going on or judges it as wrong. The vulnerable moment, which could have strengthened their connection, becomes an obstacle if Mari takes Emma's rejection personally, does not pay attention to her daughter's growth, or does not realize that their relationship has changed.

Since it would make Emma even more uncomfortable to openly express anger towards her mother, she grinds her teeth and uses the force of her anger to quietly walk away. But after a while, her self image reminds her that this might not be a good idea. She learned early on, that care is important, and she doesn't like the idea that it was mean to leave mom without saying anything. She could see that mom was disappointed. But her anger takes her back and helps her to blame her dorky mom instead of herself. Can't she just leave me alone and act like other parents and stop treating me like a baby.

If Mari had been paying more attention to her daughter shifting into a new phase of development, she would realize that things that were not embarrassing for Emma before, are very embarrassing now. Being more attentive, she might have understood that Emma needs a different kind of support than when she was younger and more dependent. Instead of blaming, Mari could have confirmed that she understands that Emma is embarrassed by the situation. Instead of trying to force her to dance, since that was what Mari herself felt most connected to, she could have stopped and seen the situation from her daughter's perspective for a moment. Without communicating with Emma, Mari could have discovered that she was blaming her daughter for what she was becoming. Mari could also have focused on her own feelings and thoughts to deal with the situation quietly within herself.

Oh, how disappointed I am with Emma. She is becoming just like any other teenager. I get so tired of everything being about fitting in. How about some personal freedom?

When Mari gets in touch with her disappointment and frustration, she can remind herself herself to take responsibility for her own feelings and what she wants, instead of focusing on how she wants to change Emma's behavior. If Mari had done that, she would have realized that she too experienced the situation of dancing by herself and her daughter leaving as a bit embarrassing, and that she felt rejected. A first step for her is to become more aware of her thoughts.

I'm disappointed, I long for the connection I used to have with Emma when she was small. When she rejects me the way she does, I feel embarrassed and stressed because I lose the feeling that I am important to her.

The situation could have been different if Mari, instead of accusing Emma of being boring, connected with what might be going on inside her daughter:

"Sorry, I didn't realize how embarrassing this is for you."

Or...

"OK, I'll stop. I'm trying to get you on board because I want to dance, but it's a little embarrassing to do it by myself. I'll get my act together to make it easier for you to relax around me. Having a moment with you is the most important thing for me."

If Mari actually wants to dance, she can take responsibility for that, without blaming or trying to force Emma to do it too.

"I understand that it's embarrassing to see me dance, you go ahead. I'll catch up in a minute."

Later, in a conversation with a friend, Mari realizes that she felt rejected and did not know how to transform this on her own. Instead, she tried to get rid of the shame by getting her daughter to dance with her and blaming her when she said no. The irritation that Emma no longer enjoyed the same things as she did when she was younger quickly subsided when Mari realized that she had her own inner work to do.

In order for Mari to be able to make more conscious choices in these situations, it is useful for her to understand both her own inner self and Emma's. With that clarity, she can manage the experience of separation in several ways, from going to therapy, to learning more ways to meet the needs for belonging and inclusion.

If she had paid more attention to Emma, she would have noticed the first signs of her daughter's embarrassment and could have reminded herself that shame is a crossroads with paths that can either lead to connection or distancing. She could have reminded herself of her understanding that adolescence is different from toddlerhood, broadened her acceptance of her daughter's choices, and been proud of her, instead of trying to get her to agree to something she didn't want.

The situation with Mari and Emma is a simple example of how shame affects us and our relationships. Although the situation ended with a break in connection, it probably played a small role in shaping their total relationship. But if Mari repeatedly relates in the way she did, it will in the long run affect the relationship in an undesirable way. Other situations are more serious. And, in the heat of shame, many of us habitually gloss over something we have done, or avoid naming the discomfort.

Even if an adult can deal with their feelings of shame in a constructive and responsible way, it takes many years for a young individual to deal with shame on their own. Marshall Rosenberg, challenged our approach to shame with the advice, "never do anything to avoid shame or guilt."[4] For Rosenberg's advice to be of value, the person that gets it, need to have undergone some physical, cognitive and emotional development. Young children's brains and nervous systems will mature with time and before that need to be protected from excessive stress in order to avoid harm. Even an adult who finds himself in a context where certain behaviors are severely punished would do well to pause for a moment to reflect on if it is wise to use Rosenberg's advice exactly at this moment.

Young children have three ways to avoid and deal with shame. They can:

- Seek and receive support from someone to help them release or reduce shame and stress.
- Adhere to the rules and norms that govern what is considered appropriate.
- Avoid strong emotions, for example by distracting themselves, ignoring how their actions affect others or that they're getting angry.

(The third category applies mainly to older children who are no longer fully dependent on adults).

If it was so simple that we could say with certainty that all children over the age of eleven can automatically deal with shame in ways other than the above strategies, there would be no need for this book. Although our brain matures as we get older, there is no exact age at which we automatically have access to internal processes that allow us to take greater responsibility for something we have done.

An individual's capacity for self-reflection at age fifteen may exceed that of another person at age thirty.

Rosenberg argued that there is a danger in using labels, whether they feel harmless or not, such as adults or children.[5] He warned that thinking of someone as a *child*, limits our ability to discover what the individual in front of us can do, wants and needs.

In this book, "child" or "teenager" is sometimes substituted for "individual" to remind us that a situation could just as easily be about an older person who has not developed beyond, for example, right and wrong thinking, or who has been relegated back to it for some reason. The word "parents", "adult" or "caregivers" are used, so as not to get caught up in the idea that only parents take care of children or benefit from understanding shame.

The feeling of shame seems to come out of nowhere (which is of course an illusion) from one moment to the next, and we stop, freeze, if only for a second. Hormones get ready, nerves dance, muscles activate or become passive. The head feels heavy and eye contact seem to send a shock through our body. All this increases the intensity of the stress, so that our eyes avoid the eyes of others. Our thoughts are grinded down in a mill of confusion that makes it hard to find words. Thoughts that we are a fraud, a failure or undesirable feel like a blow and we want to run away, but often we find it difficult to get our feet to obey.

When the nervous system puts the brakes on our biology, we adapt our behavior. In that way the emotion of shame minimizes the risk of damaging connection with people that are important to us, at least in the short term. Our brain evaluates - using information from past experiences - when it is time to put up protective barriers against humiliation and criticism.

Researcher Silvan Tomkins summarized the basic function of shame: "Shame acts as a signal and a damper on positive emotions to motivate us to repair social relationships."[6]

Shame, like other emotions, is not experienced in exactly the same way by different people and is not even experienced in the same way by the same person from one time to another. How we experience an emotion depends on need, context and how that emotion is received by the culture we are in.

The impact of shame on us changes over time. Children feel shame when they become aware (often in early school years) of the risk of not being included. When we fail to live up to our own or other people's expectations throughout our lives, shame seems to appear like a bolt from the blue.

One of the downsides of shame is that it has the power to limit our life space and our ability to communicate. The paralysis we experience during a shame attack often changes over the years, as we learn to distract, understand or calm ourselves. Although most adults rarely "freeze up", in the way young children do, sometimes shame becomes an emotion we never learn to express in words. Whether we are six or sixty years old and feel shame, it is always difficult to find words in a shameful situation.

Feelings of shame are not only physical; they are also social and help us understand the rules of the game. We gradually begin to understand when we have crossed someone else's boundaries, helping us through the important process of socialization. Whether we like it or not, shame is the communication tool of belonging. Exclusion led to death during the longest period of human history, and still does, to some extent today. So, responding quickly to the risks of non-inclusion has long been essential.

Human beings are social creatures where community is important for our development and survival. Belonging to a group not only increases the chances of access to food and safety, but also provides opportunities for care and meaning.

We often avoid shame by reducing our space and taking fewer risks. We give up on things that might reveal income in some area. Some people go the other way, pushing away feelings of shame by thinking that we don't need the acceptance of others. Shame feels restrictive, and being the freedom-thirsty creatures we are, we are tempted to try to get rid of shame. The strategies we use to avoid shame sometimes cause problems in the form of damaged relationships, distorted self-image and unfulfilled dreams, but we are rarely aware of this at the time.

Shame can be described as part of our self-preservation instinct, a reaction to a boundary being crossed. Someone has done something, or been perceived to do something, that threatens the group or its individuals. We or someone else has behaved in a way that does not involve respect for others. Whether we feel shame after someone has shamed us, or only because we shame ourselves, the feelings affect both our physical body and our inner subjective landscape.

People who avoid shame at all costs sometimes feel cold, self-sufficient or numb. The development of shame is part of vulnerability and compassion - qualities we want to maintain and deepen if we want to have close relationships with other people. When we celebrate and openly enjoy something, we become vulnerable, making us susceptible to the disapproval of others.

A child can go from excitedly celebrating an achievement to suddenly becoming quiet if they find themselves being laughed at. The child who was jumping around wanting attention for something they were proud of looks down and freezes in one position for a moment. In their physical reality, a whole host of processes are going on; joy hormones are slowing down and the parasympathetic part of the nervous system is doing its job.

The developmental level of a child affects how much they can reflect on their own thoughts and feelings. When a child freezes up, we adults we can take this as a signal, pause, and softly confirm that we see the child. Of course, the same applies when a more mature individual is ashamed, but an adult sometimes has access to more ways to recover from a shame storm than a child does.

21

Learning how to deal with shame is a valuable step towards creating close relationships and not having to shrink our life space. We seem to be hard-wired for connection and feelings of loneliness have been shown to be a threat to our health. Social isolation is estimated to be twice as dangerous as obesity, as harmful as alcoholism or as smoking 15 cigarettes a day.[7]

The Bad Reputation of Shame

Our ability to anticipate what might happen in the next moment, and create appropriate emotions to help us deal with it, has helped us survive as a species. In her book, *How Emotions Are Made*, brain scientist Lisa Feldman Barrett introduces the idea of "body budgeting" as the way you regulate energy and emotions. According to Feldman Barrett, maintaining a balanced body budget is important for your overall sense of wellbeing.[8] She uses the concept for the process that ensures that the energy in our bodies is kept in balance. This process is in short, done by the brain regulating the body's needs. It does so, for example, by using physical signals of thirst and fatigue that motivate us to drink and rest. The way we interpret our inner life of affects, feelings, emotions and thoughts affects how well we can keep the budget in balance.

It is challenging to think clearly when we feel shame. Our brain is inhibited by the cognitive shock which makes it difficult to find creative solutions. We make large withdrawals from our body's energy budget and find it difficult to concentrate. Common thoughts in shameful moments are that we would do anything to disappear, to be swallowed up by the ground beneath us.[9] Our attention when we feel shame is focused on trying to escape the uncomfortable emotions at all costs, and we sometimes behave in ways that, in retrospect, we neither appreciate nor understand. With the humiliation of not finding words or expressing ourselves in ways that we later regret, it is no wonder that we experience shame as an enemy.

Feelings of shame are often interpreted as if there is something wrong with us, as if we are broken, bad or immoral and need to be fixed, easily turning the very feelings into a threat. Because shame diminish our life space and interfere with experiences of unity, joy and pleasure, their negative image is reinforced. Potentially traumatic events to which someone is subjected to often involve shame and humiliation, which further contributes to their bad reputation. There is also the risk that the shame becomes toxic and affects us much later in life.

Fritz Perls, the founder of Gestalt therapy, called shame "the Quisling of emotions."[10] At the same time Perls described shame as an important part of our socialization, and he urged people to move away from shame as soon as possible. Psychologist and author Alice Miller also went into detail about how shame can be harmful, and rarely talked about any benefits. Given how uncomfortable shame feels, it's no wonder that, regardless of culture, we buy into the idea that it's something to be avoided. Bradshaw, Perls and Miller all experienced how unprocessed shame inhibited and made people dysfunctional during their time with clients.

Author John Bradshaw wrote about how shame becomes an enemy when we try to get rid of it; "I used to drink to solve the problems I had caused by drinking. The more I drank to release my shame-based loneliness, the more I felt ashamed."[11] On top of all that "bad press", shame usuallly feels uncomfortable. So it's no wonder that, regardless of culture, we buy into the idea that it is something to be eliminated."

Research suggests that shame in young children that is not alleviated quickly is harmful. Potentially traumatic events we haveexperienced as children, and which we have not been supported to process, at worst lead to toxic shame. Unprocessed trauma can become a component that leads to addiction or self-harm, but also to burnout and a constant striving to be perfect.

Shame has long played an important and at the same time complicated role in our relationships. Social norms affect how we respond to people who challenge the boundaries of the collective, and shame makes up the boundaries. It is easy to recognize that biological change processes take time, but so does behavioral change. In addition to personal tragedies, there is a dark history of smearing and excluding people using devastatingly lenient punishments such as the medieval pillory.

The scourge of the thirteenth century made life a shameful hell for anyone who did not join the ranks. Anyone who did not behave in a way that was considered appropriate was exposed and we may look back on the Middle Ages with horror and disgust. In our time, people are still exposed, but now with the help of social media, and the effect is frighteningly similar to that of the Middle Ages. Modern-day internet hate is, for younger people, the modern pillory.

Seconds after a humiliating situation is filmed the whole world could have access to it and most young people know this very well.

In Swedish schools corporal punishment and the right to chastise was abolished decades ago. But even today students are sent out into the corridor if they are considered too disruptive. This can be valuable in protecting learning and safety in the classroom, but it still has unwanted consequences on those who are sent out. Of course, treating even difficult children with dignity rather than exclusion becomes even more of a challenge with large classes and small staff. This might make it tempting to blame or shame when we desperately want to affect a person.

Solitary confinement in prisons is seen as one of the absolute worst ways to punish someone. Isolation cuts off an individual's ability to meet human needs such as contact, belonging, freedom and dignity. Loneliness is one of the driving forces behind suicide and, as we will see later in the book, shame is often linked to loneliness.

We can learn a lot about shame by understanding how society evolves. Parents in Sweden were until 1902 required by law to administer reasonable punishment. After that this continued to be a legal right until 1966. Then the right for parents to use corporal punishment was removed. Although there was no longer a legal basis for corporal punishment of children, it took a long time until it was integrated. The resistance to this change was maybe partly because being able to punish children in this way had been a major part of child rearing for a long time.

There were few role models and ideas on how to do things differently. This law was strengthened in Sweden in 1979 and it became a criminal offense to beat children under the Parental Code: "Children have the right to care, security and a good upbringing. Children shall be treated with respect for their person and individuality and shall not be subjected to corporal punishment or other offensive treatment."

According to a survey in 1966, violence was part of Swedish children's everyday life, but in 2000 a majority of 10-12-year olds (86%) stated that they had never been subjected to any form of corporal punishment. Unfortunately, creating a law that makes it a crime to hit or otherwise abuse children does not immediately protect all children from violence. However, laws are part of influencing norms and supports gradual change.

Even adults who, in an attempt to get their child to conform, are used to resorting to punishment (perhaps to avoid feeling shame for something the child has done), often need support to change, empathy for their own sense of vulnerability, and guidance in learning new behaviors. In the meantime, the child needs a chance for protection and support. Adults who slap their children may have had childhoods of slapping, which may explain the behavior, without excusing it.

Norm critics, activists and politicians around the world are working to widen people's life zones, to change the norms and laws that inhibit us and hold us back on a collective level. Many are fighting to create a society that supports the individual, to take away some of the pressure on individuals to stand up for themselves.

All this work is incredibly valuable and life-supporting, but focusing only on the disadvantages of shame as something to be "legislated away," risks tabooing it, making it more difficult to talk about and explore.If we only see shame from one point of view, there is a tendency to simplify its complexity.

Even a person who feels whole and has no major trauma sometimes experiences shame in situations where they make a mistake, or are involved in something humiliating. And although shame is sometimes part of a traumatic situation, the attitude that all shame is a symptom of trauma, or that something is wrong, risks getting in the way of dealing with the feelings of shame that arise in everyday life.[12]

Marshall Rosenberg, who encouraged us to never do anything to avoid shame or guilt, also warned of the consequences of blaming or shaming. Blaming and shaming often gets in the way of connection, whether between children or between adults, and becomes a burden on all relationships. The rather common expression, "You should be ashamed of yourself" or "You disappointed everyone with your behavior" can have a huge impact well into later life.

Guilt and shame arise from the context we find ourselves in, but whether or not we can communicate about these feelings or not, has a crucial impact on our relationship. Adults don't need to use blaming communication, as most children will feel shame anyway, as part of their socialization process. When we show children boundaries and make it clear that others have needs too, sometimes they feel ashamed and sometimes not.

Something adults can work on is motivating and communicating with younger individuals in ways other than shaming them and, at the same time, accepting that sometimes they will feel shame anyway. Just because we strive to take personal responsibility for our inner selves, does not automatically mean that we give up on normative and societal changes aimed at creating greater acceptance of differences and reducing the risk of exclusion. It is possible to do "both."

Even if we do not want to erase feelings of shame, it is valuable to be supported in processing potentially traumatic situations with good therapy, crisis management, or trauma processing. In addition to dealing with our own minds, we can all look at the way we communicate, shame and blame.

While the unfavorable reputation of shame seems to persist, emotions in general have received increasing attention and the importance of a healthy emotional life is supported by research in many different fields of knowledge. For example, we now know that emotions help us to remember and are important in our learning. Contrary to what we once thought, emotions do not stand in the way of logic or are the opposite of it, but rather are part of it.

To say that shame is good or bad is to oversimplify something complex because even joy in excess is harmful, and there are more ways to relate to emotions than either rejecting or celebrating them. Shame, like fire, is undoubtedly threatening if handled carelessly, but does that mean the emotion itself is something we should try to get rid of? If the function of shame is to help us ensure we belong to a group, that sounds pretty positive, doesn't it? And if shame makes us aware of when we've done something at the expense of others or our own dignity, doesn't that sound like part of a life-serving system?

2

THE CONSTRUCTION
OF AN EMOTION

What are we Going to do With our Emotions?

Which emoji should you choose? Which round face with mouth and eyes in different positions represent what you want to convey? Which expression risks being misunderstood? Which one feels exaggerated? You are not alone in your confusion. And perhaps it is not surprising, because many researchers now believe that, contrary to what was previously assumed, we do not have a universal human ability to read facial expressions. Each emotion has the potential to be expressed in many different gestures and expressions and does not look a "certain way". At least this book is based on believing emotions includes more variations that one particular one. It is also based on the approach that emotions are constructed on a personal as well as a cultural level.

When it comes to expressing emotions, words have many advantages. Those who early in life learn to put their feelings into words can reap several positive effects. First, we learn to sort our emotional state into good or bad, uncomfortable or comfortable.

But having only two opposite poles from which to work with is not very effective, and we learn a handful of expressions such as happy, angry or sad. From there, we can find more subcategories and refine our expressions. We go from concrete emotions to more subtle ones.

High emotional granularity leads to better mental health, according to several studies on the subject. When we can nuance our emotional expressions, we help the brain to anticipate and categorize what is going on. This gives us more tools that we can use to respond to the environment in a more functional way. We can use emotions to understand what we and others need and tailor our actions even in difficult situations in a more fine-tuned way. Brain researcher Lisa Feldman Barrett describes it this way:

"People who exhibit higher emotional granularity go to the doctor less frequently, use less medication, and spend fewer days in the hospital for illness. This is not magic; it happens when you leverage the porous boundary between the social and the physical. So learn as many new words as possible."[13]

With greater emotional nuance, we can make a closer connection to others, feel with them and help them feel with us. The fact that it also has a positive impact on our physical health is a fantastic bonus. One of the explanations is that when we can fine-tune what we feel and need, stress levels are lowered. We can better regulate our body's energy, express clearer wishes and adapt our decisions to feel good.

In the 1960s, psychologist Silvan Tomkins founded the Affect theory, which included nine basic human affects. It led to bigger acceptance, maybe especially in psychotherapy, that emotions and inner well-being have biological components. To describe the basic affects, Tomkins used word pairs, such as shame/ humiliation, to show that emotional intensity could vary.

Affect theory distinguishes between affects and emotions. A simplified way to describe affects is that they are physical moods and most of the time we are not aware of them. Emotion is a conscious experience of being physically affected in some way and how we deal with it.

Emotions have been described in different way by different philosophers, religious leaders, poets, psychologist and in recent time, scientists. The last category using everything from universal reactions, universal human essences, brain circuits to constructs.

A leading emotion researcher was the neurobiologist Jaak Panksepp. He proposed that mammals have seven core emotional systems originating from subcortical brain regions. His research examined the neural underpinnings of basic emotions like fear and joy in animal models. He presented a theory that our emotions arise in basic affective circular systems in the brain. The influential anthropologist Paul Ekman also advocated an approach to emotions as something that is universal. In the late nineteenth century, Ekman did research on people in isolated locations in South America and Asia to study the universality of emotions. Ekman and his team used photographs of actors with facial expressions that would reflect different basic emotions. The basic emotions were described as a common denominator for people all over the world and each emotion was attributed its own evolutionary explanation. Emojis, used instead of words, are created with the assumption that emotions are reflected in the same facial expressions around the world.

Researcher Lisa Feldman Barrett argues a bit differently from previous researchers. She agrees that we have something universal when it comes to emotions, but not that there are a certain number of innate human emotions, or brain circuits or places in the brain that they inhibit. Instead she puts more importance on our shared ability to construct emotional concepts: "Overall, the theory of constructed emotions is a biologically oriented, psychological explanation of who you are as a human being. It accounts for both evolution and culture."[14]

Emotion research can be divided into two approaches, the classical and the constructed view of emotions. The latter approach, advocated by Feldman Barrett, argues that it is more accurate to see emotions as created moment by moment rather than as innate. According to Barrett, emotions are predictions that become preparations for situations we face.

We get angry because others behave badly, we become disappointed because someone doesn't do what they promised, right? Emotions are not usually experienced as constructs. If we just look at how it feels, most people probably experience emotions as reactions, rather than something we have constructed. We experience emotions as triggered, stimulated, and that we have little choice in how or when they arise. We get angry because others behave badly, is this not a sign that we are triggered?

The idea that emotions are constructed does not imply that emotions are less important or less natural than if they are stimulated or triggered. Simply put, the experience of emotions being triggered is because in most cases, our brain works faster than our consciousness and that emotions are therefore experienced as reactions. It would be inefficient and maybe stressful if we had to consider all our internal processes before we reacted, so the brain uses memory functions to anticipate what might happen and prepares us for it.

Lisa Feldman Barrett and her research team tried to duplicate Ekman's research results (also in isolated locations). They found such large sources of error that they concluded that the theory based on previous studies needed to be revised. Perhaps the newer theory-building is influenced by the demands that are now made on how scientific results should be interpreted.

Feldman Barrett has taken the lead in questioning several theories of emotions, not only Ekman's but also Tomkins' and Panksepps.' She argues that revisions are needed, to formulate more accurate theories of emotion that include a greater understanding of how the brain works. By reconsidering the universality of emotions and broadening our understanding of emotions, Feldman Barrett argues that we can, for example, create better treatments for people with mental health problems.

While it is important to keep up to date with the brain and nervous system, we also benefit from studying emotions from more than just the biological angle. The theory that emotions are constructed, rather than stimulated, is partly based on our biology; impulses, affects, hormones, brain and the nervous system all influence what we feel. However, it is not only biology that determines what we feel, emotions are also influenced by memories, internal subjective experiences and by external social contexts. According to this view, we are not born with a ready-made emotion register and have no reservoir of emotions stored in some secret place in the brain.

In different situations, the same type of emotion can contribute to varying responses on both inside and outside of us. Or as Feldman Barrett puts it, "Variation, not uniformity, is the norm."

The view that emotions have no consistent bodily fingerprints that look the same for all people in all situations opens up a range of possibilities for how we can create emotional well-being. This book assume emotions are constructs that prepare us for challenges we face, help us communicate our needs effectively, and balance our energy budget.

We are born with a body that interacts with its environment and has a growing ability to think and understand relationships. Emotions, such as anger, have no single expression or impact on us. We can boil with anger, turn bright red, raise our voices and our pulse and blood pressure can go through the roof. But we can also experience anger as ice cold, become restrained, calculating, as our body will perceives it differently. The category of anger has not one face, but many. Intuitively, it feels like events outside of us stimulate this anger, so it is easy to question theories of constructed emotions.

The brain's rapid processing of impressions, inside and out, makes it easy to believe that emotions are more static than they are. In fact, it seems that we are not passive recipients of emotions, but creators of them.

Growing up, we inherit emotional concepts and expressions. At the same time, we learn to describe our inner selves' word by word. Shame is sometimes identified as a socially constructed emotion, but it seems like shame is not different from other emotions in his respect.

The Value of Emotions

"Your brain's most important job is not thinking or feeling or even seeing, but keeping your body alive and well so that you survive and thrive ... How is your brain able to do this? Like a sophisticated fortune-teller, your brain constantly predicts. Its predictions ultimately become the emotions you experience and the expressions you perceive in other people."[15]

LISA FELDMAN BARRETT

No matter how we explain the origins of emotions, they are important to us. The ability to understand concepts helps us sort out new information. We can learn more by connecting new information to older data. Like the notes on a scale, emotions can blend into a large number of variations. In a thousandth of a second, we receive impulses we either like or dislike, which we want to respond to or withdraw from. The impulses would be overwhelming if they all reached our consciousness, but fortunately there is an automated screening system that sorts out many impressions.

With the help of body signals, sensory impressions, memories and experiences, emotions become predictions that help us act. As awareness of our inner self increases, we can name emotions in a way that works in the contexts in which we find ourselves.

We move continuously between pleasure and discomfort in a dynamic movement known in the scientific community as valence. The emotional state varies and can be anything from a pleasurable yawn as you crawl into bed to sleep, a warm shower on a chilled body, or a stressful dash to catch the last bus home.

What we think about our affective state (our mood and energy level) shapes our emotions. Researchers basically agree that babies can feel and perceive discomfort and comfort from birth. What there is disagreement about is whether newborns come into the world with fully developed emotional concepts or not.

One way to learn to understand our emotions is to become more aware of the physical impulses that underlie them. Being aware of our bodies, we can be alert to impulses that can be of use for us.

To embody our emotions, we can start from our current energy level, discerning whether what we are experiencing feels comfortable or uncomfortable, before describing the emotion in words. So, the everyday question "how are you?" is not necessarily a superficial phrase, but can actually become an opportunity for an inner check of our valence level.[16]

Pause and reflect on where you would place yourself on the valence scale right now? Are you neutral and would place yourself in the middle? Or is your emotional state pulling you one way or the other?

◄───────── - VALENCE/ LEVEL OF COMFORT + ─────────►

The second mode of affect is our energy level, on a scale from calm, low energy to high, excited energy. Some of us prefer to be more stimulated, on the go between activities. Others prefer the calmness of chilling with friends or having plenty of time to prepare for work. Affects can be simplified by combining our energy level and valence state, so here is another scale. Use this to assess your current energy level.

Now you have discovered whether you have high or low energy, and with your valence state, whether you feel comfortable or not. You have a rough picture of your emotional state.

We can further practice fine-tuning our emotional state by using words for emotions. The danger with a certain list of words is that it limits us if the word we are looking for is not on the list and we get the idea that only those words are "appropriate." In addition, we sometimes judge emotions as good or bad. These judgements can therefore censor, exaggerate or diminish what we really feel. To avoid internal censorship, it is often helpful to start with the energy and valence scale before looking for words to describe our experience.

On the next spread is a model to help put inner experiences into words. As the model provides a static picture, there is a risk that the emotional words do not match where you would place them on the energy or valence scale. Let the model inspire you to decide where the emotional words can be placed, instead of considering it as the only or correct way.

Words for emotions are descriptions of an emotional experience derived from valence, our energy levels and the meaning we have

36

learnt to give them. The word 'anger' may lead us to believe that anger shows up in the same way for all of us. So, getting angry would feel exactly the same to me as it does to you and the same every time I feel it. But our emotional experience can be very different, even if we use the same word to describe it. We might be boiling with anger; screaming and thrashing about, our nervous system gasping and our blood pressure rising. But anger can also leave us cold and calculating, with our heart rate and blood pressure going down.

The experience of grief can range from soothing to humiliating or disturbing, and can differ from one instance to another.

We may feel aversion to certain emotions, for example we may feel ashamed of our anger, become uncomfortable when we feel sad or scared, or push any discomfort away, before we are even fully aware of them. Different emotions are more or less welcome in certain families, groups, and social settings. There are different theories about emotions, such as when we do not have inner space for our emotions they turn into shame, humiliation or anger.[17] According to the theory of constructed emotions, any emotion can change into any other emotion.

The Appearance of Shame

Emotions look different from person to person. A flushed face or red spots on someone's neck can be a sign of shame, but it can also be a sign of fear, stress, or even something non-emotional, like allergies. Like other emotions, shame does not have a particular facial expression or biological indicator, and is actually more varied than that.

A quick laugh can be a sign that someone is releasing the pressure of feelings of shame (but we can't know for sure if the person laughing is trying to avoid those feelings or is just nervous). A frozen smile can sometimes be used to conceal inner unease.

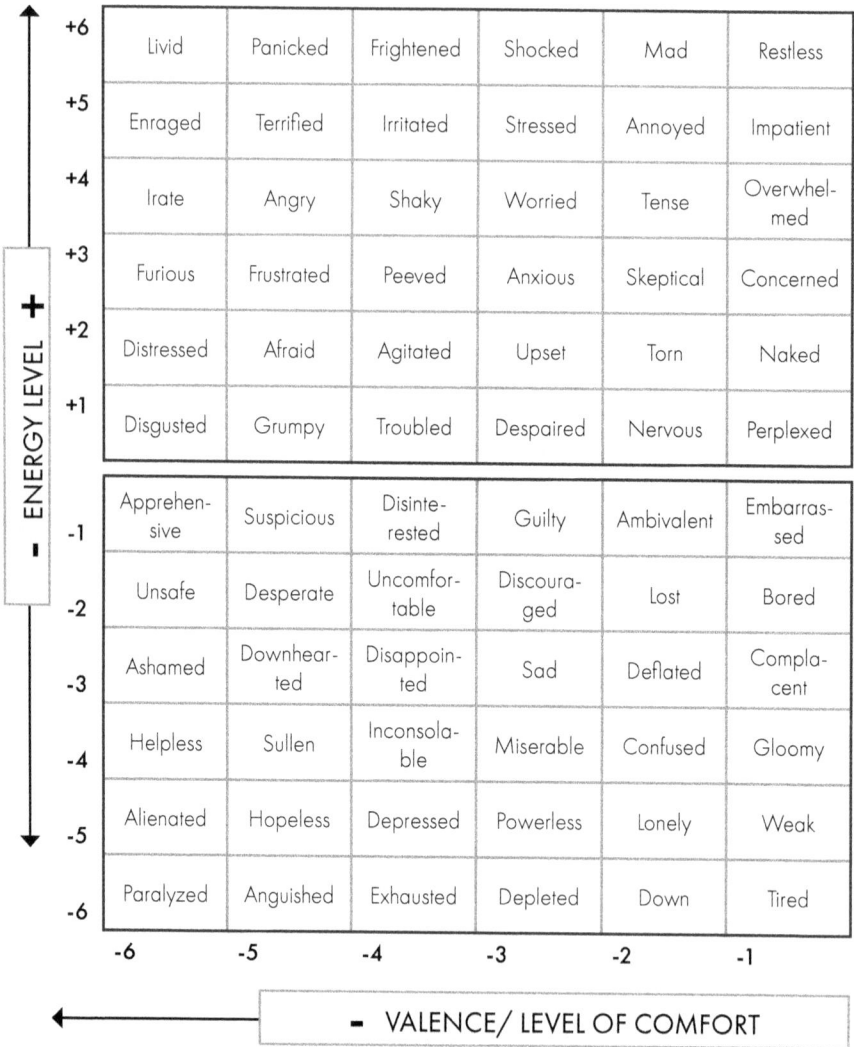

Energy Level	-6	-5	-4	-3	-2	-1
+6	Livid	Panicked	Frightened	Shocked	Mad	Restless
+5	Enraged	Terrified	Irritated	Stressed	Annoyed	Impatient
+4	Irate	Angry	Shaky	Worried	Tense	Overwhelmed
+3	Furious	Frustrated	Peeved	Anxious	Skeptical	Concerned
+2	Distressed	Afraid	Agitated	Upset	Torn	Naked
+1	Disgusted	Grumpy	Troubled	Despaired	Nervous	Perplexed
-1	Apprehensive	Suspicious	Disinterested	Guilty	Ambivalent	Embarrassed
-2	Unsafe	Desperate	Uncomfortable	Discouraged	Lost	Bored
-3	Ashamed	Downhearted	Disappointed	Sad	Deflated	Complacent
-4	Helpless	Sullen	Inconsolable	Miserable	Confused	Gloomy
-5	Alienated	Hopeless	Depressed	Powerless	Lonely	Weak
-6	Paralyzed	Anguished	Exhausted	Depleted	Down	Tired

ENERGY LEVEL (vertical axis, + to −)

− VALENCE / LEVEL OF COMFORT (horizontal axis)

	+1	+2	+3	+4	+5	+6
+6	Frisky	Motivated	Thrilled	Ecstatic	Elated	Exhilarated
+5	Stunned	Connected	Joyful	Excited	Energized	Euphoric
+4	Surprised	Giggly	Energetic	Inspired	Alert	Enthusiastic
+3	Focused	Proud	Happy	Lively	Playful	Devoted
+2	Engaged	Curious	Amused	Cheerful	Enlivened	In wonder
+1	Balanced	Optimistic	Alive	Hopeful	Awake	Moved

	+1	+2	+3	+4	+5	+6
-1	Collected	Pleased	Strong	Free	Delighted	Touched
-2	Composed	Glad	Blessed	Nostalgic	Grateful	Loving
-3	Melancholic	Vulnerable	Tranquil	Chilled	Satisfied	Wonderous
-4	Safe	Relaxed	Relieved	At ease	Content	Fulfilled
-5	Mellow	Secure	Cool	Present	Safe	Harmonic
-6	Sleepy	Restful	Peaceful	Calm	Comfortable	Serene

VALENCE/ LEVEL OF COMFORT **+** →

People can freeze with shame, making it even easier to miss the fact that they feel ashamed. In a thousandth of a second, something happens inside them that will remain there. People also freeze out of fear or to collect themselves when they have forgotten something. When someone expresses anger explosively, it can simply be a manifestation of how shame seriously influences their nervous system, although we can never know for sure what is going on inside another person.

Shame is rarely captured in the moment, because the person in front of us is avoiding, covering up, or softening the emotion that we may not even realize is there. Despite the turmoil the person is experiencing inside, the perfect surface can be barely disturbed by a ripple.

Shame sometimes show up as a downcast look, or a difficulty finding words. But also fear and nervousness can cause us to avoid eye contact and fumbling words. Other times, shame hides behind steady eye contact and a blank expression, as the person has learned to quickly push the awkwardness of shame away. Ambiguous expressions of shame pass, many times unnoticed, and the shame is relegated to the background. This affects us, mixing with other emotions and leaving us with a nervous system in turmoil. Sometimes our shame-avoiding strategies lead to actions that others have a hard time understanding as being an attempt to avoid shame.

Feelings and emotions are largely private, subjective experiences and when we have learned to put our inner experiences into words, others might be invited into that part of us. When it comes to the emotions of others, we can only guess what is going on inside of them until they tell us how they experience something.

The experience of shame is often placed on the uncomfortable end of the valence scale. But how uncomfortable shame feels, is partly due to our thoughts and memories. Those in turn, are shaped by the culture we grew up in, with its respective norms and social agreements, as well as our individual families.

Answers to the question of what shame is, are many. One way to approach the exploration of shame is to see it as an important human condition that has to do with our needs for relationships and belonging. As we develop a language that helps us name shame, we gain more freedom of choice in how we can deal with it. Since feelings of shame arise in relation to others (or others we imagine), it is also in communication with them that the emotions can be most easily transformed. An important step towards acceptance of what is going on inside of us, and with it a possible transformation, is to let others take part in what is going on within us.

In some cultures, the ability to distinguish between thoughts and feelings has long been considered important. The more we learn about the brain, the more we see that the difference between thoughts and feelings is smaller than what we might have thought. Both are important subjective experiences that shape and reshape our inner selves. Thoughts, preferences, previous experiences form our emotions. And our emotions affect our thoughts. When we feel shame, our willingness and ability to accept discomfort is put to a test, and then it is valuable to understand how we think about the experience. Often, however, such situations are experienced as an unclear inner jumble.

Feelings of shame are not bad, but they become dangerous if we get caught up in them or do destructive things to avoid feeling them. Different words are used to describe shame; Something is embarrassing, shameful, degrading, or threatening our dignity. We say that we have "made a fool of ourselves" and that we feel shamed, destroyed, ridiculous, or inferior. Or we say we're shy, feel guilty, or humiliated.

Sometimes there are no words that completely match the experience. We might not use the word "shame" to describe the discomfort we experience although someone else might suggest it is shame. Words like 'embarrassment', 'numbness' and 'fear' are often used to describe what it means to feel shame.

It is valuable to remember that a young child's cognitive development does not allow for self-reflection in the same way as when they grow older. Most young children can't put words to, experience, or understand emotions in the way most adults can. Both children and adults are affected by affects, simply described as unconscious precursors to emotions. The young child's brain "signals danger" in the event of over activation much earlier than an older child's or an adult's. While an adult has a variety of options in processing internal stress of this kind, a young child has very few. This is partly due to the development of the brain, but also to whether the adult has learned to manage internal processes in various ways.

Since feelings of shame often cause strong discomfort, we learn strategies to avoid them at an early age. And since avoidance successfully protected our young nervous system from overload, it is understandable if we continue to deal with shame in similar ways as adults. However, there are downsides to having only avoidance as a strategy to deal with shame. Let's explore this with a metaphor.

Imagine a city where there have been several car accidents. The traffic flow is analyzed. Intersections, roundabouts and other junctions where the flow is often blocked are reviewed to understand what is going on. Places where queues form during rush hour are noticed and remedied. An unforeseen increase in traffic is detected in an area at a certain time of day.

Traffic lights are installed, the roadway is widened, the permitted speed is reduced. A road is rerouted, cycle paths are created, and pedestrian crossings are more clearly marked. The measures themselves are sometimes small and far away from the accident area. But if it is the right change, even a small correction can reduce the risk of crashes in the future.

When we feel shame and don't want to acknowledge it, internal "traffic jams" easily arise. It is easy to forget that a seemingly small action in the present – such as avoiding telling an inconvenient truth – can later affect what happens if the information is revealed.

Relationships can be damaged and trust broken. If, instead, we start paying attention to what we do to avoid shame. We can pause, look at where the "traffic jams" happen, and take action. Small adjustments at an early stage can make a big difference down the line.

A young person develop into the ability to communicate about his or her feelings. They learn to calm down with the help of rational explanations, use their ability to understand time and remind themselves that the feeling will pass. Another direction to turn is to become angry at the person who is shaming them. Eventually emotions can be used as a link to human needs. And sometimes adults also find it taboo to talk about things that are going on inside of them during a shame attack. However, an adult often has the capacity and possibility to withdraw from situations that are shameful. It often takes both empathy and security for us to be able to share that discomfort with others. The more we learn to embrace our emotional state, the more we can influence it. After all, emotions aren't animal reflexes that contradicts rational thought.

One price of constantly avoiding shame is that it can prevent us from deepening relationships with others. From this perspective, it is easy to see that we have a lot to gain by getting to know emotions of shame, as otherwise they can get in the way of dreams, damage relationships and inhibit our development in any number of areas.

Even if we sometimes would like to go beyond all physical limitations, we as humans have biological conditions to relate to. When a physical discomfort intensifies, we become aware of it. For example, we have thirst that reminds us that we need to drink. Thirst can feel manageable if we manage to think that we can drink later, but the need for water continues. If we get scared that we don't have access to water, it influences us even more strongly. Basic affects and emotion both help and urge us to balance our physical and mental budget.

We don't want to get rid of signals such as thirst and fatigue, because they remind us of important needs, and shame and other emotions have similar functions even if they are not as tangibly tied to a specific concrete thing (such as food or water) or a concrete action (such as sleeping).

As mentioned in the preface, there is value in learning to accept, reshape and integrate feelings of shame. And first we need to learn to recognize and put into is words what happening inside of us. Keep in mind that this is a process that will be accessible only once we have reached a certain level of self-awareness and that this is nothing we can demand of others, especially children. Some of the things we can reap from befriending shame are:

- We will have the courage to say yes to things we dream of or long to do, even if we risk feeling shame.
- It will be easier to say no to things we don't want to do, because we are not as afraid of how it will affect us to not be liked.
- We will dare letting other people close, even if it means that they discover our weaknesses and shortcomings as we will be able to handle being ashamed if they see those parts of us.
- When it comes to us as parents or adults around children, one big advantage is that we can be role models. We can show that feelings of shame are manageable and that by processing them, we can become more aware of the dance between our own needs and the needs of others.

Shame-avoiding Strategies

Emma, 16, lies about failing a test at school (because she is ashamed). When it is revealed that she will therefore not be able to take the next course, it influences her parent's trust in her. They become angry and try to control her even more, creating distance in their relationship. Emma lies more and more often about things she thinks her parents will get angry about. The lying can be seen as another consequential error in the "traffic flow" that could have been corrected if Emma or her parents had better tools to deal with shame.

Tom, 17, expresses anger at not being invited to a party. The anger pushes away the shame of not being wanted and he says mean things to Amir who didn't invite him, expressions that make him even more unwanted. The anger is boosted by humiliation because it is never addressed, but simmers under the surface. All we see is an angry young man. Only when Tom feels sufficiently understood can he deal with the humiliation of being rejected in ways other than an attack.

Angela, 15, cuts her arms for the first time after a humiliating incident in the schoolyard. The pain distracts her from feeling the discomfort of going to school the next day. Cutting herself quickly becomes a habit, as Angela finds that the pain eases her internal pressure. Unless Angela receives support or learns to deal with the shame in some other way, she is likely to continue with some form of self-harm to relieve the pressure.

Amal, 28, has long dreamed of making a living as a singer. When she finally gets an invitation to perform at a small event, she declines because she "hasn't had the time to practice enough" or "doesn't have the right clothes." Only later does she realize that her *no* was an attempt to avoid shame. She interpreted the shame as a sign of her not being perfect.

The perfectionist in Amal protects her from uncomfortable embarrassment, but at the same time makes it harder for her to live out her dreams. Her inability to deal with shame causes an "internal traffic jam," but when she learns to deal with it, she stops giving it the permission to get in her way. When Amal learns that shame is one emotion among many and that it can be dealt with in ways other than avoiding it, she can start saying yes to offers, even if they make her nervous.

Examples of Individual Perspectives

"

– Your inner critic will be silenced when you have learnt that you are okay as you are. Straighten your back and stand up for yourself .

– With a little therapy, you'll get over feeling alone and left out

– I think you should do what I did. I stopped feeling ashamed when I realized that what happened when I was a child wasn't my fault

– No wonder you feel shame after a childhood like yours.

Examples of Collective Perspectives

"

– Why not just make what we are ashamed of legal, so we don't have to be ashamed of it?

– We need to change our norms so that we never have to feel shame again.

– Schools should teach everyone to stop shaming others. Then shame would be eradicated and no one would have to be ashamed anymore

– It's not your fault that you feel worthless, it's all the rubbish you've been told throughout life by this distorted society.

When we see links between shame and children becoming with-drawn, self-critical, acting out or inhibited in their expression, it is easy to blame it on the shame itself. What people, young and old, do to avoid shame makes it look as if they have been driving the wrong way, or that they are very bad drivers, not that they are in a temporary traffic jam. Feelings of shame are so uncomfortable that many times we are in a hurry to avoid them, which increases, rather than decreases, the number of internal "traffic jams."

The Individual and the Collective

Shame is sometimes seen only as a sign of some kind of trauma and therefore as an emotion that can always be 'healed away.' Others argue that shame is rather a symptom of the narrow-mindedness of the culture and a sign of social oppression, rather than something that the individual should have to deal with. While some blame a repressive society, others put the responsibility on the individual, saying everyone should change their attitude and learn to think correctly, grow up and stop being ashamed. Shouldn't a mature, developed person be able to use logic to opt out of shame, put it where it belongs or rise above it?

Others argue that we should all learn other ways of communi-cating and that we would then be free of guilt and shame. They might argue that it is time to eradicate all bad self-confidence and self-blame. We probably get the most out of thinking "both/and" instead of "either/or" in this case.

Each of the approaches on the last page, identifies opportuni-ties, while each also misses important aspects. Seeing shame only from a individual perspective misses the fact that we are more than individuals. Shame is also very much formed in us because we are part of a culture and a collective. We are not only part of a collective but also of a part of a story that influences our communication, our

47

actions, our bodies, and even our genes. What happens in our biology affect us continuously even if we at moments can influence it.

Having the ability to finely attune our emotions, to describe in detail what we feel, has been shown to have a number of benefits.[18] The more we can perceive signals from within and use them to adjust our outward relationships, the less we put a strain on our body's energy budget. When we can more accurately put into words what is going on within us, the clearer we become to those around us. This makes it easier for us to get the support we need.

Our emotional alertness makes it clearer to us what we need and makes it easier to balance our energy budget.[19] There is certainly value in receiving an emotional signal when we overstep someone else's limits or when they cross ours. We can also use our logical thinking to regulate emotions. The flip side of logic, though, is that it can muffle important, silent signals from within that could help us to also perceive the boundaries of others more accurately. We can act according to what we think is rational and be surprised to find that others perceive us as cold and closed off.

If shame can contribute to a better ability to relate to others in a compassionate way, it is hardly desirable to try to get rid of it. Instead, we have much to gain from becoming more aware of how we relate to emotions and how we act in relation to what we feel. Shame is socially shaped and, at best, helps us navigate norms and laws, hopes and dreams.

In addition to maturing on an individual level, we can work for normative changes and laws on a societal level that make it easier to choose more inclusive strategies in relationship to others. We can do the important work of fine-tuning social rules so that they serve us better. At the same time, we need to recognize that changes in collective norms do not reach everyone or every area immediately.

Even someone who dares to stand outside of the norm can feel ashamed of their life choices, while still preferring to live the way they do. Although feelings of shame may seem 'illogical' in some contexts, the feelings are there. For example, we feel ashamed at the thought of others thinking that we are poor or rich, careless or greedy. We can also be ashamed of what we've eaten for lunch and of things we haven't done. Sometimes we find it difficult to understand why others are ashamed of things they are ashamed of, without realizing that others think the same thing about us. However, exclusion from the collective, is a threat to us as human beings and feelings of shame help us not to forget this.

Of course, there is a difference between subjective experiences versus the actual need to protect ourselves from threats in the environment. But the difference is not always obvious.

Because of its clear limitation on our life choices, it is easy to perceive shame as undesirable. Perhaps we abdicate responsibilities of various kinds, fearing that someone will call us out as a fraud if we are not flawless. In our efforts to avoid shame, we risk becoming perfectionists. We do more than we can handle, fearing being exposed as weak or inept. We say no to exciting challenges and give up on our dreams. Not only that, but we might even avoid letting people close to us because they might see us in a light we don't want them to.

If we see shame as a sign of weakness or as a wrong approach to life, it is easy to feel even more ashamed. This can become a vicious cycle, a shame spiral, and shame will end up as the winner. Shame over shame, silencing us, and making us hide even more aspects of ourselves. Unpopular opinions are covered up, at least if we worry about being mocked for them. In an attempt to deal with situations that threaten our dignity, we shrink ourselves and our expressions to a minimum.

The price is high. We withdraw - instead of boldly taking calculated risks - selling out our needs for dignity and belonging, until we grow tired of it, rebel and break free, and at worst become isolated. Depending on our way of thinking about emotions, we try to think in way that will mitigate the emotions of shame. If that doesn't work, we may turn to alcohol, work, sex, drugs and other distractions.

Blaming and shaming are part of what gives shame an unfavorable reputation. Expressions such as "You should be ashamed of yourself" or "You disappointed everyone with your behavior" are painful and have power over us even later in life. Adults don't need to shame or guilt-trip kids; most of them will feel shame anyway as part of their socialization process. To show children limits and make others needs clear to them, at times will lead to shame in them and at other times not. Something caregivers can do is to find other ways to motivate and communicate than through shaming and then let the child feel as it does.

Learning to stop fighting shame frees up energy that can be spent on vital things like building relationships, chasing our dreams and living the life we want. We can acquire the tools to approach those uncomfortable feelings instead of avoiding them. But what do we need to do to not shame ourselves or shame itself? How can we include embarrassment, shyness, shame, guilt and even humiliation in our repertoire of emotions?

As adults, we can view shame attacks from within ourselves in different ways, at least when we have the time and opportunity to develop the ability to distinguish between ourselves and our feelings. When we make the emotions of shame objects of study, we create more inner space for choice. Emotions can be used in a number of ways, including as clues to what we and others need, and to evaluate where our relationships can be deepened.

To be ready to take greater responsibility for our feelings of shame, the brains of children need many years to mature, as we will explore in later chapters.

When we are tempted to shame someone, a combination of comments, a dismissive look or an averted face can be used to control them. Diagnoses, labels and demands are parts of a language that make it easy to shame. Shame and blame become levers of control as feelings of shame are so uncomfortable that individuals who are not able to deal with them, will adapt to subtle hints of shame.

Even the facial expression of a stranger can elicit shame in us. We want to experience acceptance, even if this person is someone we will never meet again. With a few words or phrases, someone is able to communicate who should be ashamed and for what.

Our communication skills can be used to avoid shame but also to include it. Instead of disguising the truth, we can let others know what they can do for us, or apologize when shame has made us aware that we have crossed someone else's limits. With enough safety, support and capacity, we can share how vulnerable we feel, instead of letting shame limit what we allow others to see in us. Instead of paralyzing, shame then takes on the important function of strengthening social bonds, without the need to belittle ourselves or remain silent about our mistakes.

Feelings of shame, like all emotions, have a physical component, and how they are experienced is shaped by our thoughts, memories and how we feel about them. There are different ways of describing emotions and researcher Lisa Feldman Barrett divides the approaches into a classical view of emotions and a constructed view and describes the latter as follows: "Overall, the theory of constructed emotions is a biologically oriented, psychological explanation of who you are as a human being. It accounts for both evolution and culture."[20]

We can approach feelings of shame as emotions rooted in our need for human relationships and belonging. As we develop a language to help us name shame, we have more choice in how we deal with it. It is also in communication with others that shame emotions are most easily transformed, as they arise in relation to others (or others we only imagine). An essential step towards acceptance for what is going on inside, and thus possible transformation, is to let others know how we feel. Our thoughts influences what we feel and what we feel influences our thoughts. During a shame attack, our willingness and ability to feel discomfort is tested.

Feelings of shame are not bad but become dangerous if we get stuck in them or are driven to do destructive things to get rid of them. A common thread throughout this book is the view that feelings of shame are socially shaped, based on physical functions and that they can ultimately be positive for our collective lives. The more aware we become of our inner selves, the more our inner selves are reshaped by awareness itself. Changes in collective norms as well as laws can support individuals to relax, experience the security that comes from external acceptance, and obtain a chance to make their own choices. But these changes might not take away the shame even though the norms were part of constructing the emotion. This might take some time or may never happen.

In our quest to avoid shame, we risk becoming perfectionists. Perhaps we abdicate responsibilities of various kinds, fearing that someone will call our bluff and realize that we are not flawless. Or we overachieve, for fear of being exposed as weak or inept. The stress that can be caused by trying to avoid shame will haunt oss relentlessly. With shame at the wheel, we take fewer chances, say no to exciting opportunities, give up on our dreams and let fewer people close.

If we see shame as a sign of weakness or a wrong approach to life and still feel it, it's easy to feel even more ashamed. It becomes a vicious circle where shame wins. Shame about shame, silences us or spurs us to hide even more aspects of ourselves. Emotional expressions are marooned in a culture of silence, in the hope that this will continue to keep them in the background. Uncomfortable topics are avoided, especially if we worry about being mocked for expressing certain opinions.

But is it possible to not to shame ourselves or shame itself? It is possible, but it takes several Earth years to be able to distinguish between ourselves and what we feel, and only then can we study our inner selves more objectively. Once we can do that, feelings of shame become an asset because they give us clues on how to act in reciprocity and more care for others. One dilemma is that most people do not know how to distinguish between shaming children and helping them to balance their own needs against those of others.

Feelings of shame, which children begin to express after a few years of life, make us human survivors. Shame helps us to adapt to those we depend on. While there are adults who approach their own feelings of shame with curiosity, young children cannot experience shame for more than a short period of time before they become overwhelmed. Just because we are affected by bodily affects at any age does not mean that we can register or regulate them at all ages. In affect theory, shame is described as an affect linked to sight, similar to how distaste is linked to the sense of taste and disgust to the sense of smell. As eye contact between the child and the parent is essential for attachment, a parent's disapproving gaze is thought to lead to feelings of shame in the child. Both the averted gaze of someone we want to be seen by, or a joke about one of our shortcomings that puts us in the spotlight, are stressful even for adults. We affect each other far more than we may realize.

The avoidance patterns that develop to protect our growing bodies as children, often become so effective that, as adults, we might no longer register feelings of shame. We live within the framed life space created by those avoidance patterns. These frames are like an electric fence that helps us avoid things we are ashamed of. However, if we do something outside of what is considered appropriate or normal and someone catches us doing what we "shouldn't" have done, the nervous system awakens and the heat and cold of shame sweeps over us. The panicked thought, longing for a black hole to open up beneath us, making us disappear, is familiar and tells us that a component of fear is present in our emotions of shame.[21] A simple way to explain the connection is that exclusion from the collective meant death for a few million years of human evolution. Understanding our place in that evolutionary history can sometimes ease the pressure on an individual.

Although people all over the world experience shame, the situations in which the emotion is created vary. One common area of shame is appearance, although the norm of what is beautiful or good-looking varies from cultures to culture and over time. Just think about how you react when you look at photos of yourself ten, twenty or thirty years ago. "How awful, what am I wearing?" or, "those glasses give me the shivers" you might comment. Something that was perfectly fine or even the height of fashion at a certain time can make us feel ashamed long afterwards. Something that is considered beautiful in one culture is considered ugly in another.

Dealing with shame is a moving target that looks different throughout life. We can only guess how strongly someone else feels and how much stress shame creates for them. The shame a teenager feels about not having the "right" clothes at a party, can be as uncomfortable as for an adult who has just made a mistake so serious that they risk losing their job. Perspective affects emotions more than we may realize in everyday life.

Adults may be able to remind themselves that there are other jobs, while the teenager panics about not fitting in. Therefore the teenager's shame might have a greater and longer-lasting impact on them, even if the situation is seemingly less impactful.

On Which Dance Floor Does Your Feelings of Shame Dance?

Shame dances in interaction with the environment, we take a step back or forward to adapt, create acceptance and protect belonging. Even a mild sense of shame distracts us, for a short or long moment, and shifts our awareness from connection with others to ourselves. Almost unnoticed, we close the door slightly on our vulnerability.

To assess whether it is safe to be completely open and honest, we wait and if we always withdraw, instead of at least occasionally re-establishing connection that was cut by the shame axe, we become isolated islands where important parts of ourselves are hidden.

Like other emotions, shame is constructed in an attempt to balance our body-budget and to make predictions and prepare us for what might happen. Often all of this happens unconsciously and without us actively engaging with it.

Psychologist Donald Nathanson divides the dance floor of shame into the following eight areas that are well worth exploring.[22]

1. Comparisons

2. Dependence and independence

3. Competition

4. Self-criticism.

5. Appearance

6. Sex

7. To see and be seen

8. Intimacy.

One way to study shame is to understand the contexts in which it occurs for us. Here we will use eight categories to sort it out, although for example, author and professor Brené Brown uses others, including parenting, social expectations, gender, family constellations, trauma and vulnerability.[23]

1. Comparisons

A big part of our learning happens through comparison. Weighing one thing against another helps us to understand different things better and inevitably, that strategy is also applied to ourselves.

Constantly comparing ourselves with others can cause us to get caught in feeling worse than others; uglier, dumber, slower. We can also get stuck in feeling better than others which often creates distance.

As adults, there are several other ways to handle comparisons in our favor. For example, we can take a step back and logically look at a situation more neutrally. We can learn to laugh at ourselves, perhaps exaggerate our comparisons, take ourselves with a grain of salt. Comparisons can also be reshaped by assuming that behind every comparison we can find human needs, a concept that can be read more about in chapter 10.

It is essential to remember that many of these strategies are not available until we have lived quite a few years and matured physically, emotionally, and cognitively in values.

2. Dependence and independence

In early adolescence, a sense of belonging to a group is often extremely important. Being picked last for the soccer team, or being made fun of, or being excluded from a group project at school are some of the situations where shame dances.

And it is not only children and teenagers who experience the humiliation of not being chosen and who long to feel important or wanted. When we, at any age, feel ashamed when not being prioritized or invited we deal with it in different ways: by becoming overly self-critical, getting angry at others, or by withdrawing. Some play cool and pretend that not being included doesn't affect them at all.

The fear of being associated with someone who does not look, talk or behave in a way that is acceptable and appreciated by the group we want to belong to, might make us withdraw from that person. We may be embarrassed to be associated with certain people because of their behavior, appearance, nationality or religion and worry that we will not be accepted if others associate us with them. And then we feel ashamed of not being more accepting.

3. Competition

Competition can be fun and a basis for play. But we also compete to assert ourselves or to show our independence, which can easily lead to shame if we don't perform at our best. Competition develops and encourages us, at the same time as creating stress. We want to be seen as winners or as competent and we are ashamed of big, and even of small, failures and mistakes.

Even when we lose in contexts beyond our control, we may paradoxically feel ashamed because we want to appear competent, capable and worthy. It is common to feel shame about things like telling people that we have been fooled, or revealing that we have invested money in something that turned out to be a scam.

4. Self-criticism

Self-criticism has value because it regulates our behavior to conform to group norms and to ensure our place in the group. But if we become excessively self-critical, every situation becomes like walking on eggshells. Self-criticism can even be used as a cover for shame; we cut ourselves off at the knees first, in the hope that no one else will criticize us.

5. Appearance

"My hair is hopeless; I'm going to cut it all off."

"All the other guys have six packs and I'm just fat and ugly."

A four-year-old may think they are the prettiest child in the world. A ten-year-old celebrates their beautiful eyes but thinks that other people's hair color is much nicer or that they are too fat. As the years go by, the same celebrating child has become a teenager and is the ugliest person in the world by their own estimation. Everything is wrong, hair too thin, eyes too small, nose too big, pimples disgusting, stomach too fat. It rarely works to claim that we think they are the most beautiful person in the world. A parent's words don't carry much weight with a teenager who is preoccupied with what their peers think is beautiful.

We are not only ashamed of our own appearance, but also of how others close to us (our grandparents, children, parents, friends and partners) look.

6. Sex

Sex at its best is intimate. These are moments when we let someone close and show parts of our bodies, we might not otherwise let anyone see, so we can also feel nervous and scared. Intimate pleasure can lead to sounds or words we might never let anyone else hear, which can be vulnerable.

7. To see and be seen

We feel ashamed both when we are seen and when we are not. In addition, we may feel ashamed when we see others in an unusual or embarrassing situation.

8. Intimacy and closeness

While we want to be close to others, letting someone in is vulnerable. Intimacy means risking being seen not only for our good parts, but also for our shortcomings. Will we be accepted even if we are not perfect?

Anyone who reaches out their hand to hold another, or asks for a hug, risks being turned down. This is easy to experience as being rejected or unwanted. Different cultures have different attitudes and rules about intimacy. Anyone who goes outside of these will probably feel a certain amount of shame, at least if someone will see them. The shame becomes a reminder, an adaptation, to make sure to be included.

A Childhood Story

One summer when I was six years old, I was given a pair of sandals. Using long leather laces, they were tied in criss-cross up the legs and for me they were a kind of sign of being "grown-up." My two older sisters had been wearing similar ones in the summers for some years, and now I was "one of them."

When I had insisted that I wanted the same ones, my mother said that when I was big enough, I would get them too. Now it was finally my turn. Mom helped me put on the beautiful, but difficult to manage, footwear. When I looked in the mirror, I thought they made me look grown up. I proudly inaugurated them by walking to the little kiosk near our house. But without me noticing, the laces had unraveled and tangled at the bottom of my ankles. A boy, about eleven or twelve years old, was standing there with his friends. He pointed at me and several of them started to laugh at me. Someone commented on how ridiculous I looked. It felt like shame washed over me and the discomfort spread to my arms and legs and I felt myself shrinking. A frozen state locked up my insides and even if I just wanted to escape, my legs were heavy as rocks.

The shock was terribly uncomfortable for my young brain. In my frozen state there were no words to defend myself. All I could think about was the black hole I hoped would open in the ground beneath me. I would rather die than be humiliated like this. I would rather go up in smoke than have to stand there in shame and find no way to defend myself.

I have no memory of how I got home, whether I got any candy or just turned around and left, but despite the obvious appeal of the place, I avoided it for a long time. If I thought I saw the children that had laughed at me, I went the other way to avoid meeting them. However, I clearly remember the day when my mother noticed that I had outgrown my sandals and asked if I wanted new ones and how I quickly shook my head.

As I pass the site now, 50 years later, the memory resurfaces and the swirl of shame travels like a gentle breeze through my nervous system. In retrospect, I can understand that it looked comical with a tangle of string around the feet of a part of small legs. I can understand that the laughter of the other children felt like arrows that were difficult to defend myself against. The little girl wanted to experience dignity and pride and was instead made a fool of.

In retrospect, it is easy to understand that the older children were enjoying themselves and were not necessarily out to hurt me. They didn't intend on shaming me, but I still felt shame. As an adult, I feel great tenderness for the girl who experienced such vulnerability. In her hope that she would now be seen as a "big girl", she had assumed that she would receive some respect. This open pride and desire to be seen made her an easy target. The humiliation of the moment felt terrible.

My feelings of shame at that moment had little or nothing to do with low self-esteem or a bad childhood. They were part of the human need to fit in, to belong and to be seen with respect. The event did not create any trauma, but was painful. Memories like this help me to be more compassionate about children's and adults' sometimes dysfunctional behaviors. We need to fit in so badly and if we think shame will be laughed at, we might withdraw or act in other ways that even seem counter-intuitive.

3
SELF-CENTERED CURIOSITY

To explore how shame affects us through different life stages, chapters three to five and eight all focus on different levels of development. This chapter deals with the transition from acting on impulse to becoming more self-centered and exploratory.

We are born with an immature but powerful brain, which with support gradually learns to build and sort mental experiences such as thoughts, feelings and memories. It is a wonderful process to follow.

Facing the World

Emma is sixteen months old. She moves across the kitchen floor, and using a chair, pulls herself up to standing, walks a few steps and falls on her bottom. Exploring what is around her, she sits still for only a short time before continuing to crawl towards something moving in front of her. Her father Robert smiles as he watches Emma try to catch the sun's reflections moving across the floor. The kitchen window is open to let the air in, and he is looking forward to dinner with the whole family. Robert is delighted to see his daughter making the leap from a quietly receptive infant to crawling, walking and investigating things that amuse her.

The kitchen table is set with plates, glasses and cutlery and Robert has just placed a hot pot of bean sauce on it. He turns around to hang the pot holders on a hook on the wall. For a moment, his back is turned from Emma as he rinses his hands. The floral tablecloth moving in the breeze from the window catches Emma's attention. As quickly as she can, she crawls to the table and stands up with the help of a chair leg. Her one hand reaches for the enchanting tablecloth, and she grabs it. In that moment Robert turns around, sees her, and realizes that he won't be able to get to her in time, so he shouts.

"No! Emma, no! Absolutely not. Let go!"

Emma looks up at Robert's bright red face. Her excitement ebbs, as it is uncomfortable to see her father's tense face. She barely recognizes him. The visual impression along with her father's high-pitched voice cause the exploration in Emma to freeze. The activation of her parasympathetic nervous system numbs the movements of her body, and the muscles of her hand let go of the tablecloth. The eagerness to capture the fluttering tablecloth is gone as she sees her father's open eyes. Inner discomfort replaces her curiosity and with a heavy head she looks down at the floor.

Robert takes a quick step forward and quickly lifts his daughter. As he embraces her, he is filled with fear and shame. His self-image as someone capable of protecting his family is shattered, but with a few deep breaths, he manages to calm himself down while holding Emma. The self-criticism subsides when Robert realizes that he managed to protect his daughter and that they are both unharmed. He whispers a quiet "I'm sorry, I'll be better at protecting you" in her ear, not for her sake but for his own.

Emma begins to cry, but as she feels her father's warmth and hears his reassuring voice, her fear ceases. As her tears fall, the stress is released from her little body and a smile soon spreads across her open face as she points to a reflection from the sun on one of the glasses on the table. Robert sighs, smiles back and points to yet another sun reflection, realizing that their connection calms his daughter, but also himself. His tension subsides, and he becomes grateful for the instinct to protect, even if it made him yell at Emma, which is against his own ideals of how he wants to relate to his child.

After studying the sun's reflection together for a few minutes, Robert stands up with Emma in his arms. He shows her the hot pot and the sharp cutlery and tells her again how important it is to be careful around the kitchen. She may not understand but his explaining soothes his own inner critic, who wants to remind him of his parental responsibilities. It is of utmost importance that his daughter learns to watch out for dangers, but he also realizes that she is probably too young to remember what he says. He makes an internal note to himself not to use kitchen towels until Emma is a little older and can better make risk assessments around interaction in her environment.

What would have happened if Robert had not been able to stop Emma from afar? And if she had not shifted from the open, curious stage she was in into an uncomfortable parasympathetic collapse? Perhaps she would have pulled the hot iron pot down on herself, suffered burns or even a concussion. Perhaps she would have just gotten a few small cuts from a knife or some broken glass. Fortunately, Emma was protected by the ability to freeze when her father yelled "Stop!"

Between one and two years of age, as the child expands its territory and begins to move more actively, the bond with the caregiver is tested.

During the same period, the ability to walk and to actively seek support from people in their environment develops. But before the capacity to make accurate risk assessments has developed, the young individual relies on a lot of help to safely explore what their curiosity leads them to. The child is hardly ashamed of having failed to consider the needs of others, but rather is driven by fear of not receiving vital acceptance and warmth.

There are different views on the age at which we first experience shame and this depends partly on what we call emotions and how we think they are formed. Michael Lewis in the *Handbook of Emotions* describes shame as: "... a highly negative and painful experience that causes a large increase in the stress hormone cortisol."[24]

Does shame come from stress, or stress from shame? The question is partly what comes first, the chicken or the egg? Or can they possibly occur simultaneously as they are linked to thought, experiences and memory?

It is understandable that Emma releases the pressure and cries in her father's arms, after how the stress had impacted her body. This emotional release is essential for her to feel good and relax again. Through crying, the body gets rid of stress. The intensity is further reduced by the reestablished connection with the caregiver and by Robert helping her to direct her attention from her inner pressure to the sun's reflections in the room. Emma can relax, she no longer has the impulse to make herself small because she is accepted and received by her father.

She is of course not aware that her experience, at a later stage in life, could be named shame. As she gets older, she also benefits from a supportive parent who doesn't immediately distract her with something outside herself but teaches her how to deal with uncomfortable emotions in other ways.

Born with mirror neurons (that we will come back to later in the book) children are little mimics. For example, even at a very young age children stick their tongue out at us when we show them ours.

Children learn about life from their caregivers, and the bond with them has served an important function for thousands of generations. Throughout the evolutionary history of Homo sapiens, exploring children have been regulated by a loud voice or a hand gesture.

The children who learned to adapt to adults gained a survival advantage. A disapproving look could prevent a child from falling over the edge of a ravine, disappearing into the forest on their own, getting burned or cut. Children's ability to agree to adults' rules, paired with their curiosity about their surroundings, is a survival success.

Imagine that Tom, fifteen months old, also gets attracted by an enticing tablecloth. And, like Emma, is curious to explore the moving object. Tom's father David takes a firm grip of his little hand to stop his son from getting hurt. Tom lets out a howl and begins to cry. David experiences a wave of shame as he realizes what could have happened. He is not particularly aware of what is going on inside of him, and what he perceives is a kind of turmoil in his mind and because he has such an aversion to feeling lost, he gives way to anger which he is more comfortable with.

He picks Tom up forcibly, and carries him to his bed, dropping him on it. Tom cries even louder when he doesn't feel his fathers' body against his, which increases the internal pressure in David. His job is to be the strong man, the commander-in-chief who protects his family, and it drives him crazy to see his boy crying and struggling.

Before he can think about it, he stares intensely at Tom. With a loud voice, he says that Tom has been "a bad boy and that he absolutely must not do that again." He tells the boy to stay on his bed until he has calmed down and when he leaves, he says:

"Stop it now. Big boys don't cry."

David only vaguely realizes that his explanations are going over the head of the boy, who is too small to be able to understand expectations related to time or age. Tom hasn't yet developed an understanding of how certain behaviors can lead to danger, or how to calm a runaway nervous system.

In addition, David's words, telling Tom what not to do instead of what he wants him to do, makes it even more difficult for Tom to sort out what is going on. He leaves the room, already ashamed of what he said about not crying. These were the same words that his father said to him a long time ago and that he vowed never to say to his own children. Of course, boys are allowed to cry. He blames himself but he doesn't know how to reconnect with his son.

An older child might have been able to understand more about what David was frustrated by, but Tom's imagination is not yet developed enough to understand negation. David's choice of words may not matter much in this situation, as the whole request is beyond Tom's understanding. But his action of leaving his son alone before he has discharged his stress might have had a bigger impact.

After David leaves, Tom takes a long look at the closed door while swallowing his tears. His body is itching with discomfort (since he didn't get any help to mitigate the impact of shame and stress on his brain and nervous system). He spots a package of brightly colored crayons among his toys. Quickly he gets off the bed and grabs the packet. The red crayon shines beautifully to him. His young short-term memory knows that the crayon gives color. What he doesn't remember is that Dad told him to only color on a piece of paper, so he turns to the wall. Relieved to find a way to divert his attention, Tom starts making shapes.

Painting shifts his focus outside himself and calms his stressed-out system. The wallpaper is soon full of red squiggles. A long red line ends up on the floor and it looks funny. Tom looks at the door his father left through and lets the red crayon draw a line on the floor in its direction. He likes his red artwork, but as he hears his father's footsteps in the kitchen, he freezes for a microsecond and lowers his head, and then continues to sooth himself with his coloring.

Tom's brain and nervous system are still developing, making him particularly vulnerable to stress. Unlike adults, who can calm themselves with logic or by consciously taking a few deep breaths to alleviate inner discomfort, the child is at the mercy of his environment to deal with pressure.

Emma's father Robert calmed both himself and her when he embraced her after the moment of separating shame. His immediate embrace calmed her nervous system, breaking the freeze and releasing the fear. Like Tom's father David, Robert has a self-image, shaped by culture, that is based on a man being powerful and capable of protecting his family. But Robert has worked for many years to deal with harsh self-criticism. He has thereby created some distance from the demand that as a man he should have everything under control, and the threat to his self-image does not completely control his actions. He has learned that emotions sometimes feel threatening but are actually harmless.

In fact, emotions make him more committed, so he doesn't want to get rid of them. He has realized that how he thinks about his emotions affects them. By taking a breath and putting his emotions into words, they become objects that can be studied and thus influenced. His ability to embrace his emotions in this way is particularly valuable when he needs to be there for Emma.

In contrast to Emma's calmed system, Tom's mind is still on fire when he is left on his bed, because he was not supported by his father to regulate it. It takes energy for his young body to handle the stress without outside support, energy he needs to develop other things. He notices that playing with the crayon calms him down, until he faces his father's disapproval again.

No matter how Tom and Emma are treated, no matter how different their shame lessons are, they will both be affected by emotions throughout their lives. Emma's parents can work on setting clearer boundaries, without giving up on the love they want to show her. If Tom's parents were to understand that he is not yet able to moderate strong emotions in the way they expect, they could change their approach to him. If they cannot understand that Tom does not automatically understand their intention in asking him to do something in a certain way, they will likely continue to be frustrated.

Something many of us adults miss is that children rarely remember complicated rules from one day to the next. We don't realize that the child lacks enough memory capacity to do so. The ability to think in complex contexts needs time to develop.

The Amazing Nervous system

Our autonomous nervous system is often divided into two main parts. It can be simplified into a brake (the parasympathetic part) and an accelerator (the sympathetic part). The brake helps us to stop, the accelerator activates us. The division into two parts makes it easier for us to talk about it. In fact, the nervous system and brain, when we study them, are not separate in the ways described and the brain is not divided into different parts in the way it is often portrayed. The brain is one organ that has regions that are more active in certain situations. But our brain, our nervous system and the rest of the body are constantly sharing information and are much more fluid than the separation of this into two categories can possibly describe. Therefore, we want to make sure to remember that this two-part system is a simplified description.

The process of creating physiological equilibrium called allostasis, is steered by the autonomic nervous system (both parasympathetic and sympathetic), the endocrine system (hormones) and the immune system. The accelerator, the sympathetic part, is (simply explained) responsible for the fight or flight mechanism, while the parasympathetic part, the brake, is responsible for resting and digesting functions in the body. The two parts work continuously within the same system to create balance.

With the help of the accelerator, the pupils dilate, the blood flow is redistributed from the digestive system to the skeletal muscles, the heartbeat increases, and blood pressure rises, in other words, we become ready to fight. Sympathetic activation prepares us for action by, among other things, activating the heart. When the parasympathetic nervous system has the lead, it helps us unwind from the excitement of sympathetic activation.

Reacting by wanting to escape or to defend ourselves by running or fighting, are often seen as the only choices we have, to deal with stress and are often described in a highly compartmentalized way. In fact, there are many variations on how we deal with danger, real or perceived. Stephen Porges' Polyvagal Theory introduces a third branch of the autonomic nervous system. He argues that social interaction, which is parasympathetic, simultaneously does more than just have a calming, numbing effect on our nervous system.[25]

Porges suggests that we need to better understand the parasympathetic collapse when we freeze or faun. These are common experiences associated with shame, as different from fight or flight. Perhaps we can see it as a third branch or simply recognize that there are multiple other ways where we become pacified, rather than activated, in the context of a stressful situation.

Therapists and psychologists have been studying and now know more about our bodies and our nervous system than ever before. The knowledge that we are both body and mind, (or one body-mind) can be used to find out what kind of support someone needs to deal with challenges to their well-being. Similarly, any adult dealing with children benefits greatly from understanding how children are physically affected by stress and humiliation. When we become annoyed that we are not able to connect with a child in a particular situation, it is valuable to stop and evaluate whether the child is even able to cope with the stress they are experiencing. If the child is overwhelmed to the point of "freeze," then criticism and blame probably are especially counter-productive, and the ability to take in even neutral information can be inhibited.

We humans are born vulnerable. Beautiful small creatures, unable to take care of ourselves, dependent on caregivers to meet our most basic needs, unable to move or find food and water without their support. An extraordinary being at the beginning of its development, relying completely on others to be able to experience satiety, well-being and rest.

This new little life is programmed with the expectation that the environment will give it what it needs but is also without the ability to communicate its needs through speech. We are born with the impulse to let the environment know, through sound and movement, when something is uncomfortable or pleasant. Vulnerable, but full of vitality to mature when the right conditions exist. The infant's vulnerability triggers a considerable amount of chemical and emotional processes in most of the adults around them, which contributes to the fact that in most cases care is given voluntarily.

Mirror neurons dance and ignite impulses within caregivers, prompting them to support the small, amazing, but vulnerable beings dependent on the outside world.

A newborn baby is receptive, which makes it easy to see the little life as a blank slate on which the world can paint whatever it wants. Because the thinking of children is so influenced by their environment, it is easy to assume that we can control exactly what they learn. But for the young individual in our arms, life began long before the moment of birth, and what can be called natural or inherent is not entirely obvious. Even genes are epigenetically influenced by the environment. For example, babies' vision develops normally only if their eyes are regularly exposed to light.

In addition to the fact that our genes are affected by what we encounter, we now know that our genetic material is not even fully complete when we leave the womb. Complementary genetic material can actually travel in bacteria that the child comes into contact with in his/her encounter with his/her caregivers.[26] We do not arrive in the world walking, talking or singing, but learn as we are supported to do so. We are loved into loving, smiled into smiling. We come into the world with an immature but powerful brain that, with the right support, can build and sort experiences such as dreams, thoughts, feelings and memories.

The difference between what is packed in our backpack of genes and what we pick up from the contexts we are born into, the culture, be it familiar or societal, cannot be completely separated. Or as Lisa Feldman Barrett puts it:

"We cannot attribute causes to genes alone or to the environment alone, because the two are like lovers in a fierce tango - so deeply entwined that it is unhelpful to call them two separate things like nature and nurture."[27]

Trying to separate what is innate or learned, natural or emerging from our socialization, does not seem to be the most helpful way to understand how we can be supportive of our children. Rather, the question we need to ask ourselves is, what kind of social, emotional, and physical support does the biological system best need to flourish.

Emotions such as curiosity, fear, loneliness, joy or sadness are rarely questioned in the same way as anger, guilt or shame. But all emotions are formed by our socialization process and over the decades of development our brain needs to grasp a complex world. We consider it natural for a child to stand up and take their first tentative steps at the age of one, even if they have shown no signs of walking before that. The seed for the development of the ability to talk, stand and walk is in our DNA. And in a similar way there is a base for qualities like kindness and compassion.

As the child gets older and their brain matures, different skills develop. Eventually children take steps towards compassion as they begin to take in the reality of other people. They can experience hope because they start to understand time and can visualize future events in different ways. However, even unpleasant feelings of shame, humiliation and embarrassment are important parts of relationships and cooperation and, being social beings, they gradually grow into a part of us.

If we look at a child as a blank slate, open for others to write its story on, all power is in the hands of the adults. This view suggests that when the child turns out to be talented, moral and a well-functioning individual, it is because the caregivers have done a good job. If, conversely, the child proves difficult to cooperate with, displays what we call selfish behavior, or exhibits a lack of sensitivity towards others, it is often attributed to shortcomings in their upbringing. Parents are perceived as having been overly strict, excessively lenient, emotionally distant, or providing poor role modeling. With such a weight of responsibility, it's natural for parents to feel ashamed when their child encounters challenges.

When we lack tools to deal with shame, it is easy to try to get rid of the feelings by controlling the child as soon as they are about to do something that makes us ashamed. At best, our interventions support them in understanding how a social context works. At worst, it prevents them from exploring things that could help them develop.

Through the lens of science, we're now more attuned to the profound impact of not just the circumstances of birth, but also the intricate interplay of genetics and individual chemistry on every person's journey. Each individual is a tapestry woven from a myriad of influences: the unique moments that shape their lives, the nurturing they receive, the landscapes that surround them, the spiritual values passed down through generations, and the zeitgeist of their era. Research even illuminates the enchanting bond between a mother and her child, suggesting that early taste preferences often reflect this intimate connection.

Because so many components affect everyone's life, it is far too simplistic to assume that a single context or event is all that matters. We are individuals shaped by a collective just as the collective is shaped by the individual. Different potentially traumatic situations affect us more than others, but some people are less affected by what happens, depending on what they have experienced before.

In addition to the context we are born into, the gene set we carry, not only as an individual, but as a species, influences how our life develops. A newborn horse stands up after only half an hour, while for humans, with our large brain to balance, it takes at least a year before we leave a crawling life behind. We are born without protective fur, but with the ability to develop speech, memory, morality, time perception and compassion, which means there are already lines filled in on the infant's page, but also exclamation and question marks.

In a supportive environment free from significant stress, everyone's brain and nervous system develop, accessing new brainwaves that facilitate growth at different stages. As part of their development the cultural norms that shape a young baby will later be questioned and re-evaluated by them, if we are to believe theorists such as Piaget, Kohlberg and Kegan.[28]

A baby is initially unaware of itself as a separate entity. During the first months, it gradually develops the capacity to find a way to sort color and shape, allowing it to gradually distinguish what is important, such as the face of a caregiver. Activities like peekaboo games where an adult suddenly disappears from the child's field of vision - engages them and have been shown to stimulate their visualization skills. After a while, they can see with their 'inner eye' that the important person is still near-by and only disappears out of sight temporarily.

By learning to associate sounds with an internal image, the child eventually understands that the person is in another room even when they can't see them. The development goes from being one with the caregiver to becoming their own self, which is both more vulnerable and more empowering. Although the child has physically separated from the caregiver, the emotional separation takes a few more months.

Even long after the physical umbilical cord has been cut, a sort of hormonal umbilical cord exists. The discovery of infant parents' release of the 'happy hormone' oxytocin was initially linked to breast feeding mothers. Later, comparative studies with the father or other caregivers showed - contrary to what was assumed - that their oxytocin levels also increase when they are with the baby.

It is easy to think in evolutionary terms and link how the task of parenting is supported by the happiness hormones dancing around in their bodies, since the infant's well-being is so closely linked to the care they receive. Given the pleasure and calmness the hormone stimulates, it is not surprising that adults often overlook any chaos the child creates. The sense of well-being protects the child well for the first years.

Young children are unaware that their environment perceives them as individuals who need constant care. They signal what they need, without considering that they should be less demanding.

Even if the first signs of shame develop early, it will take time for the emotion to mature or be given a name. The first four to five years of an individual's life are self-centered. Two-year-olds are small opportunists, seeing the world from their own perspective, receiving what comes their way. Their focus is on survival, and what they need and want, rather than what others need. They use other people to meet their needs. The child needs stimulation that is adapted to where they are at developmentally. At the same time, they rely on support of others and therefore submit to the power of adults.

Gradually, most children develop from being egocentric, and playmates become increasingly important. Sometime between the ages of four and seven years, feelings of shame in a child usually become more apparent.

The individual changes from only having a first-person perspective (it's all about me) to also having the ability to see something from another person's point of view, (others also need and want something). One of the effects of shame is that it can become a reminder to consider others and their needs.

Although there are many different functional variations, physical development for most children goes from learning to sit, to standing, to being able to walk, to running and eventually jumping and dancing. Young children typically learn words and concepts at a rapid pace. Cognitively, they develop the ability to visualize, to see something inside, to understand symbols and words, to think in time, all simultaneously on several different levels as in a complicated play, with subordinate meanings and unspoken relationships.

The child understands increasingly complex concepts, follows more complicated stories and can learn rhymes and songs. Emotionally, the child learns to ask for things they like, to seek support when they are sad, or comfort when they are scared, but they are still dependent on others in many ways.

At times, development appears straightforward. Other times, it resembles a spiral, where mastering one ability precedes the installation of the next, with challenges recurring at deeper levels later on.

Maturity Begins With the Support of an Inner Self

The one-year-old stands up for the first time, loses her balance and tumbles to the ground. A moment later, perhaps after a bit of crying over the humiliation in a caregiver's arms, the child is ready to try again. The sounds that come across a child's lips when they manage to take those first proud steps are wonderful to a parent's ears.

The whole world is at their little feet and every day they leave the safety of the caregivers' lap and the journey of discovery extends further. The power to create their own journey intoxicates and inspires them to look further afield. The child's happiness at having just mastered an important developmental step makes them feel invincible and adds building blocks to their temple of independence.

An infant who stays calm often meets approval and goes through the first year of life without much difficulties, at least, if they have relatively well-functioning adults around them. When the child gathers strength and stands up, the various functions of the brain and body are aligned, social connection strengthens, and the child's opportunities are multiplied. A mobile child also encounters more boundaries - and perhaps disapproval - and needs to balance this with their desire to explore.

The brain and nervous system enable us to register experiences as pleasant or unpleasant. Uncomfortable signals help us to seek acceptance from our surroundings when we are young, without even being able to put into words what is going on inside, or what we need physically. Parenting is largely about influencing children's body balance to help them interact with the environment.

Feedback from the caregiver alternates between encouragement to continue doing something and discouragement to stop doing something else. Approval comes in the form of words, sounds, hugs, and smiles. What is pleasant is balanced against what is unpleasant by the curious explorer. Disapproval is expressed in words, but also in the form of sighs, facial expressions, and grimaces, such as fur-rowed eyebrows.

Parents' - and other adults' - messages and values are step by step integrated within the child and continue to guide the child for the rest of their life, hopefully in a supportive way. Likes and dislikes are transformed into an 'inner parent' to help navigate through life. Growing self-awareness gives access to more choices to act on the internalized impulses, but it does not mean that the impulses disap-pear. Throughout life, our parents' approval and disapproval live within us, but as adults we can sometimes turn a blind eye to them.

While still in a dependent position, the child can easily shift into a passive state if a significant adult breaks eye contact with them. The muscles of the neck lose strength and the upper body becomes tense. This is a clever survival reflex but is unlikely to be a conscious feeling of shame yet. The child is in the cradle of its emotional development and will travel between phases where either the self or the collective is important and where different emotions will be central in different life situations.

Before the age of two, most children develop the ability to react to disapproval or specific tones and words. Their innate capacity to construct emotions and align their inner selves with their outward expressions enhances their sense of belonging to a group.

Vocabulary grows and provides the child with categories (such as fruit, vehicles, colors and, later, emotions) that help them sort internal and external experiences. The child perceives whether they are liked and therefore likely to be safe. Even before the age of two, most children have developed enough to react when an adult shows disapproval, uses certain words or a certain tone of voice. The innate ability to construct emotions and adapt their inner self to the outer world helps the child to socialize in a way that increases their chances of survival.

Even if a child doesn't have the cognitive ability to understand a situation where they are met with disapproval, they can perceive whether they are disapproved of, or approved of, and therefore when they are likely to be safe. Eventually the child leaves this impulse driven, receptive stage of development and becomes more self-centeredly active.

During the period when children are developing their physical abilities, learning to walk and run, they become increasingly independent, while at the same time realizing that they need adults to help them manage their emotions.

A two-year-old looks around and realizes that she is far away from her caregiver and starts crying. The panic occurs without having encountered any external danger other than distance. The child uses their caregivers to regulate any discomfort they feel at any perceived threat to their safety and survival. A hug or a kind word calms the child's racing brain. The calming support from outside supports the child's growing ability to calm themselves. Emotions such as shame, joy, curiosity, and fear help the child to learn to regulate how far they want to move from their caregiver. In this way emotions help them and gets a place in the emotional vocabulary.

Until children start walking, they often receive a great deal of encouragement. Adults rejoice in each small progress; that they are crawling, sitting, eating, standing. Young children are rarely held accountable for their actions, such as accidentally peeing on somebody or vomiting on someone's clothes. Most of it is explained away by "they were obviously not doing it on purpose."

For adults, placing responsibility or blame on an infant usually feels wrong. We don't see them as responsible because they are not able to control their actions in the way we expect them to as they get older. If they accidentally slap us with an uncontrolled hand movement, we are unlikely to think that their intention was to hurt us, even if the flying little hand hit us in a way that is painful.

Babies' impulse driven perspectives, where they grab anything that seems interesting and make sounds to let the world know when they are missing something, is rarely held against them. As caregivers, we are usually willing to take responsibility for any effects a baby's aging has on others. We might offer to wash someone's clothes if baby poop or some other kind of mess has landed on them. We wipe up the food that flew away when an uncontrolled mini-foot managed to get an unexpectedly well-aimed kick at a plate. Maybe we get the dish cloth with a sigh of fatigue, but rarely one of rejection or judgment of the child.

While a baby who knocks over a glass of juice will hear a murmur at most, an older child might be met with harsh words over spilled drinks or loud play. During these first magic months, the child is allowed to live in his or her self-centered world. We assume and accept that the young individual has no capacity to do more than the simplest of things. As soon as the child begins to talk, walk and interact with others, a period of socialization begins that shapes the individual for the rest of their life. A two-year-old child hears more frustration and disapproval than an infant. The child is repeatedly asked not only to care for herself, but also to act with growing consideration for others.

The capacity to feel both shame and compassion is nurtured and matured by the contexts in which we grow up. Shame develops as the child moves on from being totally self-centered. They slowly begin to be able to see and understand others. The child moves from being an opportunist to taking in their environment and distinguishing it from themselves.

Although shame is described as a socially constructed emotion, this does not mean that it is less important than other emotional experiences, as shame is an important part of developing cooperation and compassion. Humans are social beings who are shaped to relate to other people by innate instincts that are affected by how we are treated. Like other mammals, we develop in groups. But our brain differs from other mammals in several ways.[29]

An infant receives their first lessons in managing their mind, in relation to a few people close to them; the closest caregivers such as parents, grandparents or others who regularly interact with them. In an intricate way, they adjust their internal system to fit the contexts they face. Using signals (facial expressions, cries, or other sounds) to indicate that they need support and by accepting the support they receive, they gradually learn to manage impulses from within. Throughout life, contacts with the outside world expand to include friends and teachers, and eventually colleagues, lovers and perhaps their own children.

Child development is both about making deeper connections and growing to be self-sufficient and independent. We all understand that young children who do not have their physical needs for water, light, nutrition and air, met do not thrive or even survive. What we may not realize is that even a lack of social stimulation, presence, and touch can also lead to physical ailments, trauma, depression and increased risk of suicide. Marshall Rosenberg had a specific view of human needs that went beyond what we physically need: "I use the term needs to describe resources that life needs to sustain itself. For example, our physical well-being depends on meeting our needs for air, water, rest and nutrition. When our needs for understanding, support, honesty and meaning are met, our psychological and spiritual well-being increases."[30]

In the 1960s, the Romanian government under leader Nicolae Ceausescu pushed for a ban on contraception and abortion with the plan to grow as a nation. This led to a large number of overcrowded orphanages as many families were unable to support more children. Orphanage staff changed diapers and washed the children, but rarely had time to give them affection and attention and no one played with them. Many of the children died early, despite receiving food and basic care. Others survived but, according to follow-up studies, often went on to lead difficult lives as adults. Significant deficiencies in their social capacities led to many becoming homeless, without the ability to deeply connect with others or form a family. Several had clear difficulties with concentration and dealing with distractions, leading to learning difficulties. There was also a clear over-representation of suicide and alcoholism among them.

While ignored young children can be damaged, it is not only young children who suffer from not being connected with other people. If this were not the case, it would not be possible, for example, to threaten people in prison with solitary confinement. We humans are wired to live in groups and relationships, and we deteriorate on various levels when we have no one to relate to. In the movie Cast Away, Tom Hanks plays a plane crash survivor, landing on an island with no other humans. One of his survival strategies is to paint a face on a volleyball he names Wilson, which allows him to maintain a dialogue and thus survive for a long time. This movie illustrates how important it is for us to relate to others, to see and be seen.

A simplified description of parenting is the result of the relationships and communication a child has with others while growing up. While understanding the young individual's desire to explore and experience new things, caregivers also need to remember that children learn about boundaries and the needs of others through interaction. Caregivers help when they demonstrate personal and environmental boundaries, while expressing preferences and acceptance, supporting the child to find functional ways to relate. Shame, or the child reacting in some way remorsefully when they have crossed someone's boundaries, becomes part of parenting without having to use blaming language to blame the kids.

Researcher Silvan Tomkins claimed that "the purpose of shame is to motivate us to repair social relationships." Even if emotions might lack innate meaning in the way it may sound like in the quote from Tomkins it is a beautiful reminder of how humans interact. It is in our most important relationships that we usually receive help to transform negative shame experiences and to integrate what is at the core of them.

The Maturing Brain

Our ability to anticipate what might happen next and create appropriate emotions in response has helped us survive as a species. We continuously regulate our body's energy budget with physical signals of feelings of thirst and fatigue that motivate us to drink and rest. The way we interpret our inner life of affects, feelings, emotions and thoughts decides how successfully we move through the world.

Fear and nervousness are important emotional preparations if we sense that we are facing dangers that we need to be alert to. Curiosity about something unknown helps us learn new things. We feel and think, we understand and act. The brain receives information and transforms what we experience into memories. These memories are stored in our brain's growing conceptualizations, so that we can retrieve the information we need to prepare for the next situation.

Learning and memory functions are complex processes we often take for granted, until they don't work. Explicit memory begins to be used at around 18 months and plays an important role in all learning. To elicit memories, we need to be able to focus, think and stay curious about what we want to remember. When we meet a person we have little interest in getting to know, such as a cashier in a shop we visit once, we don't get emotionally involved and therefore forget the person after only a short time.

Emotions help our brain to associate and therefore to remember, and they don't necessarily get in the way of logic- as sometimes assumed- but can actually help it. But being overwhelmed by too many impressions can inhibit the ability to remember, as excessive brain activation motivates us to act rather than concentrate and try to retrieve knowledge. For example, feelings of shame are an ordeal for both children and grown-ups, as it becomes almost impossible to focus on what we were doing the moment before. Confused, we make decisions that are not constructive as our brain is more focused on survival and belonging than on creativity and perspective-taking.

Just before the age of two, there is an important step in the development of most individuals. The child begins to experience pride in his or her own actions but also accesses the feeling of shyness. The broadened perspective of the two-year-old also means that they can begin to feel light shame if they fail at something. Feelings of shame mature alongside the capacity to register memories and compare capacities. Shame doesn't just show up from one day to another but is part of the process of becoming a part of a group or social structure. Emotions are based on language and categories and therefore change with development and perspective taking.

Now the child walks more steadily, formulates simple sentences, and increasingly explores their environment. The capacity to observe oneself has grown, along with the ability to judge what works and what doesn't, in different situations. Even at this young age some children learn to lie. They might use plain denial to avoid the discomfort they fear will wash over them if it becomes obvious that they were the ones who ate all the cinnamon buns on the kitchen counter.

Experiences the child has at this age, and how they are treated, are stored in their memory bank even if they are unable to go back and remember. Gradually, the child's capacity to merge memories of previous positive and negative messages from adults matures, so that they can become more independent, without the risk of being excluded.

Active Two-year-olds

While grown-ups may find a child's quest for new adventures delightful, their eagerness to learn about all aspects of life can sometimes be overwhelming. The role of the caregiver goes from being an enabler to becoming a boundary-setter, a doorman instead of a festival visitor.

In the space of a few days, children at this age will hear and face more "NOs" than in their entire life so far. While limitations may inhibit curiosity to some extent, for most children the desire to participate in life is stronger than the fear of dislike. So, learning continues, and is helped by the fact that children at this age are no longer treated with the same unconditional acceptance as when they were younger.

The drive to develop causes several problems. And the child matures with the conflicts presented to them. The child wants to explore, and balance and coordination rarely develop at the same pace as curiosity. Sometimes the result is a broken vase. Other times an overturned glass of milk, or a painting ends up on the floor instead of in the drawing pad. The child, perceiving the disapproving tone of the adults' voice and seeing the raised eyebrow, hides his face in his hands as if to make himself invisible.

Confronted with a mistake, the child blurts out an "it wasn't me." The person they interact may not be angry, just stressed or worried, but the child, not yet knowing how to take responsibility for their behavior, reacts by trying to escape the uncomfortable sense of not being accepted.

We might go the other way in order to avoid meeting someone who once made us feel ashamed, in a desperate attempt to avoid feeling the same way again. We avoid going into a shop where we previously felt shame, or we might refuse to perform an act - like singing in public - if we have been laughed at previously. Memories is not only a cognitive process but an emotional one.

For similar reasons, children do not want to look at someone's face when a shard of the broken vase is held up in front of them. Even if we are able to own up to something we have done later in life, the idea of hiding to avoid feelings of shame remains. Many people find themselves covering their mouths when they have said something they regret. Others hide their face and eyes in their hands when a mistake is revealed.

One benefit of learning how our own shame affects us, is that it gives us a better understanding of how uncomfortable it can feel for others, regardless of age, when they are overwhelmed by shame. It allows for greater patience, connection and perhaps even compassion.

Remember, just because you understand that someone is ashamed of a mistake and needs your acceptance, doesn't mean you have to let go of your desire for someone (be it a child or another adult) to act differently. At what point we bring up our requests for change is a matter of timing.

It might help us cope better in a situation where a child avoids looking at some unappreciated mess they have created (a broken vase or a piece of chalk art on a wall), if we assume it is their way of mitigating internal stress. The child looks away from the scene of the crime, knowing from the adult's tone of voice that they have done something bad. This is a smart way of keeping their young sympathetic nervous system in check. They may even avoid eye contact with the adult, but this avoidance is not about avoiding responsibility, as responsibility is still too big of a concept for them.

Simply put, shame management with young children is about showing that we see them and holding them in our arms (or touching them) if they accept it. We show that we are on the "same team" as them, whether or not we are frustrated by their actions. To teach the child about interacting with others, it is important to let them know how others are affected by their behavior. An adult task is to take care of children's needs without giving up on our own, even if it means we often have to wait longer to get them met.

Touch, often but not always, helps people to relax. A hug or a peck on the cheek often does wonders for a stiff little body. After an embrace, the strongest denial (also combined with being caught with "fingers in the cookie jar") subsides. But there are exceptions. For some individuals, touching *increases* the intensity of shame attacks. Already here the individual's personality has begun to emerge.

Somewhere around the age of two, the child, with its growing sense of an inner 'self', begins to feel the first signs of pride. The desire for independence grows, and the words "I can do it myself" sometimes hurts the adults' ears. It is time for us adults to take that long breath, let the child try it for themselves, evaluate whether they actually need help, and ask ourselves whether we can tolerate something taking longer and happening in a different way than we would like.

A parent who always takes over to protect the child from making mistakes contributes to children's awkwardness or inability to start their own projects. Perhaps it is better that they are allowed to try and even fail, even if it would mean a whiff of shame?

4

INSTALLING OF THE BRAIN'S AUTOPILOT

To explore how shame affects us through different life stages, chapters three to five and eight focus on different levels of development where age and biological maturity play a role. This chapter focuses on the period when the child develops towards becoming rule-oriented and independent. We will explore the process of the parent "moving in" and the auto-pilot being installed.

The Parent Moves In

We come into the world with simple ways of relating to our environment. As mammals, we instinctively know that we need a caregiver to look after us. But now we begin the journey of making it on our own in the world outside of that safe haven. Like a butterfly leaving its chrysalis and spreading its wings, we evolve from a self-absorbed baby to a curious toddler that is starting to explore danger and safety, and concepts like *yours* and *mine, you* and *me*.

At two and a half Emma can proudly name the animals someone points to and knows that both dogs and cats fall into the animal category. She also knows the names of many colors and knows that colors are their own category. Her mother Mari has just read an article about how children's perspectives change over the years. The article talked about how children all the way up to three years of age don't understand that others see the world from a different perspective than they do, and Mari wonders if this is really true. To test what she read, Mari uses a small ball that is yellow on one side and blue on the other. She turns the ball a few times in front of her daughter, showing the blue and yellow colors. Then she stops with the yellow side facing Emma and asks which color she sees.

"Yellow," Emma says and points at the ball.

"Great! And what color do I see?"

"Yellow," says Emma quickly.

Although Mari understands that this is the usual outcome, she repeats it a few more times (although she is a bit ashamed, as she wants to treat her child with respect). Mari realizes that Emma really does not have the capacity to understand that Mari has the blue side facing her, no matter how hard she tries to make her daughter understand it. As soon as that side of the ball is out of Emma's sight, she "forgets" it and thinks that everyone, like her, sees it as yellow.

The discovery relieves Mari, as she realizes that Emma's self-absorption and limited ability to take on others' perspectives are normal for her age. She gets a little regretful when she remembers that she has blamed Emma for being selfish. If she isn't capable of understanding someone else's perspective, how can it be selfish to help herself to what she wants?

As days go by, Emma begins to differentiate more and more between herself and her mother. Her ability to observe herself from the outside also grows. The more she experiences the "you" of others, the clearer her own "I" becomes. Usually she plays alone and chooses her own games, but even if she does not understand co-play, she likes company and others are welcome to play alongside her. She gradually learns to adapt to caregivers' expectations in order to gain their approval. The more she has to balance between their approval and making her own decisions, the more vulnerable she is to shame coming in as a calibrating factor.

Her learning style has changed from infant receptive to a more active exploration of the world. With the help of adult approval and disapproval, potty training has paid off and she happily tells everyone that she no longer needs a diaper. She has learned a lot about what is considered nice or kind and what she can and cannot play with. Sometimes she protests when someone sets a limit for her but adapts if she finds another way to have fun. Progressively, she develops her own inner parent. Now disapproval comes from within if she poops her pants, but also praise if she manages to get to the toilet in time. Comfortable and uncomfortable feelings are reinforced with outside help and become part of her brain's autopilot, and shame and guilt become a big part in balancing her inner environment.

The Brain's Autopilot

Like all mammals, we humans want to ensure that we remain included in our group. As part of doing so, we form an internal navigation system to quickly access information about how we ought to act in different situations. In order to maximize the odds of safety, the thought patterns of "should" lay the groundwork for the brain's autopilot. The growing ability to use internal instructions on how to behave helps us to become independent as the parent's voice is now inside of us.

Later in life, thoughts about how we 'should' behave feel demanding like restrictive enemies and we do everything we can to silence them. But it is not very constructive to use energy in getting rid of these patterns. It is less energy consuming to make friends with the brain's autopilot, rather than spending energy fighting such a clever super function.[31]

Tom and Emma, who both got seduced by a fluttering tablecloth at the age of 14 months, eventually celebrate their third birthday. Emma is a big girl now (if you ask her anyway) and blows out the three little candles on the strawberry cake (without noticing that her mother, who is standing behind her back, is helping a little). Emma looks around for praise from the birthday party guests. As everyone applauds, she straightens her back and smiles.

With the help of adults, Emma is learning what she should and shouldn't do. This gives contours to her self-image, which increases her sensitivity to being ashamed if she doesn't manage to live up to it. When she makes a mistake, she is sometimes more disappointed than an adult would be.

Although boys and girls receive somewhat different messages about what they "should do", Tom, like Emma, has integrated his first "should-patterns." Tom picks up on the dislikes and likes he encounters from his environment and they get included in what he does and what he refrains from doing. Hopefully the demand to be a boy is not so great that it stifles all the space he needs as a person.

When Emma, at the age of three, sees the neighbor's cat, she quickly waddles over to the grey-speckled creature. She sinks down in front of it and presses her little hands into its fur. It feels wonderful. With all ten fingers she grabs it and pulls it towards her. The cat howls and Mari, who is standing behind them but not in time to protect the unfortunate animal, picks up Emma and tells her loudly that this is no way to treat animals. Emma sees her mother's upset face, recognizes the accusatory tone in her voice and looks away. Even if Mari got quite angry at her daughter, she holds her long enough for their connection to be reestablished and they have both calmed down.

Numerous similar interactions, where Emma learns the significance of respecting boundaries through experiencing shame, gradually intertwine and become integrated into her autopilot. Whether she recalls the attack on the first cat or not, her autopilot prevents her from repeating the same action. If she is about to do something that can hurt an animal, she feels some nuance of shame, perhaps guilt, as a result of the internalized "should-pattern" that slows her down. In a few years, when Emma has deepened her thinking, partly because her memory has developed, she can take the cat's perspective and realize that it needs care.

In order to be accepted by those around them, Tom and Emma strive to act in line with the should patterns that are being shaped by their family, culture, religion, social system and zeitgeist. As control moves inside, they become more independent from having adults remind them of how to behave. Through uncomfortable emotions such as fear, guilt and shame, they are alerted to when they are about to miss any expectations of their inner parent.

"Bad girl, it wasn't nice of me to tear down Tom's Lego house," Emma exclaims.

At five, she understands more about how to relate to her environment and her should patterns help her by following her into adulthood, supported by her increasingly integrated understanding of what leads to disapproval and approval. Initially, our inner "shoulds" include only us, but later evolve to include others. We are social beings and our expectations of how others should behave, think, talk, feel, dress, grow hand in hand with our expectations of ourselves.

Their maturing brains help Emma and Tom expand their language skills. They are rapidly growing their vocabulary and developing the capacity to handle time concepts such as future and past.

One day when Tom visits Emma, he spots her toy ambulance and pulls it out of her hand. Emma squeals loudly and tries to take it back. Tom's mother rushes over and tries to get him to let go of it.

Both children cry and claim that the ambulance is theirs. As Tom's mother feels embarrassed, she tries to convince him that it is not his toy and that he should return it.

"Don't you see how upset Emma gets when you take her toy without asking for permission?" she says, ashamed that her son is so dominant.

And it gets even more confusing when Emma says, "It's mine!"

Doesn't 'mine' mean its Tom's? Tom is unable to grasp the idea of ownership, since he is holding the toy, surely it must belong to him?

"You have to learn to share, you can play with all your toys later, when Tom has gone home." Emma's mother says in a quiet tone to her daughter. Mari misses the fact that her young daughters' sense of time is not developed enough for her to feel comfortable with her mother's words, so her words don't help Emma a lot at this very moment.

Since Tom's mother can't stand the conflict anymore, she pulls the toy out of his hands and gives it to Emma who smiles and stops crying. But then she sees that Tom is crying and continues to cry and that is upsetting to her. Tom turns around and walks away. When Tom's mother follows to try to get him to apologize, Emma nods and says,

"Tom bad, say you are sorry."

But Tom doesn't do as his mother asks of him and she threatens him about going home if he doesn't learn to be nice. Tom stiffens up under the threat and his mother's growing frustration and can't say a thing, let alone an apology that he doesn't understand.

Tom and Emma's ability to reflect on what they feel, and think is still at the beginning of a long journey. When Tom feels sad, in that moment he *is* that emotion. When Emma feels angry, she *is* her anger. Neither of them has enough self-distance to observe the feeling.

As part of working with others, Emma has learned to say "sorry" as soon as someone seems to want to hear it. She has noticed that this little word somehow magically calms adults' upset emotions. Their calmness affects the way they treat her, which in turn makes her less worried about them being unhappy with her.

In Tom's family, an "I'm sorry" doesn't go far, you have to mean it. He doesn't yet understand that he is expected to show a look of regret, so he rarely uses the word because it never seems to help. Tom has difficulty understanding how to behave in a way that makes adults happy. When he has done something he is ashamed of, he has learned that looking away from the mistake or a shaming adult, makes him calmer. If turning away doesn't help, he distracts himself with an object or walks away. Tom's behavior is generally more difficult for adults to tolerate than Emma's.

Other ways to regulate feelings of shame that children obtain access to at this stage is to blame yourself or someone else - one of Emma's favorite expressions is "Tom, bad." Both expressions are simple attempts to regain balance and adapt to external expectations. In order to test how different expectations work, Emma periodically becomes extremely principled.

"It wasn't nice of Tom to take my toy, he's not kind. A good child doesn't take things from others."

Emma's challenge is eventually to balance what she has learned about what a "nice child" (in this case Tom) should do with what she has also learned about "how important it is to share." She is entering a period where the friend becomes more interesting than the toy, but so far, she is working hard to integrate the understanding of yours and mine. The clash between different messages creates challenges in her young system, but also helps her to develop.

The "parent" who is integrating within the children has not yet fully moved in, so they still need outside help to deal with difficult emotions. Knowing your child's developmental level is one way to adjust to what to expect from your child.

Self Distance

In our first weeks of life, we do not feel separate from the outside world, we have no separate inner self, no separately developed 'I.' We grab a small foot and study it with interest, not realizing that it is somehow connected to the rest of our body. When we put our big toe in our mouth and bite it, however, we notice that it feels a certain way.

After some exploration, we discover that there is a difference between this foot and, say, Dad's thumb, which doesn't hurt to bite. Bit by bit, our physical identity is built. It takes some more time before we can also experience an emotional self and begin to want to play and relate to others.

Tom and Emma soon realize that they are not the center of the universe, but part of a context such as their family. They move from an *I*, and after some time understand others as *you*, to eventually becoming part of a *we*. When their inner parent can control most of their interactions, their caregivers no longer need to monitor everything. Inner structures for cooperation and caring have been built and they can start having fun together with friends.

A year after Mari first held up the blue-yellow ball, she shows it to Emma again. Now she understands that her mother sees the ball as blue, even though the yellow side is facing her. Emma has evolved from a first-person perspective (I, me, my, mine) to also being able to understand the perspective of others (you, your, yours).

Although Mari is relieved to realize the first time in her small experiment, that her daughter was at a developmental stage where this was not possible, she is even more relieved to see that her daughter can now understand the viewpoint of others a bit more.

Mari has read that this perspective lays the foundation for empathetic listening, conflict management and cooperation, all qualities she values.

Since Emma has come a long way in being able to put strong emotions into words, she can more often calm down by herself. But under stress, it is still difficult to separate herself from her emotions. When she turns five, she gets a bicycle and tries it out with her mother. They meet a neighbor on the street who bends over and ruffles Emma's hair. Unable to keep her balance, she wobbles and falls off the bike.

"Good thing you're so small that it wasn't that far to fall," says the neighbor with a laugh.

Emma gets up, kicks gravel at the neighbor and, without paying attention to her new vehicle, heads home.

"What a little thundercloud," says the neighbor.

"Excuse me, she's probably hungry," Mari says quickly.

There are still a few years to go before Emma will have developed enough self-distance to appreciate a joke at her expense. Even some adults have trouble dealing with someone making fun of them, but sometimes we seem to forget that young children have more to lose by being in that position.

Emma leaves in an attempt to get away from the humiliating situation. She might just as well have turned silent, or hit, bitten or screamed at the neighbor. Instead of responding to Emma's actions by explaining away the neighbor's behavior with expressions such as "It wasn't serious" or "he was just joking," it would have been valuable for Mari to have also shown that she understood that Emma experienced humiliation and has a need for dignity.

Emma's eleven-year-old brother Benjamin snorts disdainfully at Emma's outburst, calling her spoiled and childish. He knows he is older but has forgotten how he behaved when he was younger. Benjamin does not know that it is only at his age that an individual has developed a sufficiently stable self-image that allows them to laugh at themselves sometimes.

Self-criticism plays an important role in our development and in our ability to self-regulate our behavior. The ability to live up to what is expected of us, both from what we ourselves expect and what others expect of us, leads to pride and self-respect. When we fail to live up to our standards, it is stressful and, at best, we learn something. If the expectations of the environment are not continuously aligned with what is reasonable at a certain stage of maturity, it affects the relationship between the caregiver and the child negatively.

If adults do not recognize that the child's capacity for self-reflection or second-person perspective is limited, there is a risk that they will expect what the child is not capable of. It is like expecting someone to be able to speak a foreign language without having learned it. The task of the caregiver is to ensure that the child's frustration is high enough to allow them to learn new things but not so high that it creates harmful stress or over exaggerated self-criticism.

Self-image Provides Direction

The contours of our self-image is sharpened by self-criticism and "should" patterns, creating a container that provides an inner space to relax in. Feelings of shame are created by a mismatch between our behaviors and our self-image.

I shouldn't make my dad feel sad.

I should let other children play with my toys.

The content of the "should" patterns changes as the person matures:

I shouldn't have parked my car so that it takes up two parking spaces.

I should call my mom, she's sick.

And later on, the growing value system creates an even clearer self-image.

I want to be friendly and kind.

I want to spend more time with my family.

I want to get involved in social change.

When we learn to accept that we sometimes feel shame, similar to the way we accept hunger, even if neither one is our favorite experience, it becomes easier to live with. Even if we are hungry, we are able to wait a while to eat and in the same way, it eventually becomes possible to stop and feel shame without immediately trying to get rid of the feeling. Feeling ashamed when we have not lived up to our own expectations is part of having high ideals and values.

It does not mean that we accept others shaming or humiliating us, but only that we can be present with our inner self before deciding on the best way to deal with a situation.

Tom's older cousins come to visit. During a game, one of them calls Tom a coward and a baby and the cousins both laugh out loud. Tom, who has just turned five, has very little capacity for self-distance and feels uncomfortable with the words and the cousins' laughter. It is vulnerable to feel that one's need for dignity is not being met and Tom deals with it by lashing out. In an attempt to escape the humiliating situation, Tom kicks sand in the eyes of one cousin and stomps away.

After a moment, Tom turns around and goes to see his mother to tell her what happened. She tries to convince him to let go of the situation.

"You shouldn't care so much. And maybe you weren't so nice either? You probably misunderstood them."

What Tom needs is someone who first and foremost understands his discomfort. Maybe also someone to help him set healthy boundaries with other children or help him communicate with them. One way to approach someone who is embarrassed when their self-image is made fun of, is to offer words to describe the experience, while avoiding words that risk increasing embarrassment.

"Did you feel embarrassed when you heard what she said? Do you want to be seen as five years old now? And not be called a baby?"

While we, as caregivers, strive to communicate as well as possible, the most important thing is not to find exactly the right words, but to show that we are trying to understand the world from their perspective. The focus is on creating connection, which is supported by the choice of words, but also by tone, gestures, and timing. Eye contact or touch works in some situations, while in others it gets in the way of deeper connection.

Intriguingly, most five-year-old's start feeling shame imagining someone catching them with their hand in the candy jar and so they may avoid putting it there. Without their small fingers having even visited the jar, their ability to imagine a future scenario begins to intertwine with their imagined choices. Impulses and thoughts are regulated by the updated autopilot that creates appropriate responses. As the individual's emotional space widens, the ability to imagine, visualize and understand time perspectives grows. The idea of a parent yelling at them with an angry face can make children avoid a forbidden attraction, without the parent being around. The outside regulator moves inside, and the inside regulator shows itself on the outside.

Eventually, five and soon six candles adorn the birthday cake and Tom and Emma grasp that one activity follows another, day becomes evening, night leads to morning. They begin to cope with the awkwardness of waiting for something fun to happen later. They become familiar with feelings of guilt - an inner discomfort at the thought of something they did in the past (e.g. taking a couple of sweets from a forbidden jar ten minutes ago and suspecting that someone might discover it). There are still some years until they are ready to laugh at themselves and the self-image they hold.

Raising the Bar of Expectation

When a two-year-old struggles to learn to eat by himself, he is met with warmth even though most of the butter from his sandwich ends up on his cheeks. When the same child has turned five and sometimes fails to put everything in his mouth, he is told he is sloppy and messy. The two-year-old who couldn't wait to devour a tempting sweet was praised for his appetite. When the five-year-old can't wait for the same treat, without whining, he's called immature. This is how the five-year-old learns, but it can also feel painful and unfair.

Most adults do not accuse an individual younger than three years old of being selfish in the same way we judge older children or adults. We may even laugh at the young child's self-centeredness and find it charming that they claim to own everything that comes their way. Confident that our child will get past those phases where they focus very little on how others are doing, we accept self-centeredness as part of their development. Most adults accept the young individual's limitations and recognize that they need support to develop things like language, relationships and understanding about cooperation.

If we simply adjust our expectations only by age, we might miss the fact that there is great variation in human development and become unclear in our "you're a big girl now" or "that's not how a big boy behaves," comments. We think these are clear, yet they are perceived as vague - requests that are difficult to interpret, that the young individual needs help in coding to be able to grasp.

Young children have difficulty balancing their energy budget on their own and are best served by a strong attachment to the adults around them. The terms homeostasis or more correctly allostasis are used to describe the process to achieve balance as soon as the body lacks something. In her book *Seven and a Half Lessons about the*

Brain, Lisa Feldman Barrett uses the term 'body budget' to describe allostasis.

"You can think of the body's energy efficiency as a budget. A financial budget tracks money coming in and money being spent. In a similar way, your body budget keeps track of resources like water, salt, glucose and how they flow in and go out. Any action that uses resources, like swimming or running, is like a withdrawal from your account. Actions that replenish resources, like eating or sleeping, are like deposits... your brain guesses when to use resources and when to save them.[32]

According to Feldman Barrett we affect each other's "budget" with our actions and words. It is easy to see that a young child's energy budget is closely linked to their caregiver. If the caregiver acts calmly, it affects the child, just as upset or tiredness does.

The older the child gets, the less their selfishness is accepted by those around them. It is easy to wrongly assume that only age can help us determine a person's level of development and expect either too much or too little from the individual in front of us. Four-year-old's that are scolded, experiences a withdrawal from their body budget, but as they mature, get better at dealing with the disapproval of others. A young child may be governed by blame (you've been stupid and mean so therefore...), but as they develop more of their own will and self-esteem, their caregivers' standards will be challenged. Although we humans have always shared an energy economy with our environment, we gradually manage more and more parts of our own body budget.

The five-year-old child has begun to understand the difference between me and you, mine and yours. Gaining clarity of such social concepts makes cooperation with others possible. Friends become more important as the child enters a period where sharing is easier. The more they interact with their environment, the more they can begin to anticipate what will affect their energy and well-being later on. Children at the age of five still often blame someone else for something they have clearly done themselves because it discharges inner tension. (Some of us still do it when we are fifty-five.)

Adults may be furious with a child who has turned six because they haven't shared something (they "should understand they have to share") or treated someone else in a way "they should have understood was not okay." Most often a language of "shoulds" and "musts" is used by adults to signal that we expect certain behaviors and that children should not only focus on how they themselves feel. This is a language that is supportive at this stage and at the same time might cause challenges at a later stage.

Sometimes it is fairer to treat individuals differently, including children, because they need different levels of support. Moreover, in our eagerness to support a child, we adults may need to micromanage so that the child does everything right at once. Adults need to remember that learning is not just doing the right thing, we learn even when we fail and get the chance to try new solutions. Micromanaging often gets in the way of the child's motivation to do things themselves.

Communication Adaptation

If we shame or blame someone for not living up to our expectations, it affects the relationship. An important question that we perhaps too rarely ask ourselves is how we can best adapt our communication to the stage of development the person in front of us has reached. Besides age, experience, social interaction, psychological and mental health, emotional support and the individual's physical conditions are all factors that play a role in what the individual can do or understand. At a certain age, expectations are often linked only to age, which means that we can easily risk not seeing this particular person and their specific struggles.

"You're four now, a big girl and should understand than that everything is not just about you."

or,

"Don't be so selfish, you're actually five now and should know how to share."

And yes, of course we need to update our expectations of growing children, as the opposite would not be respecting them as individuals. But instead of calling them "stupid, mean or childish" in the hope that labels will increase their thoughtfulness and responsibility, we can say: "I don't want to do this any longer for you. I would like for you to learn to do this by yourself from now on."

A common intention behind the blaming of children by adults is to show children how to cooperate or show care. At the same time constant shaming and blaming language has a negative effect on a child's self-image and stress level. It is true that shame contributes to the learning of social interaction, but only as long as it does not overstress the young brain. And, as many adults have experienced, criticism from people in your childhood can linger for a long time and sometimes effects confidence and self-empathy decades later.

A young sensitive brain reacts more strongly to being shamed than adults sometimes realize. To get a taste of how they might feel, think about how a shaming comment from when you were a child shakes you still. Does it still make you want to withdraw or maybe makes you angry? Is the memory still a drain on your energy budget? Maybe you can benefit from the reminder and understand how deeply that kind of communication affects us. And of course, it is possible to set boundaries without pushing or humiliating anyone.

Even if we never blame or shame, but let a child know when they crossed someone's boundaries, they seem to develop the ability to construct shame. Healthy shame helps them become aware of the needs of others, hopefully without getting stuck in a loop of self-criticism. With different communication tools, we can learn to balance *you* and *me* into a *we*. In fact, feelings of shame can be reminders of when we are losing sight of the bigger picture.

The emotional vocabulary of children is filled by being exposed to the emotional nuances of others in describing inner worlds. Language summarizes the emotions of biological effects and the context in which the individual lives. The greater the vocabulary to describe emotional nuances, the greater the emotional fine tuning the child develops and the more they can cultivate that fine tuning, the more opportunities they have to influence their environment. With more nuances and words to describe their inner self, the emotions receive more ways to develop. When the shame over having done something that has hurt someone else can switch to regret or sadness, more doors are opened for the shame to be transformed into something else than self-blame.

If we caregivers want to be seen as kind and don't say no when we mean no, it becomes difficult for the child to know where our boundaries are. Our boundaries are the ones that will then move into their inner self and give them guidance on what to do and what not to do.

Obviously, it affects a young individual if the adults around them are constantly communicating by shaming or blaming, but regardless of the adults' sometimes poor communication, children are continuously striving to take in new knowledge and learn to encode unclear requests. Shame is an important tool in parenting, so stop beating yourself up if you notice your child feeling ashamed at times. If you are overreacting, remember that even very young children benefit from an apology from grown-ups. Being a role-model is not about showing up perfect.

As the child's brain and thinking develops, children can nuance not only what they do, but also why they are doing something. Eventually, the capacity for perspective matures to the point where it enables them to think and communicate in abstract comparisons.

Is it better to do it that way than this way?

Once the child is able to make those kinds of comparison thoughts, caregivers can ease up on giving absolute directives and be open to discussing change. Giving children a chance to influence changes in, for example, agreements about bedtime, without putting all the responsibility on the child, is part of learning to cooperate. Caregivers need to take the time to update their communication, give space for conversations and adjust how much responsibility the child can actually take.

A five-year-old can engage in short conversations about why they are expected to act in a certain way. They can understand that some choices impact others, like how it might increase someone's willingness to share things with them if they are also willing to share. Still it might be very difficult to live up to this when there are no adults around.

The extraordinary human ability to not only register, but also categorize what we perceive, is a great asset that starts early with children learning to understand categories such as vehicles or shapes. The next level, communicating about abstract divisions such as right and wrong, good and bad, requires more advanced abstract thinking. Being able to communicate about such subtle things as emotions, values, hopes and dreams is the foundation for being able to create deeper relationships.

To be able to divide the world into clear categories, creates a strong sense of security. To "think outside the box," as we often challenge older children to do, they first need a box.

The Magical Banana

Children's thinking develops in a number of areas, such as beginning to reflect on the role of their thoughts about what is happening around them. The child who has used words like banana enough times, with the result that real bananas often appear, has evidence of being a magician. They link an event to something they've thought and make connections to put the whole thing together.

The idea behind magical thinking is that your thoughts determine the course of events without you doing anything other than thinking. Unrelated events are tied together and given meaning in an attempt to influence them. The brain looks for connections and with our cognitive bias we see patterns even where they don't exist. Magical thinking is a natural part of learning connectional thinking. It does not disappear as we grow older, but is integrated into a thinking that takes into account more perspectives.

In any case, exploring one's share of responsibility for what happens to others is a valuable developmental step. Taking responsibility for something that happens diminishes powerlessness but also becomes a breeding ground for shame and guilt.

Emma, five years old, tries to calm her concerns about her mother not coming home with magical thinking.

If I just think hard enough about my mother coming home, she will.

One dilemma with magical thinking is that it can lead to destructive self-criticism, for example, if Emma's mother has actually been in an accident and therefore not come home. At a certain stage of development, it is difficult to distinguish between thoughts, actions and the impact we have on what happens.

"If only I hadn't thought such ugly thoughts about my mother when I was angry with her, she wouldn't have hurt herself. I am a bad girl."

Although magical thinking is attributed to children, adults also think in similar ways;

"If I just think like this, that will happen."

For adults, magical thinking can come back clearly in a crisis or to find hope in a threatening situation. Some religious and cultural systems are based on this kind of thinking. Many have promised gold and green forests to those who think "correctly."

Athletes are known to have certain rituals they just "have to" do before an important match or competition. And how many have a certain ritual when choosing a lottery ticket to find the highest prize?

5

RULE-ORIENTED AND
MORE COMPLEX

To explore how shame affects us through different life stages, chapters three to five and eight focus on different levels of development where age and maturity vary. Chapter five focuses on a phase where rules are central, from school age to adolescence.

> *For shame doesn't arise from the shameful action,*
> *but from discovery and exposure.*
>
> RUTH KLÜGER, STILL ALIVE: A HOLOCAUST GIRLHOOD REMEMBERED

Around the world, children between the ages of four and seven start school. Although they are at different points in their development, there are general similarities. Physiologically, the brain has had time to mature and handle more complex thinking. Most school-aged children have learned to distinguish between mine and yours and are able to prioritize behaviors that can lead to friendship. At the same time, any new context runs a higher risk to bringing up feelings of shame. At best, these feelings help young people find a way to fit in and belong; at worst, they grow so strong that they block what they are meant to do: to learn life skills.

School offers challenges and opportunities to grow. Rule-based games provide security, and within a fixed framework, mischief and creativity can flow and everyone can usually be included. The ability to sort behaviors into boxes of right and wrong is valuable because it gives structure to the growing children's emerging value system and makes them independent enough to manage outside the home. For seven-year-olds, it is still often a challenge to follow the rules when there is no adult watching or reminding them of those rules. But at this age, they also begin to start reminding others of what is right and wrong, good and bad, (So adults, get ready to be lectured.)

"You have to stop smoking. My teacher says it's dangerous," declares Tom as his mother Sofia lights a cigarette with a friend.

Sofia laughs at the eight-year-old's comment. When he walks away, she says to her friend:

"As if he knew everything about lung cancer. He educates both me and David as soon as we do anything that he is learning is not good, so now I usually smoke when he is not watching. It's calmer that way."

"I know. It was cute at first when my children lectured me for this and that. My daughter gets mad if I swear and maybe it's good to reflect on that, but do they have to be on you all the time?"

The adorable kids who always took their parent's side are now leaving it more and more often. Both physically and mentally. The former 100% loyalty to parents is reduced by a percent here and a percent there, and the opinions of teachers and peers complement the inner navigation system. Friends become more essential. Fitting in with peers becomes central. Previously simple expressions, such as "mommy stupid" are refined as their ability to argue grows. Eventually, they will be able to rank values and create their own life principles.

Although the seven-year-old has some time left on the journey to independence, questioning the behavior of parents and other caregivers are important parts of it. As early as eight, many (depending on traffic and other challenges) are able to walk home from school by themselves and fix a snack. A ten-year-old can cook dinner with the right support. A nine-year-old may need help getting started with homework, while a thirteen-year-old may be more ready to take responsibility for it on their own. Our ideas around age might obscure our view. As we have touched on before, it is not just age that determines what a child can do, but as body and brains develop, some things become easier.

Before testing how far the wings of independence carry, there is often a period of time when superhero stories with simple truths and divisions between good and evil fly in. Batman and Wonder Woman become role models for life principles of being there for others in need in a similar way a religious affiliation does. King Arthur manages to pull the sword from the stone and becomes an inspiration to face challenges. Spiderman fails to save his uncle's life, breaks down, ashamed and ready to give up. But even the heroes who are ashamed of their mistakes eventually take on the next challenge with a little more humility. They have often learned to accept support, trust others and co-operate.

After a short period where Wonder Woman was all Emma talked about, she moves on. She, who categorically damned anyone who uttered the slightest swear word, eventually turns twelve and suddenly she is the one who swears the most. Tom, who hid his mother's cigarettes when he was eight, soon turns thirteen and comes home smelling of smoke.

As the child takes developmental steps, it becomes possible to see their parents from more perspectives and they can see that, good people sometimes do bad things. While it can be a relief for them to realize caregivers are only human, it is not always easy to question their authority. In adolescence, their thinking is going to become more nuanced and can lead to conclusions such as: "Everyone can make mistakes and with support they might learn to act differently."

So Grown Up, and Still Just a Kid

When Tom turns ten, he and his parents decide together that he should be in bed by nine o'clock on weekdays, with his teeth brushed. Tom was okay with the agreement when they made it, but it is hard for him to adjust how far before nine he needs to stop doing other things he's doing. After a few days with continued struggle his father bellows:

"I'm so disappointed in you, why can't you ever do what we agreed to? Now go and brush your teeth."

Tom thinks it's unfair that Dad says what he says; he does a lot of things that they have agreed on. But he keeps quiet, knowing better than to argue. To feel a little bit autonomous, he walks as slowly as he can towards the bathroom. He doesn't want to talk to his dad, and when his dad later asks for a good night hug, Tom hisses at him to stop.

His dad's blaming and how Tom handled it led to disconnection between them, but neither Tom nor his dad realizes that at the time. Tom still finds it hard to get to bed the next day and now his mother's patience is running out, and she also tries to motivate him through guilt:

"No one will ever be able to trust you."

If caregivers experience a loss of control as the child develops independence and starts questioning their authority, it becomes tempting to blame, to shame. Blaming communication often makes children more compliant, at least for the moment. But blaming in the long run rarely elicits responsibility in the way we adults hope. The price for total compliance is a high one on our connection.

The challenge for the caregiver is how to communicate what they want, keep everyone safe, keep connection and to not give up. There is a difference between blaming a child for not doing what we want and using our power to protect. We adults need to learn to keep warm boundaries while maintaining the values of respect and connection. It is a sword edge all caregivers need to balance on.

"Hey, it's quarter to nine. Time to turn off the computer game and go to bed. Do you need my help, or can you do it yourself?"

How we communicate is, of course, not only a matter of the words we use, but also other things like the tone of voice and our actions, and how often we repeat something. It is not until the age of eleven that the human brain has generally developed to the point where it is able to create more distance from its own feelings and thoughts. Until then, we cannot expect much self-reflection from the child. As the brain develops, the ability to create some distance from our emotions increases. This makes it much easier to put feelings and thoughts into words, even as the young person is experiencing them. They can now start to put their inner self into words and share it with others, in a way that they previously could only do in retrospect. The child is no longer the feeling but feels it. This is the foundation of understanding that the approach to what we feel affects the emotions themselves. The experience has gone from "Emma angry" to "I feel irritated."

With self-detachment, the individual is no longer an emotional slave, and can begin to question and transform emotions using their thoughts. Glimpses of this happen when the child begins to realize that emotions come and go, usually not before the age of eleven. We begin to understand that emotions are influenced by how we think about them. With the emerging understanding of the concept of time, children can start realizing that emotions come and go, making strong emotions bearable. Gradually children can more effectively sooth themselves as they realize that their emotional state will change. Time may not heal all wounds, but it helps to let go of past hurts and difficulties.

There are many benefits to realizing that we are not our emotions. Self-distance makes it easier to take risks that we can grow from. It is easier to deal with performance anxiety and nervousness when we can step back and look at them, talk about them and reshape them. At different times, children are reluctant to challenge themselves.[33] Challenges and new things make them feel as if emotions, and perhaps especially shame, seem to threaten to swallow them up. At the slightest risk of humiliation, the child may refrain from doing something they previously enjoyed, such as singing in front of other people. They may not have been mocked or laughed at themselves, but they may have seen others being ridiculed or giggled at and that is enough to refrain. Some children won't dance in front of others, because of the fear of being judged and ridiculed. A child who is invited to be in a play turns it down, even though it seems fun and their best friends are in the play. Performance anxiety tells them that it is too difficult or that they will make a fool of themselves.

At other periods, children can become tough, put armor around all vulnerability and boldly embrace any challenge they meet. They might push themselves against the outside of the electric fence of shame (which previously kept them safely contained). Risk-taking increases, they communicate and act in a way that can stand out. One way of signaling their independence may be through a style of dress that is clearly seen as deviating from dress code norms. But more commonly teenagers dress like their peers that in some way differs distinctly from adult clothing styles.

For children in the midst of testing how far the wings of in-dependence can carry them, there is often a period of time when superhero stories with simple truths and divisions between good and evil appear. They provide role models for forming self-image and ranking values, in a similar way that a religious connection can do. King Arthur manages to pull the sword from the stone and becomes an inspiration to dare to try. In other stories, the heroes fail, break down, realize their limitations, feel ashamed and are ready to give up.

In early adolescence, some start to move beyond rule orientation and begin to prioritize rules and form them into internal principles. This may mean suddenly leaving a group if it does not live up to their values and norms. The person may join a new group, or belong to several groups at once, with a wide range of values and interests.

Children can take for granted that their parents love them, no matter what. Therefore, sometimes parents' unconditional love is not enough to prove that they are worthy of being loved. Being welcomed by a group outside our family of origin affects their self-image and sense of importance differently.

Talk to Children in the Way you Want Them to Talk to Themselves

When we as caregivers struggle with self-criticism, we are sometimes reminded of how adults in our childhood communicated.

"Oh, that's my mom's voice I hear inside me."

"That's exactly how my dad always complained about me."

"Now I sound just like my old teacher."

It is in connection with other people that children learn to communicate, not only to others but also to themselves. If adults communicate judgments, demands or threats, this is how children learn to communicate, internally and externally.

Communication is more than words and shaming and blaming also includes body language. Above all, it can also carry insinuations about who is the cause of someone's painful feelings. The words, but also the intention behind expressing something, becomes part of the communication lessons we give children.

"I feel sad when you don't care about me."

"After all we have done for you, you must understand that we are disappointed that you don't behave in school."

Blame and shame-based communication implies that the sole cause for our feeling is because of what someone else does. By connecting what's going on inside of us with someone else's actions in this way, we make them responsible for something as vague as our feelings. When children growing up with this kind of communication, as teenagers complain that they feel disappointed that their friends don't seem to like them, it becomes hollow with arguments like:

"You should not be so concerned about how others feel or think about you."

"They should accept you as you are."

"You are free to choose; you don't need those kinds of manipulating friends."

Of course, our emotions are affected by what is happening around us, but as adults we can take responsibility for how we communicate. Instead of blaming, we can express what we feel and link it to our own needs. At the same time, we can be curious about what lies behind the choices and behaviors of others. Expressions like:

"I feel sad because you don't seem to care about me. Do you realize how disappointed I am when you don't call me, even though you know I need you to call me!"

It will be more connecting if we claim more responsibility for our emotions:

"Our connection is important to me. When you call and tell me where you are, I feel calmer and can relax better. I know that you care about me, so I wonder how come you didn't call earlier? Did something get in the way or did you forget?"

In the concluding phrase above, the parent is expressing what is going on inside them. The first part of the sentence often does not even need to be spoken if the final question is asked with warmth and genuine interest. The intention is to deepen the connection, not to accuse the child. An adult who knows that their child often assumes blame, even without being blamed, can minimize the risk through his/her communication style (words, tone of voice and facial expressions). They can place the intention to connect at the front and also acknowledge any feelings of guilt and shame in the connection.

The adult can put the intention to create connection first, but also listen to any feelings of guilt and shame that arise in the contact. The caregiver who assumes that there is a reason why the child did not get in touch, which is not about them, is more likely to be successful in creating connection. If the adult can let go of the idea that they are ignored or unimportant, they may realize that when something fun happens to their children, it can be a challenge to remember to call.

Perhaps some of our connection with the child can be repaired by hearing about the fun. This does not mean that we let go of our own needs and requests but that we can maximize our ability to talk about them once we have reconnected.

What we teach our children is not only ways of communicating, but also ways of thinking and relating. Just because we don't make others responsible for how we feel, we don't have to keep quiet about what hurts us. If a child's lowered grades worry us (perhaps because we know there are dreams of education where high grades are required), it is not something we want to keep quiet about.

We can make an effort to be communication role models. For example, if we are concerned about the child's low grades (perhaps because we know there are dreams of education where high grades are required), we express our concern. In order not to make the child responsible for our worry, we take responsibility for our emotion as quickly as possible by linking it to our need to contribute, for example. We invite to talk about what might have led to the lowered grades and explore together what we can change if that is what we want.

Another parent may take the lowered grades with relief, because they have been worried about their child's performance anxiety and high standards. They can see a lowered grade as a sign that the child is letting go of some of the pressure on themselves to always perform to the maximum, and thus, their emotion is different.

Shame is Not the Same as Low Self-esteem

Emma, ten years old, pulls her hair and complains: "I'm so ugly. Everyone else is so cute."

Mom Mari's inner response is immediate, and she almost blurts it out; "But you're the cutest girl in the world." Even though the comment is completely true for Mari, she has realized that if she first listens to Emma's self-criticism, it will be easier to offer encouragement. Mari has realized that she works the same way; it is more important for her that someone hears her disappointment than that someone encourages her. She takes a deep breath, waits to say anything at all and reminds herself that Emma's self-criticism is not a problem but a necessary part of her daughter's growing independence. Mari guesses that Emma, ten years old, wants to be heard in her anxiety about not being liked. The fact that Emma is ashamed of standing out can be interpreted by Mari as a good sign that her daughter is working on finding her place in a larger context and learning how to adapt to important relationships. She can do this by reminding herself that there will be a time for rebellion as well, even later.

The ten-year-old wants her mom to listen to her thoughts of not being good enough, so the positive encouragement that worked for the six-year-old needs to be updated. Mari now shares power and influence with her daughter's peers, and she has to do the best she can with the influence she has left. This is a concern that is present at all ages, but at different stages it becomes particularly important to be accepted by peers. The ten-year-old Emma wants to be understood and heard around her worry of not being good enough, but the positive encouragement that worked for the six-year-old needs to be adjusted for her developing age.

As parents, we have the chance to develop with our children and learn to adapt our communication with them as they develop. She has a chance to show her ten-year-old how to deal with challenging emotions, in more ways than to lower your standards, look positively at things and just be happy with what you have got. Unlike the time when feelings of shame were something to be avoided in order to damage an overly fragile nervous system, Emma, who has turned ten, can now intentionally pause, feel and reflect on a situation. She still needs support to notice and articulate what is going on inside, but the inner space grows as she finds the words, and the capacity to laugh at her mistakes and failures.

As a parent, it is easy to lose our footing when we hear our child criticizing themselves. We know from our own experience that self-criticism can be challenging. Peppering a five-year-old is usually fine, but a person approaching adolescence needs other types of support to deal with self-criticism. The older child often needs someone to listen, not necessarily give reassurance and not always fix or give advice.

Sometimes we take the blame for them being so hard on themselves, especially when we equate high self-esteem with being good parents. A child who is ashamed is not the same as a child with low self-esteem. Shame is also not a sign that there is something wrong with us, it is a sign that we are human, which means having a need for community, acceptance and dignity.

Maybe we criticize ourselves and take full responsibility for the child being self-critical. We wonder if we have set too high standards and try to make the child see that their performance is good enough. Important questions to ask. But even though we play a role in influencing how children talk to themselves, we need to be careful not to equate high self-esteem with the support we give them.

International twin studies suggest that upbringing actually has less influence on the personality someone develops than we might think.[34] This means that the extent to which we are self-critical or not is partly genetic. Perhaps the most important thing you can do as a parent is to relax and be there with your children as they explore everything from self-criticism to life goals.

The Conventional Teenager

Becoming a teenager often feels like the middle ground. You are not a child, neither are you an adult. You are expected to take responsibility, sometimes more than you can handle or understand the reason for, and in some contexts, you have no rights. Adults may find it challenging to realize what is easier and what is yet difficult for their teenagers.

What do Swedish teenagers feel ashamed of:

The following is a list of some of the things that teenagers in Sweden said they were ashamed of, in interviews on Swedish Radio.

> Blushing in front of the class or someone you like

> Having pimples

> Failing a test

> Stuttering

> Being forced to do something you don't want to do, for instance singing, dancing, talking in front of a group

> Being caught doing different things they are not supposed to do

Tom has turned 14. He is no longer the one moralizing about what others should do or not; on the contrary, he is usually fed up with all the prohibitions his parents have laid on him. To his father's annoyance, Tom breaks almost every agreement they have made about when he should come home in the evening. On a few occasions, he has been summoned to the principal's office after playing rough in the school hallway, but he just sighs at his parents telling him to shape up.

The smell of smoke in his clothes does not come from his own smoking, but he would never dream of outing his friends' smoking habits and ignores his parents' questions and shakes his head when they tell him he can't smoke. Prohibitions become tempting to defy, as rebellion offers a sense of independence and freedom. The autonomy that comes from having some distance from his parents gradually allows him to question rules and explore his own values. Even if it seems contradictory, he is becoming more rule-oriented as he makes the rules his own. He begins to be able to rank what is more important than something else and his life principles become clearer, helping him to act with greater integrity.

When Emma's parents remind her of the time she has to come home at night, she finds them harsh and that they can't understand the fact that she is no longer a child. She ignores the question of what she and her friends are up to and grunts at the threat of a curfew. The humiliation Emma feels when her friends mock her for being the only one who needs to be home at ten o'clock on a Friday night has become more uncomfortable than her parents' frustration when she arrives at eleven. She wants to be seen as mature enough to make her own decisions about her time and what she does with it.

When her mother Mari points out that Emma has "borrowed money" from her purse, she retaliates. "I'm the only one who doesn't have any money. It wasn't much, I'll give it back to you as soon as I can." Where did the righteous little eight-year-old, who knew it was wrong to take money without asking, go?

When Tom's friends try to get him to drink alcohol, it feels silly to say no, but up till now the thought of his father's anger has been too real. Eventually, though, he drinks beer with them. Being a bit drunk, he accepts a cigarette being passed to him. He holds it between his lips without inhaling the smoke. It tastes really bad anyway and a child's voice in the back of his head reminds him that smoking is dangerous. A few quips later, about how anyone who doesn't dare take a puff is a coward, he coughs up the smoke. Belonging and acceptance are high on the priority list of teenage needs.

Gradually, Tom withdraws from his parents. He is present physically but more and more his warm feelings towards them become locked up. This makes him less dependent on their approval and he can more easily ignore their criticisms. He used to feel compelled to be loyal to his parents' values, but now he can shut out both them and what they value, at least partially. In situations where he used to feel uncomfortable lying to his parents, he now does so without blinking, simply turning his back on any attempt to shame him.

Contrary to what he previously felt was unthinkable, Tom makes out with his friend Armin's girlfriend and Armin breaks up with him, Tom shrugs. There are others who want to be his friend, what does he need Armin for? "He's just a pompous ass who wants everyone to like him."

In fact, it hurts Tom to lose a friend, but he doesn't tell anyone. Who would he tell, no one understands what he feels anyway? When his father points out that he have not seen Armin for some time, Tom mutters something inaudible in response. If Mom and Dad found out what Tom has done, they would only be angry and of course take Armin's side. Out of integrity, his inner voice tells him that what he did was wrong, and he promises himself never to do it again.

Tom's strategy of keeping his distance from his parents also affects other parts of his life. A lot of energy goes into proving that he is independent and can manage on his own. But the price he pays for staying detached is high, because it often makes him feel numb and bored. At the same time, he becomes more independent, able to do things on his own, and better able to decide what he really wants. To numb all signs of dependency, he invades any sign of vulnerability. He mocks others who are not independent.

Cool and self-sufficient, he becomes open to risks that could potentially affect the rest of his life. Forbidden substances can be particularly attractive because they become a demonstration of autonomy. Drugs can also be appealing because they - at least temporarily- break down unwanted internal walls and make room for spontaneity and emotions that would otherwise be suppressed.

Although the way he does this varies, Tom is far from being the only teenager to put up a barrier against his parents. The exploration of how independence is regulated by feelings of shame is mostly unconscious, and caregiver boundaries are still important, even if they are not respected by such teenagers' actions.

Some teenagers go through periods of loneliness without any problems. At the same time, the risk of isolation and alienation are cited as a reason for suicide among young adults. Even for parents, constant rejection can be difficult to deal with, and we may stop showing how much we care.

One important thing grown-ups can do for young people is to recognize the right to development. Caregivers can show that they value and see the journey the independence warrior is making, without accepting or even liking the specific expressions the development takes. It is probably less about a specific conversation but about how we as caregivers can create conditions for a continuous dialogue. As a caregiver, it is valuable to keep a cool head and remember that eventually most individuals will relate in a more reciprocal way, even if it takes a few years.

For many teenagers, the adult world seems boring and demanding, and even if they realize that there is no other way forward, they may think about how to delay their entry into it. At the same time, most teenage cultures are difficult to navigate. External attributes and appearance, and to a large extent achievement as well, are central and are largely driven to avoid shame. The pressure to fit in is great and teens often dress in similar styles and colors of clothes and shoes, and have the same hairstyles, regardless of what they liked a few years earlier.

There is a huge fear to stand out and risk not belonging or being accepted. In Judi Picoult's book *19 Minutes*, one of the characters says, "if you find a thirsty teenager in a desert and offer them either to be popular or a glass of water, the teenager is guaranteed to not choose the water."

In early adolescence, many move beyond rule orientation and start to prioritize what is important from which they form their inner principles. This may mean suddenly leaving a group, if the group does not live up to the values and standards of the individual. Instead, this person might join a new group, or may belong to several groups at the same time, with a wide range of values and interests.

Many teenagers spend more time with their peers than with their family, which shapes their way of being. Having friends and communities outside the family, where they get the support they need, can actually become a lifeline for some children. It can give them an important "second chance" to get experiences they didn't get during childhood. To keep up with the child as they grow in independence, the parent can take their own journey through some of these areas:

- Expanding their fields of knowledge, daring to be a beginner.
- Reflect on, question and reshape their own opinions.
- Learning to let go, getting in touch with their own independence and developing it.

- Finding new ways to support the teenager to find their own path and being open to conversations about what their choices might mean.
- Regularly talking to others about the realization that their children are not them and have their own life journey.

Rather than putting ourselves in the shoes of our teenagers, we are on a slippery slope if we try to force them to give up their participation in areas that are important to them. Such demands increase the risk that they will withdraw from us. We can express opinions and stand up for what we value, without demanding that our children agree with us or give up important group membership.

If we remain interested in what attracts the teenager to be part of a group that is unattractive to us, we can maintain connection with them, which increases the chance that they will understand that we are there for them when they need us.

Fact and Knowledge Resistance

In an attempt to influence our children's opinions and behaviors, it is tempting to present facts and if they argue against us, we pound away with even more numbers. Maybe because we as caregivers are not willing to face the shame of having teenagers with radically different values?

We urge our teenagers to be careful about sources and to question things that are not scientifically proven. But what effect does this have? Professor Mikael Klintman writes in his book *Knowledge Resistance* that: "Belonging is so important that we are inclined to stop listening to facts if they risk jeopardizing our place in an important group."[35]

It seems smart to follow Klintman's suggestions and take advantage of the survival conditions that have shaped humans, if we want to get information across.[36] The basic human need to belong to a group has a huge impact on our choices and actions, more than we may realize.

When a child moves beyond their family of origin and seeks out other groups, they are not necessarily accepted. But if they are welcomed, their self-worth is affected in a different way than if they receive the same acceptance from their family. It is sometimes taken for granted that our parents will love us no matter what, so this does not count as proof that we are worthy of love.

Throughout human history, group affiliation, loyalty and consensus on right and wrong have increased the chances of survival for both the individual and the group. Religions have emerged and different creation myths have created cohesion among those who believe in the same thing. Shared beliefs make it easier to come together in defense against external threats.

We have always been dependent on others for our own security and belonging to a group often times feels much more important than having an accurate perception of reality. According to Klintman, no matter how good we are at packaging information or presenting scientific evidence on an important issue, it rarely causes anyone to reconsider their views if it means that they need to question their place in the group.

The resistance of teenagers to new facts can feel incredibly dense. Instead of expecting them to be interested in taking in information that challenges a group they belong to and is valuable to them, we can start by understanding why this is so important to them at the moment. If we want to reach a teenager, it is more constructive to first accept their desire for belonging to this group than to bombard them with the importance of correct sources of information.

"This is what I believe, I don't care about the facts you point out, science has been wrong before" reflects an attitude many people have had for quite a period of time in recent history. This attitude can be seen as an attempt to find one's way of relating to research instead of just blindly buying all research results. Another approach is to "pick the raisins out of the cake." It makes it possible to acknowledge that research is good, while only those research results that support one's own views count. Later still, the young adult can become almost obsessed with facts and measuring things, where only what is measurable counts.

A test for caregivers, parents and teachers is whether we can express our opinions and requests in a respectful way. Can we express ourselves without blame or shame and put connecting with those young people first? After creating connection, can we articulate our concerns about the risk of drugs, certain actions or a particular group affiliation, for example, without demanding or belittling in a way that challenges the teenager's desire for autonomy? And as caregivers, what happens within us and to our way of expressing ourselves and listening, if the children do not share our views? Do we have the tools needed to deal with our own sense of alienation, frustration, fear or powerlessness?

While adolescence can be a time of play, joy and exploration, it is also a time of adjustment. The focus is on freeing oneself from dependence on the adult world, while the desire to be accepted by one's peers grows stronger. The young, and conventional person has evolved towards greater freedom. And there is still some way to go before true independence. The pressure to fit in, to keep up, to be cool, to be one of the gang influence most of their actions. It is an important time to learn to stand up for yourself and sometimes give in to, to support cooperation. Author and honorary doctor Lasse Berg suggest that we remember that, "For millions of years, alone meant not strong but dead."

Your Child is not You

"When I was your age, I had already started working, earning my own money."

"At your age, I already knew how to build rooftops."

"When I was the same age as you, I walked all the way, three kilometers every day, to and from school."

How many of us adults felt frustrated when our own parents (or grandparents) tried to teach us something, or lectured us by telling us about their own childhood? And hand on heart, how many times do we communicate in a similar way with our children and teenagers? What do we hope to achieve? Is the message getting through or are we missing the mark completely? Let's examine some problems with the above quotes.

First, they are based on comparisons. We compare what children can do with what we could, and we do it to our advantage (perhaps oblivious to our own difficulties or how long we needed to master this). Comparisons are good for some things, such as determining which of two routes to the beach is shorter, which pants have more stretch so I can use them for physical movement, or which house paint is cheaper per square meter. But when it comes to human connection comparisons are rarely the most efficient. Instead of bringing people together, comparisons often create distance. Moreover, comparisons are clumsy or simplistic; they focus on one dilemma but ignore another, such as how times have changed or how knowledge that was important when we were young no longer matters that much. Knowing how to churn butter is simply not as important as it was 100 years ago, as regular grocery stores sell at least 10 different types of butter and margarine. We may think it is inspiring to hear about how good we were at something at their age, but is it really?

"In my day, we didn't even have calculators. How hard can it be to learn this stuff with all the help you have nowadays?"

In the above expression, we might guess the hidden longing in the caregiver to be heard, either in their pain or in their celebration. Perhaps they want to be seen, or they have a desire for the teenager to understand that life hasn't always been so easy for them either. So, why not tell the young person about that? Or is the grown-ups we more likely to be heard if they ask a friend to listen, instead of trying to be heard by a teenager whose focus is on getting through their teenage life?

If you find that your "When I was a teenager..." is actually an expression of joy and pride in something you've achieved, the same applies. Celebrate this with someone that is open and interested in hearing it! After all, who wants to hear someone else celebrate their successes when they themselves have failed or are struggling to do something challenging? Another downside of comparative comments is that they are sometimes perceived as blaming, mocking or bullying.

Hypocrisy, Procrastination and Embarrassing Parents

Emma, who at the beginning of the book distanced herself from her mother's dancing to their favorite song in the store, has grown a few years older and her reluctance to leave the house together with her mother has as well. It is a bit easier with her father because he has the sense to stay a little more in the background and seems to understand how embarrassing it is to do things with him as if she couldn't take care of herself.

Emma despises the way her mother talks, dresses and moves, and even if she feels guilty about thinking that way about her own mother, the thoughts help her keep some distance. So, she pushes back the self-criticism on her tongue, using the impulse control she has built up.

Tom despises his father. He has a lot of thought like, "You think you can tell everyone else what to do but you can't even cook your own food or take care of mom when she is sick." The threat of a curfew or withdrawal of allowance, when his father gets angry at his son's words, is judged by Tom as another sign of weakness, a silly attempt to regain control by acting like an idiot.

Both Tom and Emma have a difficulty understanding the complex decisions and time frames an adult needs to consider and they find it hard to accept what their parents want or need. This does not mean that they don't care. They are just so busy getting ready to enter the adult world that they have little space for anything else. Emma calls her mother, who speaks kindly to the neighbor that Emma knows her mother actually despises, a 'traitor' and a 'phony.' But later, she is also embarrassed when her mother loudly objects to the same neighbor's desire to cut the hedge between their plots.

One of the challenges adults face, is to see teenagers as mature as they want to be seen, while understanding that they have limitations on the perspectives they can take. Their focus is on finding their values and life principles and they will test them on their immediate environment.

Shame upon Shame and Blush over Blush

Blushing is a physical sign of increased blood flow in the skin. Blood vessels dilate and cause redness of the skin during vigorous exercise, hot temperatures, alcohol intake or in reaction to strong spices, or sometimes to allergies. Some people blush when they feel strong emotions such as shame, joy or anger.

Blushing is not dangerous: But for many, and perhaps especially young people wanting to appear cool, there is little comfort in knowing that blushing is "just" a physical reaction. Some blush daily and others never, which can feel unfair. For some it is very visible from the outside and for others not as much. The self-consciousness of the red, warm face is often uncomfortable and can make everyday situations hell. The threat of the red face can make people avoid certain situations that they would like to take part in. The person that blushes might feel ashamed because of that, and become even more red, making it easy to feel like a prisoner of their own physical reaction.

Blushers are often most helped by others ignoring it. Not putting attention to it allow them to find a way to calm down. But if a teenager in your life blushes repeatedly and seems to be bothered about it, ask them if they want any support, so they can have a say in the matter.

Laughter Serves Many Purposes

Laughter is with us throughout our lives. We crack a smile at five weeks, giggle at ten and laugh that first ringing laugh somewhere between 16 and 20 weeks of age. Many adults still remember laughing in their teens and how connecting it felt to laugh at the same things as their friends. A giggle of embarrassment or a bubbling laughter can, almost miraculously, transform a tense atmosphere into a warmer and more accepting one. The discharge makes "the forbidden" easier to talk about. The embarrassment is affecting us, but does not threaten to destroy or separate us as shame does. We are no longer inclined to withdraw and can talk further about things like love, taboos and sex. As the charge increases, the next giggle erupts, and the tension is re-calibrated to a manageable level. Sometimes a real big laugh is needed to fully melt away embarrassment and dare to talk more intimately.

A good comedian combines the forbidden and the taboo with humor. The most embarrassing topics can be talked about if they are followed by liberating laughter. The more surprised we are by the point of the joke and the more embarrassed we get over the conclusion we had imagined, the greater we experience the joke. The stand-up comedian engages with our inner beliefs and gives us a chance to release the tension with a laugh. Without a surprising punch line to release the tension, the joke falls flat. Sometimes we laugh at jokes we don't even find funny just to discharge of uncomfortable embarrassment. Teenagers sometime laugh at things that an adult or younger child doesn't see the humor in.

Laughter is not always about something being funny. Sometimes laughing together is about a confirmation of the connection between two people or in a group.

When a group laughs at something that outsiders do not understand, it becomes a kind of code for the community. Those who do not know the secret may not be excluded, but they are not fully included either. Research has shown that laughing is a precious tool for enhancing learning and integrating information. The fact that teenagers' jokes are about creating community does not mean that we should keep quiet if the jokes cross a line. But if we want to influence the teenager's values, we need to connect it to their deep need of belonging and inclusion. If adults blame teenagers instead of openly discussing the boundaries the jokes have crossed, it leads to different things. One is that the laughter stops as soon as the adult is around. The adults think they have made their point, but they have only shown that with them there is no room for the laughter or maybe even for humor. A second scenario that occurs among shamed teenage jokers is that they become angry and accuse adults of being narrow-minded or controlling, sometimes directly in their face and other times behind their backs.

Making jokes about a person can be offensive and painful, and adults can help teens reflect on this. It is easy to be horrified and, as an adult, say something like: "How can you be so insensitive as to joke about this. So heartless and disgusting. If you continue like this, I will have to talk to your parents." The adult is more likely to connect if they express themselves differently, perhaps along the lines of: "I understand that you are having fun together and I like that. At the same time, I am worried about how the joke affects X, who I also care about, I wonder if you have thought about that?"

And if X really doesn't seem to care; "Great to see you laughing and having fun. At the same time, I'm worried about the contents of your joke, because I want everyone to feel respected. Did anyone reflect on what you are actually making fun of?"

When adults show that they see teenagers as humans, and not as monsters having fun at the expense of others, connection is possible. It is easier if they communicate in a way that shows they understand how important it is to sometimes not take things so seriously. And why would the teenager take the step of opening up to an adult who doesn't understand the essence of belonging? They would rather turn to peers who understand them, perhaps by making a joke about the adult. A humiliating joke alleviates feelings of shame because it lowers the other person's status.

And remember, it is possible to ask questions without demanding a direct answer. A challenging question leads to a plethora of internal reactions in the teenager, that they need time to sort out. They may never answer the question to the person who asked it, but that doesn't make the question any less important.

Self-medication

If childhood was a training in dependency; adapting, following rules and forming deep bonds with people, adolescence is about exercising the ability to break free and act more independently. Just as it was important to give younger children rules to follow, it is equally important to support teenagers in questioning the caregiver's moral map and finding their own principles to live by. A group affiliation may seem vital one week, only to be replaced by another the next. Belonging itself is important, but which group fits your values can vary.

Throughout life, we continually balance between dependence and independence to create mutual relationships. We need to move to the next step without giving up on the previous ones because this is how the possibility of reciprocity is built.

The graph on next page created by Kay Rung, is an attempt to highlight the relationship between time and development in thinking in complex terms. Human development begins with a period of dependency. It is human nature to need adults to take care of you from birth, but the challenge of evolving past that dependency starts early on. Until we can take care of ourselves, we would do well to cooperate with those we depend on.

After some time, it is time to question the dependent position. Now is the time to explore ways to be independent. Once we have integrated independence, we no longer need to be so distant from those we have freed ourselves from, but can allow ourselves to start acting more interdependently.

Complexity

INTER-
DEPENDENT

INDEPENDENT   INDEPENDENT

DEPENDENT   DEPENDENT   DEPENDENT

Development over time in phases

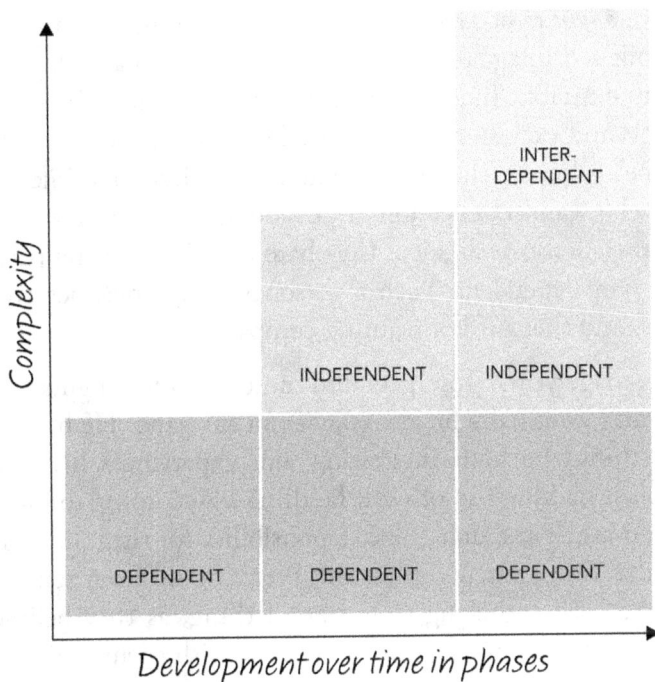

Interdependence can be described as a stage where we consider both our own needs and those of others. When we have integrated mutuality, we can accept that we sometimes need help from others, that we are still partly dependent. If we are told no to something we ask for, we can use the capacity to act independently to turn to someone else and ask them for help. Interdependence occurs when the two previous stages are accepted and integrated.

As adults, we can sometimes forget that it takes a while to be able to think in complex terms: *"If I do this, this will probably happen, except if X chooses to do this at the same time, because then it could be like this."*

A common cause of shame is not being able to do things that we think we *ought to* be able to do, according to ourselves and others. When our self-image takes a hit, the search for total independence can seem desirable. Independence leads to shame if it is perceived as loneliness and exclusion. "I don't need anyone" is nice, "but no one needs me" is lonely. The humiliation of exclusion sometimes leads a person who wants connection, to paradoxically withdraw, so as not to risk their sense of dignity. They hate the idea of being perceived as clingy or dependent. Such a person is sometimes perceived by those around them as not wanting company.

In his teenage years, Tom gets into more and more fights with his friends and eventually breaks away from his gang. He has tried to discuss things he finds interesting, but experiences his so-called friends just making fun of what he thinks. According to him, they drink too much and don't take responsibility for their actions.

At first Tom's parents think this breaking up from some of the groups he used to belong to is a good thing, as they believe this will mean he is going to spend more time with them again. But he withdraws more and more, even though he actually doesn't want to be alone. Feeling like an unwanted outcast, loneliness is eating him alive, but going back to the old gang seems unthinkable. He struggles to find something meaningful to do and with a group of people in whom he can recognize himself and where his values and needs can be accommodated. Even though it is he himself who has withdrawn, he has a sense of being ostracized. The balance between belonging, acceptance and dignity is really hard to find. And during this period, he values dignity more than belonging, as he doesn't want to sell himself cheap.

For a while, he tries E-sport but soon loses interest, and the same is true when he starts working out at the gym with a group from school. Inspired by Emma, he participates in a poetry slam that ends with so much shame the he decides to never invest time in poetry again.

Tom's father David calls himself a recovering alcoholic. He describes the first time he drank alcohol at the age of seventeen as a flash of love, *"I could finally relax and be that charming, cool guy I knew lived inside me."* After that a lot of things went wrong for David so it is no wonder he's nervous about Tom going down the same path as him. It took him a couple of decades to realize that alcohol was his way of self-medicating, numbing self-criticism and avoiding the shame that ate away at his self-respect. That David remained for many years in a certain community where, despite his addiction, he was accepted, has little to do with his son but, like many parents, he confuses his own process with that of his son.

It can indeed be seen as an expression of healthy independence when someone manages to opt out of a community where their life principles are not acknowledged. It is actually common that teenagers belong simultaneously to different groups, looking for a place where they can experience fitting in. Sometimes a teenager withdraws from a group because the behaviors and values of that group are not conducive to meaning or self-respect. Other times, they just don't find it meaningful. One thing that adults can do for young people is to acknowledge their right to development, supporting them becoming more autonomous. Adults can show that they value and see the journey that the independent warrior is making, without accepting or even liking the specific outcome of that development. As a caregiver, it is important to keep a cool head and remember that eventually, the vast majority of individuals will relate in a more reciprocal way, even if it takes a few years.

Sometimes we forget that teenagers do not automatically have tools to deal with strong emotions. We miss the fact that they do not have the ability to deal on their own with the self-critical thoughts that come with shame and the painful isolation that comes with withdrawal. When feelings of shame are stronger than young people are able to regulate without support from others, this sometimes leads to self-medication.

Self-medication includes anything that can numb internal stress and anxiety. It can be anything between alcohol, drugs, food and self-harm behaviors but also things like sex, exercise and gambling of various kinds. There is a freedom in being able to regulate your inner self. A sense of control and autonomy that is so appealing that any side effects are not a concern for them until long afterwards. Both children and adults are affected by blunting their emotions. Numbing works to get rid of the internal pressure but only short-term. Many people who self-medicate have realized that their drug not only numbed the feelings of shame but also other emotions. When shame is silenced, joy is also silenced, and the nuances of life are blurred. Bottled-up self-criticism often overflows when someone stops self-medicating their long-standing habit, and it can become overwhelming.

Alcohol and drugs expedite rebellion against what is uncomfortable. The substance numbs, dulls our presence and makes us less attentive to signals from within and without. We no longer constantly worry about how we look; our self-image is blurred and the one we see is just fine. Worries about not being funny enough are gone, we crack jokes and if no one else laughs, we laugh at ourselves or get annoyed. We sing and dance in a way we don't do on a daily basis and it is only embarrassing the next day when someone sends us a recording of our moves.

Rich or Poor can Both be Shameful

Areas such as money, appearance or achievement can create big anxiety in teenagers and, as adults, we may want to alleviate that anxiety. The best we can do is to remind ourselves that they are exactly where they "should be" in their development and that we can support them but not live their lives.

Emma's friend Angela suggests that they go to the cinema to see the latest Avatar movie. Emma doesn't have enough money for the movie ticket but doesn't say anything because she feels embarrassed about not having money as if she were some small baby. She dislikes the feeling of being dependent on her parents so instead of telling her friend that she can't afford it, she makes up another reason. Angela replies that she finds Emma boring, and that she will ask Mika instead.

Emma goes home and when she meets her dad in the kitchen, she snaps at him when he tries to talk to her. He doesn't understand what is going on, gets annoyed and tells her that she shouldn't speak like that to him. Emma ends up going into her room and slamming the door behind her.

Later, when Dad knocks on the door, Emma's stomach clenches with discomfort and she tells him to leave. The discomfort in her stomach goes away when he does, but she feels extremely lonely and confused. Nobody seems to understand.

Money is a dilemma in many young people's lives. Not having any money is shameful but coming from a rich family can be, too. In some circles, wealth and money are idolized, while in others, money is demonized and the rich are seen as taking advantage of others.

Those with money may worry about not being seen for who they are because they have realized that others see rich people in a certain way. Those without money can feel extremely vulnerable and devalued.

The fact that money is also a loaded topic for many adults can make it even more difficult for teenagers to figure out how to relate to it.

6

LIES, MORAL MAPS AND CONFABULATIONS

This chapter examines lying. It focuses partly on the way shame affects the ability to stick to the truth, but also on alternative ways of understanding lies.

What is a Lie?

Have you ever questioned the real meaning of a lie? Can we call it a deliberately presented untruth? And is it a lie even when we have not checked as to whether what we're saying is really the truth? What about withholding information that we suspect someone might want to know? Are we lying then?

According to the Swedish Academy's dictionary, lying means "deliberately telling an untruth, usually to gain an advantage." However, as we will see in this chapter, we can consider "lying" from a wider perspective. Let's start with a story about Tom and Emma's families and how they deal with lies.

Tom and Emma's families are having dinner together. Afterwards, when the children have gone off to play, Emma's father tells them that Emma, who just turned five, refused to participate in a children's gymnastics class earlier in the week. He and Emma watched while sitting on a bench as the other children rolled around in somersaults, stood on their hands, and jumped on trampolines.

"And then she lied to me about the experience," Emma's mother added. "She has a really vivid imagination. She described to me how she had done this and that, and I believed her of course. I couldn't believe it when Robert later told me that they had been sitting on a bench watching the whole time."

"You even had trouble believing me when I told you," Robert said. "Exactly! I believed everything she said. She's a terrifyingly good liar. I get angry at her. It doesn't seem to help much."

Sofia, who has been sitting quietly for a while and nodding, can't keep quiet anymore.

"Tom is the same. He lies all the time. I tell him not to, but before I even have a chance to notice it, he has lied to me again. I have to make him stop."

For an adult who has learned the importance of telling the truth, it is tempting to focus on the fact that your child is lying when talking about perfect handstands and high jumps. You want to raise your index finger and make sure the child knows lying is wrong.

But didn't Emma actually take part in the gymnastics class? Her entire attention was focused on the movements. Her brain took in how it was to be upside down in the exercises. Her stomach was churning as she watched all the somersaults and she realized that it was important to concentrate to keep her balance on one leg with her eyes closed. Should Emma's story be considered a lie because she did not physically take part in the gymnastics class, yet all her senses were so involved? Are her imaginative memories of the class the same as lying, and if so, where do we draw the line?

Discussions about what should be considered truth can often wait until after we have listened to a child and acknowledged our children's excitement about an experience. Surely it may be more important to be present and listen, rather than punish someone for something that doesn't match how we see the world? At least as long as the lies don't contribute to endangering themselves or anyone else. Or does it lower moral if we fail to correct their lies right away?

Both Tom and Emma's parents are concerned about their children's lying. But how they approach the dilemma differs.

Emma's parents quickly realize that their daughter lies more often than they have a chance to notice, despite their attempts to get her to stop. Only afterwards do they realize that she hasn't changed the cat's water or done her homework as she claimed. After visiting their grandmother and coming home with a silver ring that she claims to have received as a gift, their concern increases because they know it is not true since their grandmother was looking for it.

Robert and Emma know that lying is normal, but they worry that they might miss bigger lies that could have complications. As long as Emma is in the phase where she is egocentric, focused on "becoming her own individual," communication can sound one way. Individuals at that stage don't always realize the difference it might make if they say this or that. Later on, as Emma matures, the conversation may focus more on reciprocity and connection and on finding appropriate boundaries.

Before a conversation the year Emma turns eleven, Robert prepares himself to bring up a touchy subject. Previous to this they have had some kind of "family crisis" where he was very upset about some things Emma has been lying about that happened at school. Now he has calmed down and is trying to understand how he can contribute to trust. He wants to know what's behind Emma's choice to not talk to them about the things that have surfaced.

Nervously he ponders ways to start the dialogue and wonders if it is a good idea to first check with her to see if she knows that he cares. He tries different ways of expressing himself in front of the mirror in the hope of restoring connection with his daughter:

"Before you say anything about what happened, I wonder if you want to tell me if there is anything I do or say that makes it difficult for you to share certain things with me?

He worries that this sounds demanding. But the exact words are hard to find, so he tries out another entry point:

"I would really like to support you in this. We can do it now or later. I prefer now, but what works best for you?"

Robert realizes that the most important thing for him is to contribute to trust and connection. He can't control what Emma will tell him, but he can maximize the odds of staying connected. After some awkward attempts on his own he decides to start like this:

"Emma, I want to feel confident that you are telling me the truth about what happened. I care about you and that's why I want to know what happened, so that maybe I can help set things right. Is there something I can say to assure you that I care?"

Emma does not answer, but stares down at the table.

"Perhaps I can help to put things right or help you with something? Do you understand why it is so important for me to know what is happening to you?"

Emma is still sitting quietly. Robert realizes that it may be difficult for Emma to find words to describe what she is feeling. He ponders: *"Maybe she's ashamed of something. I wonder if I can help her by guessing what is going on inside of her?"*

"Is it so that when you are looking for words to describe what has happened, you feel uncomfortable to tell me about it? This is not an easy thing to talk about, is it?"

Emma nods slightly at his last question and Robert guesses that her words are stuck in internal discomfort, so he tries a new approach.

"Would you like to nod again if something happened yesterday that is difficult to talk about?"

He still gets no response, but he tries again as Emma is now looking up at him.

"Do you want me to know that you feel nervous about talking about what happened yesterday? And you want to be confident that I will listen to you no matter what you say?"

Emma's father shows that he is aware that what and *how* he says something affects their connection. It is not a big deal that Emma is stretching the truth sometimes. He can even be amused by it. At the same time, he is worried about missing important information about what is going on in her life.

Tom's mother, meanwhile, is determined to make her son realize that it is unacceptable to ever lie. She is worried about how it will affect his future if he does not learn to stick to the truth. Moreover, she actually isn't that aware that she feels ashamed herself every time she discovers that her son is lying. Raising him to behave the way she expects him to, becomes more important than how her way of communicating about it affects their relationship.

"Lying is bad. You absolutely must not lie to me or anyone else. Go to your room and come back when you are ready to tell the truth."

While Tom's mother, Sofia, sets boundaries for Tom, which in itself can create safety, the way she does so risks eroding trust rather than building it. The inability to show interest in what lies behind the young individual's lies blocks the dialogue. The challenging communication and demands stress Tom, who is unable to calm his own nervous system on his own. It makes it even less likely that he admits to something he thinks he will be punished for. At one time in human history, the person who said the earth is flat would not have been accused of lying. What is "generally accepted truth" in a culture varies and changes, which makes talking about lies and truth even more complicated. Are stories about imaginary friends lies, even if the child is not aware that their experiences can be seen as such from the adults point of view?

The author and family therapist Jesper Juul believed that pre-schoolers don't lie, but are simply unable to distinguish between fantasy and reality, arguing that parents and the family can there-fore turn children into liars.[37] Others, such as researcher and profes-sor Michael Lewis, claim that there are many more reasons for lying than culture and family. Lewis divides the reasons of why we lie into four categories:

- To protect others.
- To avoid punishment and protect oneself (or to avoid losing a reward).
- For our own benefit (fantasizing, having fun and having imaginary friends).
- To hurt others.

Lewis's categories help us to distinguish between lying to avoid taking responsibility and lying to create a parallel universe through fantasy. Simplifications such as "lying is always wrong" or "the truth always comes out" provide direction, but lack important nuances.

Playing with the brain's capacity to think in concepts of time and symbols is appealing to adults and is a skill developed and used for example by novelists, architects, arborists and filmmakers. There is nothing unusual or bad about a young individual with a vivid imagination creating alternative realities, as it gives them some sense of power to influence a situation.

A black and white approach to lying is often counterproduc-tive. The fear of being punished for lying can make someone lie even more. The desire to calm a stressed nervous system sometimes makes it easier to construct a lie, even if we value the truth.

Children's Lies, Adults' Responsibility?

"Look me in the eyes," says Tom's father David, grabbing his son's shoulders.

The boy keeps his eyes on his hands. His face flares and the words seem so far away that he wonders if he will ever be able to say anything again. The thoughts run around in his head like a roller coaster.

"I said, look me into the eyes and tell me the truth about this."

Tom makes an effort to lift his head, but it feels extremely heavy.

"You have to look me in the eyes so I know if I can trust what you tell me."

The shame is accelerating as Tom tries to lift his head and do what his Dad is asking him to do. To be able to relax, he would have needed some sign that David understood his fear. Missing that confirmation, Tom clenches his jaw and the fear turns to anger, mobilizing his muscles and helping him to lift his head and stare into his dad's eyes.

"Good! How can anyone trust you if you can't look them in the eye? So, did you do it or not?"

"No, it wasn't me."

Tom holds his gaze in his father's for as long as he can. The lie and fear swim in the background, but the anger gives him the strength to resist. Anger is good, Dad likes him when he stands tall, claims it shows strength. Tom doesn't understand why David seems so uncomfortable when Tom gets scared, he just knows it's the case.

"Good. Then I know."

Have you ever been forced to look someone in the eyes? Did the coercion create more connection? or less?

The Appearance of a Lie

Probably, like most people, you have been incorrectly told that we can tell what someone else is feeling by reading their face or looking in their eyes to see if they are lying. When we notice that someone is avoiding our gaze and assume that their actions are the result of an attempt to relieve the stress on their nervous system instead of assuming that they are hiding the truth, it can help us connect.

If it is really connection we want, why not let the other individuals decide when, and if, they can handle the uncomfortable feelings that increase in intensity from meeting our gaze? Or maybe we can just put a warm hand on their arm - if they are fine with touch- and talk to them without forcing eye contact?

Even if a child's lie is an attempt to regulate stress and create inner balance, they are usually not aware of that intention. Leaving out details or distorting the truth can mitigate the strong emotions that come up every time something stressful or embarrassing is mentioned.

Shame is like an electric fence around vulnerability. If we want to encourage children to have the courage to approach what they are ashamed of and tell us about it, we can show them that we will not put more stress on their already stressed nervous system. Only then can the electricity of the fence be turned off and not leave us outside.

The movie "The Invention of Lying" is set in a parallel world where people have not developed the ability to lie. They simply can't tell anything but the truth, but the main character, played by Ricky Gervais suddenly discovers that untruths are possible. His mother lays anxiously on her deathbed so he fabricates a truth about where she will go after death, and it helps her pass away in a soft and peaceful way. But the staff have heard him and now he is faced with a dilemma, should he tell the truth about not knowing what happens after death at all and let people continue to act as they have until now? Although the protagonist's unique position gives him a lot of power, he is soon overwhelmed by being the only one lying.

Children of a certain age may have imaginary friends that they wholeheartedly believe others can see. They have difficulty distinguishing between what others see and what they themselves experience.

"Did you steal this from Emma?"

"No, it's mine. I got it from a friend I was playing with."

"Now you're lying. You've been alone all day."

"No, Yoki was here with me."

"There's no one else here."

In less than a minute, the child is accused of both stealing and lying. However, the child is in an egocentric stage and is not fully aware that the friend is someone only they can see and has difficulty distinguishing between concepts such as yours and mine. They have no, or very little, idea of what others experience or need.

Some parents worry that a child who sees an imaginary friend has some mental defect or feels lonely. In most cases, imaginary friends are not something to worry about, rather the relationship with the invisible friend is a way for the child to develop his/her imagination. Dialogues with the perceived friend stimulate the imagination and give the child a space to control their own life.

When we argue that the child's beliefs are lies, we build a barrier between their world and ours. If we deny them the freedom to imagine, we create an unnecessary barrier to their choices. If we instead show interest in the imaginary friend, without making them think we see their friend, we can be invited into their secret world.

From a young age, humans are capable of lying, which distinguishes us, for example, from chimpanzees who do not have the ability to use a third-person perspective and think: "I know that the other chimp knows that I know" or, "If I just add a smile, Dad will think it was someone else who ate the banana."

As soon as children learn to control facial expressions and tone of voice, they can become small actors. To be really good at it they need to become mind readers. Presenting variations of "the truth" stimulates their capacity to see the world through the eyes of others. Concentration skills and the ability to create an internal image enable the individual to adapt the lie to the context.

In experiments conducted over several decades to understand why children lie, children are asked not to look at a toy that is behind them. The child is promised a reward for not looking and then the experimenter leaves the room for a while. The child is filmed and some peek at the toy after a few seconds, which many deny when the experimenter returns. The experiment has been repeated a large number of times with similar results. 65% of three-year-old children who peeked denied it, while 80% of four-year-olds and over 90% of six-year-olds denied looking.

Denying something requires less effort than making up a lie of your own. To lie successfully, we need to be able to create a parallel universe, where our lie is the truth, while also being able to imagine what someone else might know. We need to remember what we and others have said in the past. Paradoxically, many of the skills that adults appreciate in children - planning, remembering, controlling their emotions, and taking into account other people's point of view - are the very skills that make children successful liars.

Different types of body language have been suggested as signs that a person is hiding something. Eyes that don't meet ours, fingers twirling a strand of hair. Increased knuckle movements when we push the person to tell the truth. Light taps on a table surface, a tapping foot, mumbling and a lack of arguments are all said to be signs that we have a liar in front of us.

All this, and then the gaze which has stopped at a point in front of the child, and which remains lowered even when we ask them to look us in the eye and tell us what has happened. Words are whispered and red flames spread along the little neck. Terrified, we study our children; are they lying? Why aren't they honest with us? Is it their faulty character or is it our fault?

Sometimes a lie is hidden behind certain body language, but more often than not, we are unable to tell a lie from gestures or a facial expression. A lie can just as easily be hidden behind steady eye contact and a steady voice, as behind the opposite. But whether the child is blushing or looking away, lying or not, what we see is tension, excitement or signs of shame, anxiety and insecurity. Signs that we want to take seriously if we want to create connection.

The child may be squirming out of fear of being punished. Stuttering and fumbling words does not necessarily hide a lie but can be a fear of not being accepted. Will they be believed? This is the moment when trust and connection can either be built or destroyed. Slowing down and reminding ourselves that we can't know for sure what we are seeing is a first step if we want to create connection with a child who we think is lying or withholding information. A second step can be to invite a conversation by saying something informal that expresses empathy or understanding like:

"I'm guessing that this situation doesn't feel entirely comfortable, is that right?"

As caregivers, we have a certain responsibility for our children's lies. In cases where the child is actually hiding something, a degree of reassurance is needed. When they trust that a challenging truth will be received with respect and interest, it becomes a little easier to express.

Whether it is our child or our boss, we are all generally worse, more than we think, at judging whether someone is lying, or stretching the truth. The reason why someone scratches behind their ear may actually be because they were bitten by a mosquito, even if some book on body language tells us that it is a sign of lying.

When the Child is Lying

Since lying is very human, it's not surprising that children say, "I'll be home in a minute" (even though they know it will take much longer than that to get home). How many of us adults regularly come up with little white lies, such as about how fast we ran a mile, how often we clean? And how many have said we are on their way home even though we are still at the office?

While we tell children not to lie, we, at the same time, tell them not to make others sad. They shouldn't tell grandma if they think the food is disgusting. Nor should they honestly express disappointment about a gift they don't like, but rather kindly say "thank you."

Children will hear a father say on the phone that he can't talk now because he's playing games with the family, even though that's not true. Their mother may have asked them not to tell the other parent about the extra sweet they had together while out on the town. All this becomes challenging for kids, if they are verbally told that the truth is always the most important thing to consider.

Since the norm in most contexts is to stick to the truth, our child's lies might make us feel ashamed and wonder what others will think of us. Is it our fault that they don't tell the truth? Most likely, the moment we judge our child's lying, we forget our own childhood lies or ignore the fact that we regularly slip up on the truth ourselves.

Even if morality signals that lying is not okay, humans are said to lie or tell so-called white lies up to a hundred times a day. Whatever the figure for the number of daily lies, it is part of most people's communication to occasionally give ourselves a little leeway with the truth.

If we think that everything a child does depends on their up-bringing, it may feel tough to reflect on the role we as parents play in our children's lies. However, we may strive, there are hundreds of situations where our weaknesses as parents will be revealed. To quote Marshall Rosenberg:

"Hell is being a parent and believing there is such a thing as a perfect parent."[38]

When we ask ourselves to be perfect parents, we need to be prepared for the many occasions when evidence of the contrary is presented. Perhaps it is less shameful to think that our child was born with a weak character or is hanging out with the wrong company. Or maybe we counteract the uncomfortable feelings of shame by blaming the school or the other parent. As long as we see lying as wrong and immoral, the places to look for a scapegoat are abundant.

Some of us will try to get our children to stop lying by telling our own stories of how we lied as children and bitterly regretted it. Carlo Collodi's tale of Pinocchio's growing nose is meant to scare children into telling the truth. Then there is the fable of the boy who cries "the wolf is coming" so many times that no one responds anymore, and where he eventually falls victim to the wolf's jaws. Nobody came to his help when he finally really needed it. This is another way to try to moralize truth telling into our kids.

But if all people lie, and if it even stimulates our child's imagination, how do we want to react to our children's lies? At the same time, there is a difference between children exploring what it means to stretch the truth, and them lying because they do not trust that they will be treated with dignity if they do tell the truth. Those who have previously expressed a truth they were punished or shamed for, may not be willing to endure it again and instead choose lying. The confusion of being told that "the truth always wins," and then being punished for telling the truth, can be big.

The Morality behind Telling the Truth

Morality develops within us during a period when our thinking is not governed by processes that are entirely logical or linear, but magical. A clear conception of morality is based on simple categories such as right/wrong, good/bad, normal/abnormal, appropriate/inappropriate. While this simplification helps, dilemmas arise when we eventually discover that it is rarely possible to say that a certain behavior is always good or that lying is always inappropriate.

As young adults, we can think in more complex ways, such as "if I do that, this can happen, but only if I also do it this way or if someone else fails to do it."

We soon discover that it is rarely possible to say that a certain behavior is always good or always bad. For example, if we still hold on to the idea that lying is wrong, and at the same time we have grown morally and see value in protecting other people from harm, something that helped us earlier in life can now become a dilemma.

An example used to discuss morality is to imagine a person running past you, screaming at the top of their lungs. You think the person looks terrified and stands there in surprise. Shortly afterwards, a man comes rushing towards you with an axe in his hand.

You think the person looks terrified and stands there in surprise. He asks in a loud voice which way the first person ran. Are you going to tell the truth? Does it matter what the man's intention is, or do we want to play it safe and tell the man that the first person ran in a different direction than what you saw?

In this situation, most adults are likely to see it as more important to protect, rather than absolutely adhere to the truth. We have been taught that it is always best to be truthful, but also to be considerate of others, and the latter principle has become a higher-ranking principle as we have matured. Even if it is clearly a lie to say that the person ran in a different direction than we say, we want to use "protective use of an untruth."[39]

152

Moral researchers generally seem to agree that we evolve from a basic ability to sort behaviors into categories such as right and wrong, to eventually being able to nuance our responses. American psychologist Lawrence Kohlberg's research on morality assumed (similarly to Piaget) that as children's cognitive development progresses, there is a change in the child's ability to make ethical considerations.[40] To nuance our understanding of lying and morality, we can use Kohlbergs three levels of development.

1. Pre-conventional level

At the first level, one's actions are based on impulses from the environment and, by extension, reactions to the actions of authority figures. Am I being punished or rewarded? Liked or disliked? The immature individual needs support from adult caregivers as morality at this level is regulated from the outside. The individual's behavior is governed by authority's approval.

At the later part of the pre-conventional level, bartering occurs: "You can borrow my bucket if I can play with your stuffed animal." The individual is motivated by things that lead to personal satisfaction in the short term.

According to Kohlberg, the pre-conventional level covers the period up to the age of ten, but some critics argue that it ends much earlier and can last much longer.

2. Conventional level

Gradually, the young individual's behavior is directed from being regulated by relationships with people in the immediate environment to also being influenced by the rules of the surrounding culture. Relationships with siblings, friends and peers influence the child's behavior more than at the previous level. Now adaptation is about managing expectations and personal relationships.

Individuals in this phase perceive the intention behind a certain action and not just the consequences of it. They do not automatically judge themselves or others as careless if they accidentally break a toy, especially if it is clear that the intention was not to do so. However, if a person deliberately throws a fragile toy to the ground, they are judged as mean because they had the intention to damage or destroy it. The thinking here has developed and is different from that at the pre-conventional level, when the individual could not see that there could be different intentions behind the same kind of action.

At the conventional level, the individual adapts to different roles, but gradually gains greater understanding of the rules that extend beyond each person. Individuals at the conventional level, children and adults alike, are usually loyal to the system they live in, do their "duty" and follow rules, motivated by the fact that laws are there to prevent certain behaviors that harm others. Acceptance of rules enables the child to take part in games they did not understand before maturing to the conventional level. The maturing child can also accept and understand that adults may have different rules than themselves.

3. Post-conventional level

At the post-conventional level, the individual begins to question authority. Rules are no longer taken for granted but can be criticized and discussed. The individual's morality is more and more controlled from within. The maturity from the earlier stages is there, but because morality has been integrated within, the individual does not need to be constantly reminded of what applies.

Self-direction makes it possible to deviate from established norms and choose one's own path. The individual gradually realizes that laws and rules are relative and different, depending on the cultural or social community. People who answer "yes" to the question of whether it is wrong to lie give varying answers as to why. With morality at the pre-conventional level, someone could answer like this:

"Yes, it's wrong to lie."

"Why?"

"Mom told me." (Alternatively, "because it is right according to my teacher, my religious leader, culture" and so on.)

"Is it wrong to lie?"

"Yes."

"Why?"

"Dad has promised me that I will get an ice cream every time I tell the truth, even though it is hard."

Kohlberg divided each level into a couple of sub-stages, so even though the answers below are nuanced which is a sign of some development, they are still based on the pre-conventional level:

"Yes, it's wrong to lie."

"Why?"

"My friends get angry with me. I don't want to lose my friends."

Or,

"My teacher has said that there is a rule we have to follow in our class, and I don't want to make him sad."

Further maturation produces responses that reveal that morality has been integrated and fits into the conventional level:

"Yes, it's wrong to lie."

"Why?"

"It doesn't feel good, I want to be able to stand by what I say and not have to worry about things I have lied about."

The answers change further as the person's ability to take in more aspects develops and their thinking and morality moves towards post-conventional.

"Yes, most often it is wrong to lie."

"Why?"

"It is wrong to lie if it becomes more difficult for people to trust me. I want them to be able to trust me."

Especially in the later part of the post-conventional level, individuals act according to their own ethical principles, guided by their conscience:

"Yes, lying could be called wrong, but it depends. It is wrong if it influences other people to do things based on my lies. Since they trust me, they might invest time and money in our project and I don't want my lies to negatively affect them or their trust in me or even the outcome of our cooperation."

In the last dialogue, the focus is on whether someone might be harmed by a lie. We are ready to lie to the axe-man in order to protect someone from getting hurt, because the importance is how our truth affects the situation, more than about always telling the truth. Because we generally feel good about telling the truth, honesty is not necessarily driven by concern for others. Revealing the truth is sometimes a relief for someone who has been holding something back. It is only later in development that an individual can reflect on how a truth might affect others, and then decide how, if, and when to present it.

One downside of lying is that it becomes more difficult to relax around people we have lied to. Especially if we know that they believe that lying is always wrong, we may withdraw or hide aspects of ourselves. We face the dilemma of protecting the truth and balancing it with care. Caring is one of the reasons why we resort to white lies when our friends ask if they look tired, or when they ask if we like their new jacket. We may become withdrawn and hide aspects of ourselves, if we meet people that have strong judgments about lying.

The claim that the ability to lie is an important part of our development may be difficult to digest, as it is considered reprehensible in most cultures. But it is possible to embrace both, supporting moral maps that claim that telling the truth is valuable, as well as accepting lying as an important element in our evolution from pre-conventional to post-conventional thinking.

Peer Pressure and Retrospective Constructions

For millions of years, belonging to a group has been a prerequisite for survival. So, no wonder we want to belong, as being included in a group makes it easier to meet physical needs and gives us a psychological sense of safety and meaning. Feeling lonely sometimes seems to be part of being human, but at other times it is very challenging. At different stages of our development, we are particularly vulnerable to exclusion and loneliness can become excruciating.

Different individuals are also differently affected by loneliness. Some are fine being outside of a group, while many others are ready to give up certain values to ensure their place in the group. Even if there is little tolerance for difference and the jacket of conformity becomes too tight, it is sometimes more difficult to not belong.

Scientists have used what is named "the Cyber ball task" to study social pain in different ways. In this task, participants play an online ball-tossing game with two or three other players, in which the other players throw fewer tosses to him or her.

This experiment has been carried out in different ways, measuring the pain, sense of exclusion and even loneliness that shows up as the participants are no longer included in the game. In some experiments the participants were told that the other 'players' were not people, but digital devices and the game involved throwing a ball between them. However, after a while of throwing the ball, the human was excluded while the digital figures continued to throw the ball between themselves. After even a few minutes of not receiving the ball, the subjects reported feeling alienated and even lonely.[41]

With our strong drive to belong, it is no wonder that it is sometimes difficult to tell uncomfortable truths. In Solomon Ash's mid-20th century experiment, it becomes clear how easily we adapt to the 'truth' of the group. Each member of a group of seven to nine people was asked which of three lines was equal in length to an original line. It was obvious to the eye which line was equally long, but everyone except the subject had been instructed to choose another one. In many cases, after a few rounds, the subject also switched to the wrong line.

In newer experiments, led by Petter Johansson, a researcher in cognitive science at Lund University, subjects were asked to look at portrait photos.[42] The photos were shown in pairs and the subjects in the experiment had to choose which of the two people they thought looked more sympathetic. The photo of the person they chose was sorted into a special pile.

What the subjects did not know was that the researchers had been trained by a magician. With a structured trick, the participants were sometimes shown the photo they had chosen, sometimes the one they had rejected. When asked what they found sympathetic about the person in the photo, the vast majority were able to answer, even when the photo was not the one they had chosen. It usually took them a fraction of a second to find an answer. They said things like "I liked that person's hairstyle better," "that person's smile" and "that person looked more likeable or charming than the other."

Very few of the participants in the experiment protested when the wrong photo was held up. Most stated afterwards that they did not realize that the photo was different from the one they chose. They assumed that the person holding up the photo would not try to deceive them and easily came up with reasons for why they chose that photo.

A few noted that they had discovered that they were being tricked, but chose not to say anything. Confabulations seem to come easy to us. A common behavior when someone receives a wrong dish in a restaurant is to refrain from pointing it out. We don't want to be 'awkward' or 'make the waiter uncomfortable.' This might still be seen as a kind of lying, but with a motive to avoid shame and uncomfortable communication and maybe to protect others.

Lies are Hard to Catch

Some parents think that it is possible to tell if our children are lying because they don't meet our eyes, answer our questions in a mumble, or can't stand still while we are talking to them. While we can learn what a particular person close to us usually does to avoid discomfort and shame, we are generally poor at detecting other people's lies (although many of us think we are the exception).

Researcher Tim Levine studied adults from different professions and backgrounds to find out whether some professions are better at detecting lies than others. Social workers, teachers, police officers and judges were asked to watch videos of children and adults, either lying or telling the truth about something. To the surprise of the experimenters, the ability to detect lies was consistently low. Most studies give an average of about 55%, which is slightly higher than chance. Levine argues that a central part of our inability to determine whether someone is a liar is that we assume people are telling the truth.[43] Trusting that someone is telling the truth makes us feel more comfortable.

There is a link between economic security and increased trust between people, perhaps because when we are free from the pressures of poverty we can "afford" to trust others. The insecurity of constantly worrying about being deceived is something few people are willing to live with.

A person with paranoid traits can be very useful, for example in detecting a spy in the way Malcolm Gladwell describes in his book *Talking to Strangers*.[44] Reg Montes was the only person in the CIA who was paranoid enough to question even the most trusted person. His suspiciousness paid off, but the constant paranoia created stress and illness on him.

We are simply better off trusting people than not. At the same time, it is of course important not to blindly trust people as this makes us gullible and can put us in danger.

According to the aforementioned researcher Lisa Feldman Barrett, it is not surprising that we miss our children's lies, because emotions do not have fixed facial expressions. She argues that it is misleading to say that emotions are aroused, triggered or stimulated, because emotions are not passive states that come to life at a particular moment. There are no physical "buttons" to press to make someone feel or express certain emotions in a certain way.

Feldman Barrett doesn't question that emotions are reflected in people's voices, facial expressions and gestures, but mean that does not mean that everyone's anger or nervousness looks the same. Additionally, the ability of different people to show a neutral facial expression, if they want to hide something, varies.

Sometimes we get feedback that our guess of what others are feeling is correct, but Feldman Barrett says we should be careful not to make too much of it.

"Perceptions of emotions are guesses, and they are correct only when they match the other person's experience; that is, both people agree on which concept to apply. Every time you think you know how someone else feels, your insight has nothing to do with actual knowledge." [45]

Emotions are constructed to balance our energy, to help us focus, and to create meaning. They prepare us for different situations and challenges. Therefore, a blushing child's face could just as easily be a sign of concern about what might happen to their friend if they say it was the friend who scraped the car or ate the last cookie, as about the actual withholding of the truth. We can guess, but never know what we see in someone else's body movements or facial expressions.

Because children's lies cannot be detected from the outside, ongoing conversations about telling the truth about things that can be dangerous are important. If we also want to create connection when children express information that is uncomfortable for us, we need to use our impulse control skills and not shame them. We maximize the odds for an ongoing dialogue when we can show up ready to accept an uncomfortable truth. It is not up to us to decide if the child is lying or not, but we can do some things to influence the situation.

There are contexts and times when there are real, (not just moral) challenges with a child not telling the truth. If their safety or that of others is at stake, it is valuable if they feel safe enough to tell an uncomfortable truth. Bullying, self-harm, or being a victim of any kind of abuse or violence is vulnerable to talk about and adults need to be aware of this. But how do we support children so that they can talk to us about what is important? What helps children overcome resistance, and perhaps denial, even though it is extremely uncomfortable for them to talk about something?

Threats and demands to tell the truth, coupled with shame that lying is wrong, can get in the way of scary honesty. When someone feels insecure about how their truth will be received, they sometimes use further lies to escape punishment. If a child has become entangled in various lies, a usually secure relationship can suddenly feel insecure. Trust between people is built by keeping our promises, seeing the intention behind mistakes and being willing to repair what is broken. It might also be about admitting that we have not been truthful, but also admit to actions that lead to the broken trust.

There are situations when it is particularly important that children dare to tell an inconvenient truth. A person of any age who is being bullied, abused or sexually assaulted needs help, but is often ashamed, making it difficult for them to express themselves. Whether or not someone logically realizes that the blame does not lie with them, logic doesn't necessarily ease feelings of shame; the emotions are embodied and therefore perceived as personal. It is only later in life, when we have developed a certain awareness of emotions that we can separate the two. Until then we usually need warm support from others to deal with shame.

A person who hesitates to reveal something is anticipating that strong emotions will wash over them, if they uncover what they have been subjected to. As soon as words or thoughts approach the memory, they are paralyzed, their thoughts become a mess and the words get stuck in their mouths. Is it really safe to talk about something that feels so threatening?

Creating the moment of Truth

When we as caregivers realize that we have treated the child in a way that has not been helpful, we can do a re-take. This can mean anything from getting support to deal with our pain, apologizing, listening to what the child has to say about how they were treated, or asking for support to talk to the child again.

It is valuable to remember that it can be challenging to listen when someone talks about something that we also have perceived as shameful. Even if we put the blame on ourselves, we risk building barriers between ourselves and the child. One way to get out of it is to remind ourselves that we feel guilty because we care and to remind ourselves to make sure that we are heard by someone else.

A shared history influences whether someone dares to open up to us. Past deposits in the trust account become an important security buffer. If people, young and old, can recall times when they have been accepted, included and treated with respect, it can open the door to greater honesty.

For adults dealing with children who express difficult things, it is valuable to have an understanding of how we humans express shame. Shame discharge takes the form of a laugh, an angry comment, a distracting game, a silent withdrawal, a diversionary prank, or a shrug. Sometimes it is difficult to connect a certain behavior with what is really going on inside the person.

Mentioned earlier was the concept of secondary shame, which is the shame we feel when embarrassed by what others do, often people we are closely associated with. As early as the age of four, the ability to feel contempt and discomfort towards other people and even towards ourselves begins. Usually it takes a while before some children feel full blown shame over their parents.

The behaviors we are uncomfortable with depend largely on the morality of the context in which we find ourselves. Culture and family members show us what the norms and boundaries are and what is appropriate behavior.

One of the most difficult examples where secondary shame plays a role is when a child has been abused by an adult. Often children who are sexually abused are shamed by their abuser. They are told that they are disgusting and that no one will believe them if they tell what happened, because no one really cares about them:

"They will like you even less if they find out."

Victims of abuse also face threats such as:

"If you tell on me, I will ... (kill you, hurt your friend, family, etc.)."

The threats and insults lead to the encapsulation of the experience and the child or young person may withdraw from connection with their family as well. Presumably, adults who abuse children do not have a straight-forward relationship with shame. They may numb their inner critic with alcohol or drugs and often carry within them potentially traumatic events (which of course is never an excuse for harming children).

Whether or not the abuser feels shame for what they are doing in the moment, they are likely to be avoiding shame, which allows them to cross their own and the child's boundaries. If the perpetrator's inner critic is silenced or never supported to develop, it cannot stop harmful behaviours either. Tragically, the child then carries the shame of the perpetrator.

Self-harm is a strategy to numb overwhelming emotions associated with abuse or other potentially traumatic situations. Self-harming strategies range from things like cutting oneself, taking drugs or even selling sex. Paradoxically, self-harm often provides a temporary sense of control in an otherwise powerless situation.

There was a time in Europe when not only the perpetrator, but also the child victim of incest was punished for it. The child was considered partly responsible. Although the view of the child's responsibility has changed, children who are sexually abused are still faced with dealing with what has happened, an experience of humiliation, but also sometimes with the seeds of doubt planted in them by the perpetrator.

Many adults realize that it is seldom constructive to pressure a child to tell what has happened in a difficult situation for them. When and if they do tell someone, they will, even if only for a short time, "re-feel" the shame that comes with talking about the humiliating things that have happened to them. The memory of what they have been through, and the words they remember the person who hurt them saying, become overwhelming to remember and express. The slightest sign of disapproval and questioning from the listener can cause them to withdraw to avoid more shame and stress.

For a child to experience trust and dare to talk about situations that feel shameful, the adult needs to listen emphatically and receive what is said, before questioning the truth of what is said. On top of this, children also remain silent out of strong loyalty and to protect the person who has hurt them. If the adult listens and avoids either questioning the child, defending the perpetrator's behavior, or threatening to harm the perpetrator, the child can often more easily talk about what they have experienced.

It is valuable for an adult who encounters a child carrying a difficult secret to recognize that the child may be silent and numbing the stress within. Their withdrawal is not necessarily a sign that the child is rejecting support. The withdrawal can be a sign of overwhelm and fear at the thought of approaching the vulnerable or shameful talk about what has happened. This takes a lot of self-awareness both for the child and the adult, and at the same time is well worth working on.

Additional pressure is put on the children when caregivers gets embarrassed that a child has not confided in them, or who takes the child's silence as a personal rejection. In such a case the best option might be that they themselves seek support first, from a third person. Anyone who has been in such a vulnerable situation can attest to the importance of someone listening and believing in you. Stress is relieved when we feel that someone is there for us, and that we are not alone.

The first time someone talks about an abuse they suffered is not necessarily more crucial than the second. But *how* the person is met the first time is crucially important. According to the Canadian family therapist Allan Wade, "one of the things that most accurately predicts how difficult a violent situation will be for a person to deal with is how they were treated when they later talked about it." Wade says that how they are received "is a greater determinant of stress levels than the level of violence and the person's relationship with the perpetrator."[46]

When caregivers hear about something painful their child has experienced, they may react in a way that is difficult for the child to understand. Often, the caregiver feels shame for failing to protect the child. In an attempt to avoid the discomfort of shame, the adult may do anything from withdrawing, blaming, or even trying to persuade the child not to 'take it so seriously.'

Integrity Tastes Good

Psychologist Angela Evans has done experiments similar as Lewis, showing that children are less likely to peek at the toy when the researcher leaves the room if they have promised not to. Even young children who do not have a clear understanding of what exactly the words "promise" and "lying" means, understand what it is about.

The ability to see alternative scenarios reduces feelings of powerlessness, both in children and adults. With a growing capacity to understand time, symbolic thinking, and the understanding of how people express emotions, children are ready to edit "the play of lies." Acting as the director of an experimental play with power over both plot and characters, and where the ending can vary each time the play is performed, a young individual becomes a little more mature.

Nevertheless, continual lying can sometimes bring anxiety, especially when we lie to someone we care about or about something that is important for us to stand for. Of course, a young person who withdraws or becomes aggressive over small things can do so for a number of reasons. One might be to avoid being reminded of past lies and the shame associated with them. Teenagers often dislike duplicity and posturing but do not always know how to deal with it. As mentioned earlier, young adults mature by integrating core values and eventually start to be able to stand up for them. This can become so important that over time, they can gain the courage to stand up against injustice, even if this means they become excluded themselves. Paradoxically, being able to lie, and still sticking to the truth is good for us.

The Superpower of Impulse Control

We sigh, but smile, when we see a two-year-old painting stick figures on the wallpaper. If the child's teenage sibling did the same thing, we would probably stop smiling and call it irresponsible or immature. When the fourteen-year-old doesn't behave, we demand impulse control and threaten with punishment if they don't come home at the time we ask them to, or do something else we don't approve of.

In his book series about the Kalahari, Lasse Berg describes how in history individuals in most hunter-gatherer societies constantly gained and lost weight.[47] When a mammoth was killed, the human body was able to store energy in fat, the extra layers of which provided heat and energy that slowly burned during the following mammoth-free weeks or months. Without refrigerators and freezers, the body's ability to hold fat reserves was a major asset and was far more important than impulse control.

Contemporary man, with supermarkets in every neighborhood, is constantly facing a mammoth feast. As soon as we visit a grocery store, we are overwhelmed by sight and smell. The instinct to eat remains in us, driven by our will to survive. With the constant availability of calories, the ability to regulate the temptation to eat sugar and fat becomes vital. The capacity to regulate satiety and hunger is of greater importance to human health than ever before in human history. It is not uncommon to shame yourself and others for having a bad character, in order to create motivation in gaining better impulse control, an attempt that usually has a bad payoff.

The foundations of our impulse control have been laid in the early levels of development. Children learn to wait their turn, follow rules and eventually refrain from cheating even when no one is watching. Some learned behaviors include always saying "no" or "yes" immediately and impulse control may be used to give oneself some time to think over your answer.

If we always want to have time to think a little longer, the impulse control might be used in pushing yourself to answer more directly.

Both children and adults may find it difficult to hold back a chuckle in an inappropriate moment, but as we develop, most of us learn to control laughter if we understand that it may hurt the person we are laughing at.

Lewis's experiment, where children are asked not to look at a toy while the adult leaves the room, becomes easier for the children the older they get. Generally, a six-year-old can resist temptation longer than a three-year-old, because they understand more about how time works and can regulate their behavior accordingly.

About 35% of the six-year-olds in Lewis's experiment used their impulse control and refrained from looking. At the same time, their ability to deny looking at the toy increases as they get older. They can more easily determine whether the adult is able to detect their deception than before and have developed the ability to lie more thoughtfully.

When we get upset, it is easy to say things we later regret. If we stop and reflect when we are angry, we can act and express ourselves differently and protect important relationships, apologize and repair broken trust. In a situation with strong emotions, the ability to control one's impulses relies on being able to regulate the intensity of emotions. This will happen through the way we think, or by breathing, distracting ourselves, expressing ourselves, or asking for help.

If we assume that impulse control is needed to refrain from harming others, it is easy to believe that without it we will be overwhelmed by violent inner urges. But we don't have a beast inside us that needs taming and is driven to hurt others. A small child who hits us over the head with his little toy car has low impulse control but does not act out of malice. They simply cannot determine how painful it can be to get hit with a plastic toy on the nose.

As adults, we face daily challenges, such as refraining from having that extra cookie, remembering to ask for a break to think about an important decision, or forgoing another episode of your favorite TV show in order to get enough sleep. Impulse control is often linked to the ability to stop oneself from doing or saying something. But it is often more advanced than that, as it is also needed in order not to give in to an overwhelming impulse to always restrain oneself, or to overcome resistance to addressing a difficult family dilemma. Someone who constantly has the impulse to stay in the background can, with the right support, often break that pattern and choose to act more directly. The few children in the Lewis and Evans tests who were able to completely restrain themselves from looking at the toy were, according to follow-up tests, generally the smartest.

Walter Mischels' well-known Marshmallow test, which has been running for decades, studies how children deal with delayed rewards.[48] Mischels' tests began in 1970. Tim, five years old, sits alone in a room at the Stanford preschool. In front of him a fluffy marshmallow is placed. He knows he is allowed to eat the tempting sweet, but also that he has been promised more if he can wait a while. Tim avoids the temptation by not looking at the piece of candy. He lets his eyes wander and study the room around him.

Other children in the same experiment distracted themselves by making a humming sound. Some repeated a word like no, no, no, while others focused on rocking back and forth on the chair they were sitting on. For a longer time than many others, Tim refrains from eating the candy. When the experiment was followed up, children who, like Tim, abstained, were found to be more stress-resistant, better able to concentrate, had higher grades, lower BMI, better jobs and more sustainable relationships in adulthood than those who did not persevere.

While we can learn a lot from past experiments, young people face a challenge that did not exist in the seventies. Put a smartphone in the hands of the child and let them swipe through colors and sounds and most will have no trouble letting go of the idea of eating the sweet in front of them. Dopamine and other feel-good hormones are released when playing computer games and swiping on social media, making it almost impossible to put the phone down. When children are finally forced to leave the screen, they might be grumpy, not only because they are prevented from continuing with something fun, but also because the flow of dopamine has been cut off. They are in a state of mind that many adults find difficult to deal with as well.

Children are often praised when they wait to take another cookie before everyone gets one. We appreciate that they let someone else choose the toy before them and admire their self-control. Paradoxically, at the same time, spontaneous people are described as delightful. Controlled or restrained people do not have the same positive connotation. But perhaps controlled is not the opposite of spontaneous? The concern that impulse control will turn us into controlled perfectionists is in most cases unfounded.

Moreover, a person suffering from restraint can use their impulse control by acting on their first impulse instead of following the impulse to abstain. People who usually give in to their first impulse may do the opposite and carefully choose the moment when they say or do something. The ability to embrace one's emotions or divert attention from them, rather than letting them take over, is an important part of an individual's development.

Children and young people who have difficulties with impulse control are often scolded or shamed for it. We assume that they are able to refrain from suddenly screaming or throwing another cookie and try to shame them into taking more responsibility. But there are individuals who do not have the impulse control we expect from them. For example, people with different diagnoses, such as ADHD or autism, often have a greater challenge with impulse control, a difficulty not related to their level of intelligence but to the way their brain works.

Moreover, people who have gone through potentially traumatic events may have impaired impulse control skills, temporarily or permanently, and even if they are told endlessly to stop doing something, they find it difficult to refrain if the action mitigates the experience of the trauma.[49]

Opinions and Observations

When we combine observation with evaluation,
people are apt to hear criticism.

MARSHALL ROSENBERG

Honesty, based on our thoughts and opinions, is valuable when we want to debate, discuss specific topics and compare them against each other. According Marshall Rosenberg, when we want to connect with other people, build trust and strengthen our cooperation, it is more valuable to express ourselves honestly based on what we observe, feel, need and want. He claims that this is not about how we, "... remain completely objective and refrain from evaluating. It only requires that we maintain a separation between our observations and our evaluations."[50]

So, for example when someone asks if you think that their new jacket is nice and you don't like it, what do you say? First of all, you can think about whether you think the purpose of the question is to receive a compliment, an opinion or if the person just wants to start a dialogue?

One way to choose which part of the truth to express is to distinguish between what we observe and how we judge what we observe; whether you say the jacket is ugly or whether you call it stylish (regardless of if you like it or not), both are your opinions. An observation could be that it has the same yellow tone as the person's hat or that you see that it reaches the person's knees.

But what does the person really want? To be seen? To be appreciated? Or to get your opinion? Is it honest to say "I think green suits you better than yellow" or "yellow makes me happy" even if I don't like the jacket or how it looks on them? When is something caring and when is avoiding expressing our opinions damaging? When is it valuable to be what is sometimes called "straightforward" even if we imagine that it might hurt the other person? Of course, this communication challenge is not limited to situations with children, but may actually be particularly problematic between adults.

Mari sighs when she receives an invitation to lunch with Angela's mother, Cornelia. She hesitates because she has little desire to spend time with Cornelia. At the same time, she wants to have a good relationship with the parents of Emma's friends. Today, she doesn't feel up to it, so she tells a lie that she doesn't have time. Cornelia then asks which day would work better. If Mari were to be honest about her thoughts, there is a high risk of damaging the relationship, as the answer would be something like:

"No thanks, as I find our conversations so boring, I don't want to have lunch any other day with you either."

If Mari, instead, were honest about her needs, there could be a chance of growing the relationship, at least if Cornelia could hear Mari without feeling insulted. But there is no guarantee, and such communication often takes longer than a simple yes or no. At the same time, effective and connective communication often saves time in the long run, as we avoid breaches of trust. Honesty with a focus on needs, instead of on opinions, can sound like this:

"I'm not sure how to express myself and I want to know if you are willing to hear my honest answer - are you willing to hear?"

"Okay. It sounds a bit uncomfortable, but sure."

"The last few times our conversation has basically been about interior design and I'm not particularly interested in this but haven't told you that. The thought of us having a similar conversation again makes me hesitate. What is it like for you to hear this?"

Notice that Mari takes a lot of responsibility here, not lying or judging Cornelia. Sometimes this might be seen as tiptoeing but remember that the purpose is to maintain contact when expressing what may be easy to hear as criticism. At least now the conversation has started.

"But why didn't you say something?" Cornelia asks.

"I didn't want to hurt you or be the one in charge of the conversation and couldn't find a way to tell you that. At the same time, I wish I had found a way to say it earlier, because I guess it's not fun for you to hear this afterwards?"

"Exactly. It feels very uncomfortable."

"I feel stupid for not having said something earlier, especially when I realize that you probably would have wanted to hear it."

"I'm still glad you're saying it at all. And I'm curious, what would you like to talk about?"

"That's another reason why I didn't tell you. I don't really know what I want to talk about, so it has been difficult for me to suggest anything."

In order for Mari to be able to have this conversation, she needs to dare risking that Cornelia becomes annoyed or disappointed. Mari needs to be able to deal with her inner discomfort and the guilt that is sprinkled on top of it. Her self-image, as a kind and generous person, clashes with the desire to say no because she judges it as selfish.

7

SEX AND INTIMACY

Since intimacy and sex are often affected by feelings of shame, this chapter touches on it. Hopefully, in its simplicity, this chapter can provide some clues to the sometimes nervous conversations about sex between caregivers and children and create acceptance of the differences that make us unique.

Let's Talk about Sex

Sex sells. Newspaper articles and TV spots have extra impact if they highlight or imply something sexual. News about the sexual habits of celebrities increases circulation. Half-naked bodies have been used to promote everything from cars to cigarettes. However, what is rarely exposed in the media, is that our first experiences of sexual interactions, in addition to excitement, intensity and pride, are often tinged with insecurity, powerlessness and a sense of failure. Moreover, many people, teenagers and adults alike, feel embarrassed to talk about sex, ask questions, share their sexual preferences, and listen if someone else shares theirs.

Sex is a multi-leveled strategy with the potential to meet many different needs. It is therefore not at all surprising that some people are fascinated by everything related to the subject. Sexual experiences can satisfy needs for acceptance, being seen and acknowledged. Also needs such as warmth, belonging, and dignity can be met by sexual encounters and, of course, love and closeness.

Relationships involving sexual expression can strengthen connection and provide meaning and pleasure in a way that contributes to the experience of freedom and excitement in a wonderfully vulnerable mix. Sex can be exciting, enticing and sometimes secret, shameful and taboo. In addition, sex can be fun.

Preschoolers often develop curiosity and interest in their own and other people's bodies. Children at that age can show and examine their genitals with their peers. Many children under five starts looking at their own and other people's bodies and become curious about what happens when you go to the toilet. Also common are masturbation (without orgasm), erection and lubrication, and the use of sexual or genital words.

Later, when children start school, they may become curious about adult sexuality and animal reproduction. Sexual games may become more prominent, and it becomes particularly important for adults to convey the importance of everyone participating voluntarily. The games occur most commonly with a child they know well, or siblings close in age. At this age, shyness about being naked may increase, while looking at naked pictures is exciting.

Tom, like many of his sixteen-year-old friends, thinks about sex, jokes about sex, blushes when sex is mentioned, giggles about sex, dreams about sex, worries about sex, lies about sex, imagines sex, denies his interest in sex, listens to music about sex, and watches movies about sex. Since Tom has only made out with a few girls but hasn't had what he calls sex, he's trying to figure out what sex really means.

During giggly science lessons, the teacher focused on what happens in the body during intercourse and on contraception, but that was about it. Tom would have appreciated being able to ask more specific questions, such as how to get close to someone, how to show that you want to have sex with someone, and a lot more. The lessons only answered some of Tom's questions and talking to his parents about sex is out of the question. Tom has gotten some of his answers from the internet and others from listening to his friends although he knew that some of them were lying, maybe all of them, or at least exaggerating. Other information he got from watching porn movies online, but it felt charged and stressful, because he worried that his parents would catch him watching pornography.

One evening at home on the living room sofa, Tom sees a book that his mother, who is a teacher, had shown him earlier and said she got from a visiting lecturer at her school. The word sexuality blazed out on the cover, and he picks it up to flip through it again.

"The World Health Organization (WHO) defines sexuality as a central aspect of being human throughout life. It encompasses sex, gender identities and roles, sexual orientation, eroticism, pleasure, intimacy, and reproduction. Sexuality is experienced and expressed in thoughts, fantasies, desires, beliefs, attitudes, values, behaviors, practices, roles, and relationships."[51]

Tom reads the text, a couple of times before putting the book down. The description seems good, but how does the sexual arousal that sometimes consumes him, go together with falling in love with someone? It cannot possibly be a sign that he is in love. He hates that this feels so awkward to talk about.

With a sigh, Tom picks up the book again, turning the pages at random, and thoughts that often circulate in his head come to mind. He has felt aroused or sexual excitement around a couple of girls at school. But he has also gotten excited when a certain guy has come close. Is he gay? Or bi? But what do these words really mean? He doesn't know anyone who is open about being bi-sexual, even though everyone uses the term. The biology teacher assured him that it was perfectly normal to be attracted to someone of the same sex and that it could vary, but he sounded so dry and matter of fact, that Tom doubted that he really knew what he was talking about, so he keeps reading.

"According to the Discrimination Act, everyone living in Sweden should have equal rights and opportunities, regardless of sexual orientation, gender identity or gender expression."

It sounds straight forward enough, but if he were to tell his friends that he gets horny looking at both boys and girls, he wonders what they would think. And Tom doesn't even want to imagine what his dad would say. Once, Tom tried to recount that a lecturer at school had said that gender identity should be seen as something fluid that can change over time. But when he told his Dad about this, he had just laughed and joked that fluidity only exists in bottles. Tom understands that when his dad was young, terms like non-binary, cis or trans-gender were rarely or never used, but still thinks the joke is absurd. What Tom hasn't reflected on is that many adults find it challenging to articulate and define what sex and sexuality is.

Some time ago Dad asked if Tom knows how sex works, and when he said yes, Dad let him be. That Mum has never mentioned sex at all, is not something Tom has reflected on.

Over the last few years Tom has gradually discovered that he can satisfy himself. At first it was embarrassing, but now he knows how it works and it feels good to know how to deal with that inner pressure. He often wonders about what it would feel like to have sex with someone else.

Sex and Gender Identity

It is valuable to understand the difference between sexuality and gender identity. Our sexuality is about so much more than who we fall in love with or feel attracted to. Our gender identity is about how we experience our identity in terms of gender and gender expression. Here it is helpful for adults to gain knowledge and/or explore these issues together with children. One option is to help the child find a safe place to talk to someone else about it if they want to.

Sex is portrayed in different ways in media, porn, fiction, music, and film. This reduces it's charge. But it also makes it easier to get lost in different interpretations of what sex "is" and what place it can have in our life. Is sex an intimate soft encounter? A place to be cool and independent? Fiercely challenging? Or tender and warm? An opportunity to express your unique personality? Is there room for breaks? Room for tears and other emotional expressions? The questions are many, and the power of sexual energy rarely leaves anyone indifferent.

Sexual exploration affects our body chemistry and can regulate stress. The degree of sexual interest varies greatly from individual to individual and during puberty there are major bodily changes to be balanced and integrated. Forging sexual bonds sometimes provides a sense of belonging beyond what the teenager has with their family of origin.

As a parent, it is sometimes difficult to see your children as sexual. In our eyes, they are still small, and we fail to adjust our vision and see them for who they are now. Maybe the lessons we got were mostly about using condoms or came in metaphors about the flowers and the bees.

With the impact of media it is easy to get caught up in the idea that a healthy teenager 'should' be interested in sex, and if we don't see it in our teenager, we get worried. We generalize without realizing that interest in sex varies and comes and goes throughout life. Sexual exploration doesn't necessarily start in the teenage years, yet the rearrangement of hormones during that time is one reason why sexual interest often becomes central to adolescents.

Parents and other adults who want to talk to teenagers about intimacy and sex would do well to remember that teenagers (and probably most people of any age) want to feel free to choose with whom they communicate about intimate matters. We can make it clear that we are open to talking to them about sex, but that we do not expect them to confide in us. A young adult has the right to privacy.

Depending on personality, habits, norms and social context, the level of embarrassment during conversations about intimacy, consent and sexual preferences varies. Perhaps the best advice is to show your own vulnerability and get personal only if the young adult wants to talk to you about the intimacy of sexual relationships.

Think twice before you share any of your own experiences and really check with the young one if they want to hear. Being open and vulnerable doesn't mean you need to tell stories; on the contrary it is more about listening.

One way to approach the conversation is to show interest even in things we don't understand ourselves. In recent decades, for example, many young people have been reflecting on the pronouns they want others to relate to them by, a reflection that many previous generations have never done. A caregiver who shows genuine interest even in things they don't understand can help lower a young person's guard, thus creating opportunity for connection.

Remember that not everything needs to be said all at once. If the teenager in front of us squirms at the mention of sex, we can remind ourselves to give them space to choose how much they want to ask or share with us. Or perhaps we ourselves come from a background where sex was shameful and where adults avoided talking about it, and we need to learn to be mindful of our own embarrassment as it comes through. The teenager's insecurity may be about the topic itself, or it may be that talking to us is the source of their discomfort. Either way, it rarely helps if the caregiver bluntly suggests that "sex is perfectly normal and not at all embarrassing to talk about."

It is valuable to be able to distinguish between shame and embarrassment. They are often linked to similar needs, but there are important differences. Shame feels private, and is seldom accompanied with an impulse to share about it. Embarrassment is almost always related to feeling uncomfortable with other people, but might be followed by an impulse to be shared with people we feel safe with. What distinguishes these feelings is, among other things, the intensity of their discomfort. Another thing that distinguishes them is that embarrassment doesn't tend to create the same confusion and difficulty of expression as shame. A person that feels shame might need much more safety and support to share what they are going through than the person that is embarrased.

Many teens can stay in the conversation even if it feels awkward, especially if joking, circuitous routes, and moving at an easy pace in the conversation are allowed. When we get a "no" from a teenager to our invitation to talk about sex with them, it is important not to prioritize our desire to be part of their life, over their need for privacy around this often-sensitive issue.

As adults we can use this opportunity to show that consent matters to us, that it is possible to handle a no, without getting caught in thinking that we are being rejected or that we can handle those thoughts in a non-demanding way. A no can also be heard as an invitation to further dialogueue, in finding ways to also include the needs of the person saying no.

There is much to talk about in how to support our children when it comes to the body and sex. Almost everyone thinks about these questions, which can feel embarrassing and secretive. There is a whole plethora of thoughts about how things work.

To feel good about your body, it is good to know more about how it works. Even though these topics are covered in school, some children find it easier to talk with their parents about things like puberty, periods, ejaculation, and appearance. Others would not dream of sharing any of this with parents.

Talking about puberty, for example, is a way of normalizing a challenging period of life that for most people starts somewhere between the ages of ten and thirteen. The hormonal changes cause some people to develop pimples and blackheads, plus hair in new places. The amount of sweat and body odor may change, voices may darken, moods may fluctuate. It is common to feel tired and hungry more often and to start thinking more about sex. Remember that whatever you talk to your child about, it doesn't need to cover everything about that topic in one conversation.

One helpful thing to inform both boys and girls about are such "private" things as the first menstrual period, which can come as early as ten years old or even so late as after fifteen. Eventually, the period comes about once a month and lasts for 3-6 days.

There can be different amounts of bleeding and different numbers of days. Some people suffer from menstrual pains, and while it can be annoying, it is not dangerous. It can be shameful to ask about how to deal with menstrual blood. Regardless of whether the young person wants to talk about bodily changes such as menstruation, the adult can make sure to provide needed help about the practical matters of this change.

Sex is a positive force with important health benefits such as reduced stress, increased intimacy, and better sleep. Children and teenagers are at risk of getting one-sided images of sex from mass media and may be relieved to hear that sex can be pleasurable, fun, challenging, emotional, vulnerable, and awesome, sometimes all at the same time.

The nervousness in talking about sex, often decreases with age. Later, as a young adult, it is not the end of the world if mom finds that condom in the trash or someone accidentally opens the door and sees something that was not meant for their eyes.

The summary below offers different topics that are worth addressing. However, do not treat it as a list of items to be discussed as at a board meeting, but as an inspiration for different conversations.

A Parent's Focus in Conversations About Sex

1. Highlight that sex has positive health benefits, including reduced stress, increased closeness, and better sleep.
2. Talk about sex as something that can be pleasurable, fun, challenging, emotional, vulnerable, exciting, and sometimes all at once.
3. Emphasize that sex needs to be done with mutual respect, open communication, and consent.
4. Explore how they can say no to sex they don't want to participate in but still would like to stay in connection with the other person.
5. Reflect on how they can accept, understand, and respect a "no" from someone else.
6. Share your understanding of how sexual preferences are personal and can vary from person to person. There are many ways to have sex and explore sexuality. Be attentive if your sharing is not supportive or connective.
7. Share your knowledge on how we protect ourselves against unwanted pregnancies and sexually transmitted diseases.
8. Bring up the question of what sexual identity is? We all benefit from understanding concepts such as homosexuality, bisexuality, queerness and more.

Taboos, Norms and Laws

Norms are unwritten rules that we all relate to. They set limits and are a prerequisite for us to function together.

PUBLIC HEALTH AGENCY OF SWEDEN[52]

In many cases, norms are positive. They provide a basis for order, security, and predictability. One everyday example is when we stand in line at the supermarket checkout and don't need to fight to be first. Another example is when we help a stranger who has fallen or support someone who is lost. Some norms, which lead to acceptance only of certain appearances or sexual expressions, have a negative impact if they lead to disrespectful treatment or discrimination. Norms both allow and restrict, support, and hamper behaviors.

Fortunately, norms are products of people and are thus open to challenge and modification. Laws play a role in determining societal acceptance of sexual expression, leading to variations in acceptance of bisexuality or homosexuality in different places. Homosexuality is considered a crime in countries like Russia, Uganda, and Saudi Arabia and recently also Iraq. Altering or removing a law usually follows a long-term change in societal norms. Normative change is an important step towards the creation of new laws or the modification of old ones.

Anything that goes beyond our description of what is normal, is seen as outside the norm. In Sweden, homosexual intercourse was illegal until 1944. When it was no longer an offense, the law shifted to view homosexuality as a mental illness that should be treated accordingly, until 1979 when that law also shifted.

Even though almost fifty years have passed since that law was changed, homosexuality is still sometimes perceived as outside the norm and in some situations, difficult to talk about. This reinforces the challenges of talking about LBGTQ and the concerns and experiences our children and young people have about gender and sexuality.

Norms seldom change overnight and as we see, they keep evolving both before and after new laws. The way society views gender and sexuality has varied throughout history and changed depending on the context. In Sweden, for example, popular movements, both global and national, for LBGTQ rights, mental health and improved living conditions have played a major role in changing the norms around these issues.

Masturbation was taboo in Europe for a long time and still is in some places. The reasons why it wasn't okay varied, but proclaimed risks such as hair growing under your feet, getting pimples, or going against God's rules, all made it shameful to satisfy yourself sexually. In adolescence, many people discover the joy of sexual self-gratification and the pleasure and freedom it brings. Enjoyment, independent of another person, gives the teenager access to their body in a way they haven't had before and with it, a certain self-confidence. Even though self-pleasure is accepted, masturbation is perceived by many as extremely private. For most it is not something that we share with others, not even friends, partners, or parents (and even less so on social media and such).

Because adolescence is so often associated with an interest in sex, it is easy to miss people who feel sexually disinterested. In some cultures, and groups, young people are expected to wait until after marriage to have sex, while in other cultures abstinence is unimportant. In some contexts, and cultures, sex is assumed to help people fall in love with each other. In other contexts, the connection between love and sex is not central or even logical.

Whether or not the norms around sexuality are spoken about or not, they are agreements about what is considered to "be normal." The individual is impacted by the collective. Let us assume that you are okay with the norm that other people express their sexuality as long as they do not harm themselves or anyone else, and that it is consensual. If you can accept those sexual expressions, many different behaviors fall within the norm. Feelings of shame will occur earlier if your definition of what is okay is narrower. Your boundaries may be that you require marriage before having sex, or you only view sex with someone of another gender as acceptable. Perhaps you can only envision having sexual encounters with someone who shares your religion. Perhaps you perceive sex as happening in a specific place or position, like a bed or a bedroom.

The boundaries your norms create, at best, provide safety and support to clarify your sexual preferences. If you want to broaden your experience of what is normal and acceptable, the previous norms will determine where you encounter feelings of shame and where you need to put in some work to expand your sexual horizon. The feelings of shame do not mean that you should stop there, but that you need to pay more attention to what you choose to do, and why.

One way to understand how norms and shame affect our sexuality is to imagine that our sexual fantasies and preferences are publicly revealed. Imagine that information about what makes you most aroused becomes available to everyone. Probably the idea that this intimate information about you would come out, feels vulnerable or even humiliating. You feel embarrassed whether what comes out is true or not.

"I'd rather die than find that my most intimate information is revealed", you might think.

At the same time, a cocktail of vulnerability, intimacy and arousal helps to make sex and sexual impulses exciting, vibrant and enticing. You may choose to share your sexual desires with someone close to you. Sharing can be awkward and vulnerable, but when accepted, it can often lead to deeper intimacy and pleasure.

Sexual humor is based on what is inside and outside the norm, the culture and nationality, which can be seen by what jokes were considered funny fifty years ago, but not now. At best, joking helps to process what is embarrassing. A dark side of jokes is that they sometime cause misunderstandings, separation, and preconceptions that prevent us from being vulnerably present.

According to psychologist and author Donald Nathanson, shame often precedes a pleasurable moment. He claimed that shame wil "come in" when we are open and in touch with something that makes us happy. He said we might also experience shame just after having felt pride or connection with someone else.[53] Other emotion researchers would probably question whether this is always the case, as variation is the norm for emotions, rather than emotions always showing up in some particular order.[54] At the same time, many people have experienced intense shame after pushing their boundaries, expressing themselves more freely, stepping outside of their usual space or taking the risk of letting someone see them up close.

Shame then pauses the joy, the sense of unity or the pleasure, as a reminder to check in with the risks involved in unconditionally saying yes to the experience. It can be valuable to sense if there was a moment of joy, openness or a sense of pride, just in the moment before shame showed up. This insight can provide some self-acceptance of why the feeling feels so chocking and helps us to gain understanding and warmth for ourselves.

Consent

In intimate relationships with others, it is particularly important to listen to the other persons's signals. If you are unsure, it is best to ask what they mean and what they want. Listening to your body's signals is equally important. In what way can you tell if you don't want to engage intimately and how can you communicate that?

In 2018, a Sexual Offences Act was introduced in Sweden. Like most other laws, it was preceded by a long debate. Among other things, there were concerns that victims would face even tougher and potentially abusive questioning to find out whether or not they had agreed to sex. The #MeToo movement probably had a strong influence on the creation of the Consent Act. In 2020, Brå published a report stating that the impact was far stronger than critics had predicted.[55]

The Consent Act gave the criminal classification of rape a different meaning. In simple terms, it means that sex must be voluntary and consensual. Previously, violence, threats, coercion, or a particularly vulnerable situation were required for something to be called rape. Not resisting is not the same as giving consent. Anyone who wants to have sex should clearly show or say yes to sex. This is why in Sweden it is illegal to have sex with someone who is asleep or unconscious, for instance, because of alcohol intoxication.

Paradoxically, victims of sexual abuse of any kind are often ashamed of it. It feels shameful to have ended up in a helpless situation. When victims tell someone about what they have been subjected to and are met with words that are meant to be supportive, such as "it is not you, but the person who subjected you to this who should feel shame," it is not always helpful. It becomes yet one more thing they should be able to deal with, another thing to be ashamed about: the idea that they could just get rid of the shame by thinking in a certain way.

But the feelings of shame don't automatically disappear by thinking that they "should" not be ashamed. At worst, the struggle can leave them even more isolated because they feel that they cannot make themselves understood. Without support, a traumatic experience can be a process that takes years to heal.

Psychological trauma is often the result of a shocking and painful experience that creates so much stress and overwhelming emotions that they become difficult to deal with. Difficult events affect us both physically and emotionally. However, it is important to recognize that no matter how uncomfortable the feelings are, they are often positive signs that someone is beginning to recover from something that happened to them and is now able to cope with even feeling them.

In his book, *The Mind Body Code*, neuropsychologist Mario Martinez divides potentially traumatic experiences into three main categories.[56]

1. rejection
2. being shamed, humiliated;
3. being abandoned, left behind.

In everyday language, the word trauma is sometimes used to describe a dramatic event that has changed someone's life in a negative way. There is a before and an after. However, not all difficult events lead to trauma, nor is trauma always caused by a single dramatic event. What is traumatic to one person may not have the same impact on another person. People's reactions to crises are usually transient, especially if they have people around them who care about them.

Although everyone is affected by all three of the categories above, they affect us in different ways. Trauma is a complex matter than can arise from one individual situation, but also from a prolonged neglect of basic human needs. When someone suffers a trauma, the usual shame avoidance strategies are reinforced and exaggerated to avoid further stress. What the best support is varies. Sometimes talking about what has happened is best; at other times hugs or light touch is more supporting; and at other times therapy of some sort is what is best.

One aspect of traumatic situations is that they affect our nervous system. Trauma sometimes leads to over activity, a feeling of stress. Pencil tapping on a table, an inability to sit still, constant visits to the toilet, these are all sometimes signs of trauma. Severe mood swings or difficulty in expressing oneself are further symptoms. Some people become passive and disengaged as the parasympathetic part of the autonomic nervous system works overtime.

Nothing feels fun or engaging, no relationships are particularly important. And the social isolation that follows withdrawal risks delaying trauma processing. Sometimes great reliance is placed on logic, "Those people who did that to you, they don't deserve your thinking about them, so just stop. What happened was not your fault." Or, "Let shame land where it belongs, it's not you who should be ashamed." At times, such comments are supportive, as it feels like someone is on our side. It is nice to be reminded that logic sometimes has the power to get us out of a paralyzing situation. But logic and emotion are not as separate as we might think, what we feel affects what we think and what we think affects what we feel.

With awareness, we can learn to focus our attention on the physical discomfort we experience when we feel shame just by thinking about the traumatic situation and reminding ourselves that this is not now happening. This can make the shame melt away and, along with a range of other measures, make the trauma fade.

But anyone who has dealt with their shame knows that we rarely experience a shame attack logically or as something we have full control over. So, while comments such as leaving the shame on the person who has hurt someone else are meant to be supportive, they are sometimes perceived as a demand that feels impossible to achieve.

A few Words About the Clitoris and the Myth of the Hymen

Emily Nagoski, author of the book *Come as You are, The Surprising New Science That Will Transform Your Sex Life*, argues that how we feel about our genitals affects more about how we experience sex than how the organs themselves function.[57] Whether this is a general truth or not, it speaks volumes about the importance of understanding and knowing our bodies. Since taboos around our bodies and perhaps especially our genitals are common, there is a considerable lack of awareness in this area. For example, the lack of knowledge about women's genitals contributed to the myth of a "hymen" spreading for centuries, and unfortunately, it still perpetuates. For just as long, in areas where this mythical membrane is supposed to be the proof of their virginity, young women have lived in fear of this non-existing membrane being ruptured. Women, as much as men, need to get to know that the hymen is a constructed idea with no biological basis.

Some women do bleed a little the first few times they have sex, but it is not because there's some opaque membrane that's been penetrated. Rather, it is an abrasion of sensitive mucous membranes that causes the bleeding, and it's far from something that all women experience.

Until 1998, there was little understanding of the anatomical structure of the female clitoris. In ancient times, the philosopher Aristotle described the woman as having a 'tube' like a penis but turned inside out and inside the body. The Greeks called it the 'little hill' - the kleitoris.

Leonardo da Vinci, amongst others, began dissecting the bodies of executed people - almost all men - to better understand our bodies. Man was man, and since women were not allowed to study in European universities, there were no women there to protest any obvious inaccuracies. Perhaps the clitoris was described only as 'a bit of extra tissue,' because it was not important for reproduction.

A prominent researcher who has recently investigated the structure of the clitoris is Dr. Helen O'Connell.[58] She is an Australian urologist and surgeon, and her work has been ground breaking in better understanding the anatomy of the clitoris. Dr. O'Connell published a study in 1998. It described the complete anatomy of the clitoris, including internal structures, and her work contributed to a deeper understanding of the role of the clitoris in female sexual function. O'Connell made it clear that the clitoris was not a small hill, but a much larger structure than can be seen from the outside.

In her work, O'Connell discovered that in prostate cancer surgery, great care was taken to ensure that male patients retained as much of their sexual ability as possible. In her experience, similar considerations and knowledge were lacking when surgery was performed on women, which got her thinking.

The clitoris wraps around the vagina and urethra and parts of the bladder. The outer part of the clitoris is connected to a larger part on the inside and O'Connell found that it is connected to several other organs. Her research shows the importance of choosing the right approach in cases such as gynecological surgery, cancer treatment and uterine prolapse.

Shame probably played a role in why it took humanity so long to figure out the structure of the female genitalia. It makes you wonder what else we have avoided taking a closer look at in order to avoid uncomfortable feelings of shame.

8

THE YOUNG ADULT

This chapter focuses on a developmental phase where young adults want to be good at something, become experts and to stand on their own two feet, something they can explore for the rest of their life or eventually develop from. By late adolescence, most young adults have developed such a clear identity that actions and values they previously ferociously defended, now can be questioned, and discussed.

Becoming an Expert and Finding One's Identity

The young adult often enters a phase where what is happening inside of them becomes of more importance, (although the age at which this happens varies greatly). When this happens, subtle matters like feelings, thoughts and needs take on a deeper meaning than they had before, when the focus was on more concrete things outside of themselves.

As an understanding of the subtle inner world develops, the individual no longer needs to focus so much on becoming independent and starts to value interdependence and connection. This individual usually finds it easier to receive support, at least from an expert in the field. It is only when feelings can be renegotiated or reshaped that the advice mentioned before, "to never do anything to avoid shame," can be seriously explored and learned from.

In most people's lives, there is a period, shorter or longer, when the pursuit of achievement and expertise in a particular field takes center stage. Some people may spend most of their lives with this focus. This means that young adults at this stage may find themselves at the same level of development as their parents and they might even start to collaborate with them.

Excelling at something feels great. Success fuels pride, and pride feeds self-worth, even if that success is not always obvious to the outside observer. Expertise can be anything from being good at your sport, a music instruments, having read more books than those around you, to becoming an expert at burglary. It can also mean being a person who has visited many places, accumulated a lot of knowledge on a subject, or is successful in protesting against societal injustices.

Emma plays football, and her team has won the biggest junior cup in the country. They celebrate the victory with a dinner together. When the coach stands up to make a speech, everyone shushes each other and turns their attention to him.

He begins by saying how proud he is of them, praising how hard they have trained, praising them at length for their successful play. The players respond with a cheer for everything he raises and feel seen and celebrated. But then the coach concludes by saying something that diminishes the cheers:

"Remember, the most important thing is not to win, but to participate."

In a moment of open pride in her achievement, Emma can't help but stare at him. *Participate?!! We're not little kids, are we? We've proven that we are the best. Doesn't he get it?*

Emma's coach wished to emphasize the importance of participating and not on results, because as an adult he has come to value that. But he forgot who he was talking to and what might be the best support for them. The coach's intention was good, but not adapted to the developmental level of the individuals of the group. Emma, and probably the others in the team, wanted to focus on their performance, celebrate their achievement, and had little interest in inclusive values at that moment. Eventually they will move on, but the more we understand what is important to the young person in front of us, the easier it is for us to stand by their side, rather than creating distance by claiming that they should value the same things as us.

Of course, we want our youth to be successful, but we also want to see them grow up to be caring, wise people or at least team players. If we as adults no longer see achievement as the most important thing (perhaps because our focus is on seeing people regardless of their results), we risk underestimating the value of success for those who enjoy being really good at something. We might also come out of worry that our children will become self-righteous monsters, or worse, that they will think we will love them only if they perform.

The quest to master or become an expert in a certain field can be seen as a sign that someone has moved on from the period when it was all about fitting in and being accepted by peers. Now it's easier to stand out, make priorities that feel right to you and take up your own space. If it doesn't suit the group, the young adult is of often prepared to leave communities and find new groups to belong to. A desire to be seen as capable, knowledgeable, or extraordinary grows. One's own individual perspective becomes as important as being accepted by the group, or even more important. Sometimes the young adult steps out of a group that was previously essential to them, because they want something different from what that group allows.

The group may no longer represent values or actions the individual wants to be associated with. Belonging and acceptance are still important, but at this stage the person may be willing to sacrifice some of that to stand up for their own values.

They start being able to distinguish between human needs and the different strategies that can meet those needs, which gives them more freedom to act than when they thought that the only way to experience acceptance was to submit to parents, teachers or peers.

A person in this phase can visualize their goals, and project their dreams into the future. The magical thinking of childhood, where they believed that they were influencing their environment just by thinking in a certain way, has evolved further.

The young adult has realized that becoming good at something also requires effort, perhaps on their own, like spending a lot of time at the piano, or in a team where their performance is an important cog in the wheel.

A limitation in their imagination means that they often fail to realize how much of an impact achieving their goals will have. They may think that everything will be fantastic, if they get together with the right partner, find the right job, or lose weight. They might exaggerate the importance of their goals. Often it is very hard for them to imagine the impact of what reaching their goal will mean. They might be disappointed when they achieve it, as it all might seem quite empty in the end, and not as fantastic as they thought.

As we saw in the example of Emma, performance-based pride is important to support as caregivers. Eventually, the young adult will move on and appreciate things that are not based on results. Untimely moralizing rarely creates the change it was intended to create. Of course, Emma's football coach did not want to take away the team's joy but chose a poorly aligned time to express his own values.

Dignity, Honor and Pride

She held up her drawing,
described it,
pointed out every detail.
Chirping and singing about the chalk lines
that covered the paper
seemingly without plan or context.

And I,
idiot that I am,
couldn't help but let my mockery pull
at the corners of my mouth.

Couldn't help but let my words contaminate her pride.
"That doesn't look like a horse. Horses have four legs and
a tail and a mane. And they especially aren't green."

I wish someone had stopped me. Told me to shut up.
Told me to look up and protect the little one
who crumpled the paper, threw her crayons in
the garbage, never to pick them up again.

LIV LARSSON

The six-year-old has just cycled her first hundred meters without training wheels. The many words describing her achievements and her eagerness to show what she can do with the bike makes her pride obvious. She seems to have grown not only inside, but also in height. Descriptions of how far she was able to cycle, how easy it was, and the enormous speed achieved, bubble out of the child as soon as she meets an adult who seems willing to listen.

The desire to be seen (as opposed to being swallowed up by a hole in the ground, as is so often the thought when there is shame around) helps a child, with dignity intact, to raise their head and meet the eyes of others. A comment from an older child or an adult can easily raise or lower the level of excitement.

The cycle of pride can be simplified into four stages:

1. Someone wants to reach a goal.
2. The person does things that move them towards the goal.
3. The person succeeds and wants to be recognized for their achievement.
4. The person is received in their celebration and is nurtured by it. Or they are ignored or even scolded for their pride, which often leads to isolation, frustration or withdrawal.

Pride can be seen as an expression of the need to celebrate and be seen, but also of dignity, acceptance, meaning and belonging. The person has reached some kind of standard (at least partly their own) and wants to be seen in it. When an adult shows that they see and appreciate the drawing the young individual proudly displays to them, they quickly rush off to create a new one.

Sometimes we borrow pride; surfing the success of others, basking in the glory of those we associate ourselves with. Even if we are ashamed of some shortcoming in our own life, we can keep the shame away if we stick with the winning team. When Lionel Messi switched teams from FC Barcelona to French team PSG, after about twenty years, the new club's revenue from club shirts sold with his name on it were said to be in the six figures. One of the reasons why sportswear with a big star's name on the back sells so well is that people want to be associated with someone who is successful and feel like a winner themselves.

Borrowed pride also has a tragic downside. A group of supporters of a Portuguese football team crowded into the dressing room after an important match. Their team had just lost. It was one loss in a long line of many, and the fans abused several of the football players. The opposing team could shower and dress in peace because it was the home team whose pride had been borrowed by the fans.

In another tragic example, domestic violence against women after soccer losses typically rises in the UK (and probably it is the same in other countries and sports).

One way of borrowing pride, is by distorting information or inventing things that elevate us. The Washington Post kept track of President Donald Trump's lies (or gross exaggerations) during his 828 days as President of the United States. They calculated that he knowingly or unknowingly lied 10,111 times.[59]

It is possible that Trump did not lie more often than others, but since we have a truth bias, a detected lie by such a high-profile person has a different impact than when the average person lies. We assume that other people (perhaps especially selected officials) are telling the truth because it is hard to imagine that anyone would take the risk of being exposed and so we project our values onto them. Behind false pride, made-up stories and exaggerations, there are human needs: the longing to be seen or heard, to be respected, or to feel important. Despite Trumps lying, many people have become great fans of him as they feel he is reflecting their values.

Sometimes we pretend that we are okay with a certain result, but pretending gives us very little energy in the long run. Or we don't want to gloat, and avoid celebrating, to avoid hurting someone else who hasn't done as well. Joy and genuine pride make us vulnerable. The openness that comes from excitedly showing how happy we are makes us open targets for others' comments. Questioning comments can be harsh when we have openly displayed our pride. The joy is easily diminished if we discover that the standards we have set for ourselves are not the same as those of others. Also sometimes we don't want to gloat, and avoid celebrating, to avoid hurting someone else who hasn't done as well.

Attitudes vary between families, social groups and cultures about what is considered appropriate for a boy or a girl or what someone of a certain age is expected to be proud of. Those who go 'outside the box' soon find out where the boundaries are. Group norms are integrated into our individual self-image in such a way that we overlook being strongly affected by them.

When someone transgresses group or societal norms, whatever they are, it is noticed. Sometimes the transgression is rejected, viewed with skepticism or even disgust. In other groups and situations, transgressing norms is celebrated, seen as inspiring and giving others the courage to change. In adolescence, challenging the norm sometimes becomes a norm in itself.

In one context, the expressed pride in an achievement is accepted; it can be okay to be proud of succeeding in school, while succeeding in sports or music may not be seen as something to be proud of. In another context, it is the other way around, and academic scores are seen as silly to be proud of, while running fast or winning a basketball tournament will obtain gold stars.

Sometimes pride is seen as bullying or bragging and is not welcomed regardless of the size of the achievement. In some contexts, humility is what is considered good and appropriate. And even healthy pride doesn't stand a chance if all self-appreciation is seen as being arrogant and self-absorbed. The fear of being seen as a show-off can easily lead to false humility. At times receiving appreciation can be embarrassing and may be hard to take in. Not necessarily like when we are ashamed and at a loss for words, but even if the shyness is not as intense, it can be uncomfortable to be praised. It is clear that someone is watching us. For young adults it might be extra sensitive to feel 'unprotected', and judged, even in positive terms.

For sure it is okay for children to claim the right to shout out their happiness at having achieved something and celebrate their own abilities. And surely, at least from a certain age, we can ask them to wait for the right moment, to consider others who have not done as well. Of course, if we are happy about something we are satisfied with and bubbly about something we are proud of, it does not have to be compared to another person's achievement.

Aspects like restraint and judgment do not always go hand in hand with celebration. But it is possible to celebrate an achievement without putting someone else down. Celebrating without expressions like 'better than' or 'worse than' might seem desirable, but can be difficult for young children. Comparisons are a big part of their everyday life and schooling, and sometimes celebration comes out in expressions like "crushed the opposition," which can be tough for the opponent to hear.

If our children only seem to be able to connect to their celebration when they talk about how much better they were than everyone else, or that the others were bad, we can help our children to wait for the right moment. We can also help them to find joy by understanding why this success was so important to them, by guessing what needs of theirs were met by it.

Performance Anxiety

Self-criticism up to a certain point is creative. Up to a certain level, excitement, and even nervousness, can also be useful in helping a person perform at a high level. But there is a point where a certain level of stress can feed strong self-critical thoughts and get in the way of performance, energy, and creativity. Balancing stress is something that many adults struggle with throughout their lives, and in adolescence a caregiver can still play an important role in helping their charges learn more about how to handle this.

Performance anxiety can be described as an excessive drain on our energy budget, that makes it difficult to focus on or tackle an important task. The stress increases in a negative spiral when the shame of non-performance becomes a bitter icing on the cake.

Emma has invested a lot of her time and energy in getting good at soccer and her schoolwork is becoming heavier and heavier. She looks forward to the end of high school because she would rather play ball or write poetry than do her math homework.

After failing three tests in a row, she feels powerless and under enormous pressure. The pressure seems to come from all sides; from within, from her dream to be a master at her sport, from the shame of failing and from outside, with the seemingly unreasonable demands from the adult world. Both before and after a test or match, she has trouble falling asleep, feels anxious, and can't stop her mind from spinning. During her menstrual period, she starts feeling nauseous and has heart palpitations that make her anxious.

Her father helps her get in touch with the school counselor, whom she immediately trusts. The counselor seems to know what he's talking about. It is a relief for Emma to hear him confirm that she is not going crazy, just needs support to manage her stress levels. She has forgotten that her parents have been saying the same thing for months.

As mentioned earlier, young adults, in the phase of life where they are increasingly in touch with their inner selves, have a great deal of trust in experts. This is one reason why a counselor or other expert is sometimes a better support than a parent or friend, even though they don't know that person as well.

The quest for results and achievements is sometimes unconsciously driven by the hope that if you were just perfect, all self-doubt will fall away. It's just a matter of getting smarter, thinner, fitter, and succeeding in all areas of life. The desire to be perfect is an attempt to escape the feelings of shame that come when our shortcomings are revealed.

Performance anxiety is rarely overcome by trying to convince our children that they are good enough as they are and that everything will turn out all right. Sure, the teenager may have the confused idea that they are only valuable or accepted if they perform, but this rarely happens on a conscious level. As well as reminding them that they are good enough, they need support on how to work towards the goals they long to achieve. Only when they trust us to really hear what they are dreaming about can we have a good conversation about whether it's time to lower their goals or to keep trying to get there. While balancing stress is something that many adults struggle with throughout their lives, a caregiver can still play an important role in supporting young people in adolescence.

Of course, the desire to escape shame is not the only driving force in the pursuit of excellence. A young person may want to master every aspect of basketball because they love the sport. They may want to get the highest grade in a subject because they want to get into a dream university. Also, they may want to be sure to make that desire team, and their identity is strengthened by being good at something.

Not all young people are like Emma, who strives hard to reach her goals. Some seem to have no goals at all. The reasons can be many, and some are happy with that, while others would like to have goals but don't have enough support, or don't know if they dare to go for it. If the desire to avoid shame is the drive behind the quest to always get top grades, win medals in their sport, or become a celebrated musician, it becomes extremely difficult to keep up the motivation if a crack appears in the facade.

Self-criticism up to a certain level is creative. But it's also healthy to not always strive to be the best at everything and to be able to sometimes laugh at your mistakes. Silvan Tomkins did research with a hypothesis that laughter arises from a rapid shift in emotional intensity. His approach, which (simply put) was based on the idea that laughter calibrates mood, is easy to understand for everyone that has laughed hard. In addition to helping us mentally cope with challenging situations, laughter stimulates powerful breathing and provides a kind of internal massage with proven physical health benefits. Laughing together also has the potential to strengthen bonds between people.

One clue to finding out if shame is driving something we are doing, is to look at the way we deal with mistakes. Do we have difficulty letting go of criticism for singing off-key in the choir and become overly self-critical when someone points it out? Do we resent something we think we should have expressed differently? Do we furthermore criticize ourselves for being too self-critical and think we should have more self-distance? If small mistakes lead to agonizing, we can assume that shame is part of our motivation to some extent.

Thoughts and Emotions can be Altered

As mentioned earlier, from around the age of eleven, it becomes possible for most people to hold two contradictory concepts in their minds at the same time. The development of the brain and thinking means that most teenagers realize that things change over time.

This makes it possible to adapt their view of the future by thinking in terms of 'what if' or 'even if I can't do this now, I will probably do it better if I practice it.'

This way of thinking allows us to see something from multiple perspectives, which was difficult before (and sometimes led to adults calling us selfish).

Eventually, the young person can step back and reflect on what is going on inside of them at that moment. They can talk about the butterflies in their stomach or the creeping discomfort, and they learn more words to describe their inner self. The words turn the feelings into objects to relate to and study, making it more possible to reconstruct them. Self-reflection skills vary greatly and take different amounts of time to develop.

One of the things Emma appreciated about the counselor in school, is that he was able to help her with performance anxiety by thinking about her emotions in a different way. Having played soccer himself, he embraced her love of the sport and suggested that she approach the nervousness in a way similar to how her team approached the next game.

Together they came up with code words such as 'quick passes' which helped Emma to let go of a disturbing lingering thought. Another code word was 'create more space in between the players,' which helped her to take a deep breath and create more inner space to find (a good) better decisions.

The more Emma realized that her emotions were affected by how she thought, and her thoughts by how she related to them, the less anxiety she felt when nervousness crept in. She enjoyed experiencing control over thoughts that had previously kept her locked up inside. This way of thinking created self-distance, which gave her the space to joke about the times she had made less than stellar choices.

As we discussed in Chapter 5, those who find a level of joking that suits the group they are in have a great social advantage. Being able to joke, especially about ourselves, makes us more resistant to shame attacks, more flexible, and ready to see things from more perspectives. To see the humor in our own human mistakes, we need to be able to step back and look at ourselves, which helps us be more effective at dealing with feelings of shame.

Of course, this kind of joking is not about looking down on ourselves or allowing others to treat us unworthily. We can't expect that ability from individuals (children or adults) who don't have access to this kind of thinking. To joke about ourselves we need to be able to take a step back and remind ourselves that our identity doesn't need to be protected at all cost.

Thoughts to Help with Shame Attacks

Here are some approaches that young adults can often relate to. For some people, it takes decades before they have the self-distance needed to study their thoughts in this way, so use these approaches with care.

- Just because I feel shame doesn't automatically mean there is something wrong with me, even if my mind is full of arguments to that effect.

- It is possible to accept myself, even after making a mistake. I don't always have to do the right thing or strive to be perfect to like myself or be liked by others.

- How I choose to think about a situation and an emotion affects whether I feel shame or not. How I relate to the emotion (with for example empathy or judgment) will affect it.

- Instead of trying to get rid of uncomfortable feelings, they can be seen as a signal of human needs, needs I want to get in touch with before I think about what to do with the emotions.

9
JOYS AND CHALLENGES
OF PARENTING

And a woman who held a baby against her
bosom said, Speak to us of Children.
And he said:
Your children are not your children.
They are the sons and daughters of Life's longing for itself.
They come through you but not from you,
And though they are with you yet they belong not to you.
You may give them your love but not your thoughts,
For they have their own thoughts.
You may house their bodies but not their souls,
For their souls dwell in the house of tomorrow,
which you cannot visit, not even in your dreams.
You may strive to be like them, but
seek not to make them like you.
For life goes not backward nor tarries with yesterday.
You are the bows from which your children
as living arrows are sent forth.
The archer sees the mark upon the path of
the infinite, and He bends you with His might
that His arrows may go swift and far.
Let your bending in the archer's hand be for gladness;
For even as He loves the arrow that flies, so
He loves also the bow that is stable.[60]
KAHIL GIBRAN, THE PROPHET

It is easy to draw simplistic conclusions about how parenting shapes children. But the link we have made between parenting and child development may not be as straightforward as we have thought. Research, for example on separated identical twins, suggests that personality is largely a matter of genes. Children are not building blocks for us to put together, nor are they a lump of dough we can shape into something we like. Or as geneticist Robert Plomin provocatively writes, "parents matter but they don't make a difference."[61]

In saying such, Plomin is warning us that while parents are important, we can easily overstate our power to shape our children's personalities, which seem to have much more to do with their genetic make-up. He argues that our power as parents lies in creating good relationships and a safe environment for our children."

However, Plomin quickly adds that while parents are important, we can easily overstate our power to shape our children's personalities. He argues that our power lies in creating good relationships and a safe environment. If children's personality has as much to do with genes as gene research on human claims, what does that leave us as parents? What is in our nature and what is it up to culture to provide, and how are they connected?

Whether children are shaped by their genes or by culture or environment, parenting a child is a central task as it forms the relationship with them. The fifteen to twenty years we spend with your children can be a struggle or a joy, depending on us. Still, if we can influence the relationship with our child, but have little or no control over the outcome, how does that affect us? For some it might come as a relief, for others a disappointment. Others will not believe it at all.

Some parents of young children are bursting with life and energy. Others have a rough start with sleep deprivation, financial pressure, insecurity, or other tough challenges. For most people, interpersonal communication becomes challenging under this kind of stress. Most modern societies are structured differently from the small groups in which humans evolved over hundreds of thousands of years. Many people in modern societies have only one or a couple of other adults to share responsibility for their young children with, and it can be a challenge. In general, we have greater physical comfort, but less family support in parenting than in the past, in hunter-gatherer societies, and later, in agricultural societies. At the same time, we feel strong pressure to be 'good parents.'

Not getting enough rest during the infant years affects parenting. It is no wonder that parents sometimes suffer from self-doubt. Many feel ashamed to show anything other than being overjoyed with the new life they are holding in their arms.

Parents are often aware of their children's need to sleep and eat well. But if caregivers themselves constantly give up on their own needs for recovery, they are likely to sometimes act in a way towards their children that they later regret. The airline's notice to "put on your own oxygen mask on first before helping others" is a good reminder in this context.

With the responsibility of young children, it is easier said than done to constantly check one's own energy budget. Most parents realize how their patience is affected by not getting enough rest, good food and perhaps some exercise. In addition, if it is possible to spend time with friends or get some time alone, energy levels are replenished, and parenting can be more satisfying. Author Haim G. Ginott sums up what can happen when we can't find an opportunity to take care of our own needs as parents: "First I am so permissive that I begin to resent my children, and then I am so punitive that I hate myself."

Here are some questions we can continually ask ourselves throughout the two decades our children are maturing by our side:

- What could help my child mature through their early self-centered years and on to greater independence and connection with others?
- What is my part in helping the child to install a well-functioning inner guidance system?
- If I am the one teaching children the basics of communication and interpersonal relationships, what do I want to teach them?

What do I want to be open about so that my child has a role model in being open as well? As mentioned above, stress often contributes to the escalation of conflicts. Why not learn to act while "the iron is cold" instead of waiting until the situation gets overheated? This could mean talking over Sunday lunch about what to do when bedtime approaches in the coming week. Or to figure out have a relaxing evening talk about what to do for the weekend? And maybe another conversation about how to deal with recurring frustrations? Maybe the morning is a good time to talk about what time in the afternoon you should do your homework together? And maybe important sensitive issues are best dealt with in the car or on a walk with the dog? What works best is related to age as well as the maturity of the child.

One thing that adults seems to have a hard time remembering that a young child will not remember agreements that have been made too far in the past.

"I have something I want to talk to you about, shall we do it now when we're not in a hurry?"

"Sure."

"It's about how we don't get to doing your homework until it's so late and we're all really tired. I'd like to change that somehow. Would you be willing to look at some ideas about this with me?"

"Okay."

"Great. First, I would like to hear how it's for you that last week we did the homework at nine o'clock in the evening and then both you and I were annoyed and tired. Do you want to continue with that schedule or how do you feel?"

"It's not great, but homework is so boring. It kind of ruins the whole evening if we start it earlier."

Depending on the age of the child, one way to build trust is to show understanding of the child's resistance. As adults, we can still set times and stick to them, while understanding why the child may be resisting. Acknowledging that we hear the frustration goes a long way in easing this.We don't have to think about whether or not they have the right attitude (adults tend to find homework interesting in a way they didn't as children); it's enough to just listen, so that the child sees that we are willing to understand their perspective. For example, a dialogue with focus on connection might start with something like this:

"You really like to have fun and do things that are meaningful, don't you? And homework is hard to find fun in, right?"

Or,

"When you come home from school, you want to do something fun that you've been looking forward to, and want to put off homework for as long as possible, is that what you mean?"

You can maximize the odds for connection if you bring up recurring difficulties at a time of the day when there is space to talk in. And you can bring up the topic several times, such as when you're driving to soccer practice, or walking the dog, and can really take time to listen. A conversation about life is never "finished," and does not necessarily lead to decisions, but is part of building a solid relationship where you can also communicate about things you don't agree on or understand.

Parenting means that we are challenged to take on at least two perspectives: our own, and the child's. When we allow ourselves to see the world from the child's point of view, we can more easily attune to their level of development. This means that as parents, we can go through a long and sustained training in balancing our own needs and those of others, and in making conscious choices to meet those needs.

How much we get out of the journey we as parents are invited to take, is partly based on whether we are willing to develop our own capacity to communicate, both with others and within ourselves. The kind of support we get from outside is also influencing the experience. As a parent, it is valuable to reflect on what opinions we have inherited from our own childhood about emotions and about shame specifically.

We all benefit from being open to adjusting the parenting we were taught by our parents. These adjustments are not done not because our parents were necessarily wrong, but because the world has changed, and we live in a different time and context. Remember, we also have much greater access to information about parenting and communication tools than previous generations did.

Why do we Shame Children?

- We shame children in the hope that it will influence them to change their behavior. We hope that a change of behavior will help them to be accepted and included in different groups.
- We don't have access to any other tools at the moment. We don't have the support or clarity we need to communicate in a different way.

- We hope that shame will influence the child to change their behavior into one that is less shameful for us. We want to be seen as good parents who can showcase caring and well-functioning children.

- We have crossed our own line and given up on our own needs for far too long. Our energy budget is stretched, and we are desperate, worried, or scared and have a need for understanding as to how the situation has affected us.

- When our children cross the line or misbehave, we might feel shame and therefore blame them to avoid feeling the shame ourselves. This might be out of habit or unawareness. Every parent was once a child with grown-ups who employed the parenting skills they had learned in their upbringing. If we were shamed or blamed, that was the communication style we also learned.

- We have not updated our learned style of parenting. Until a certain age or level of development, the child accepts that it is the adult who sets limits and creates rules. As the child becomes more mature, they might not be so pliable anymore and we might resort to shaming to regain power and influence.

- We want to be seen as good parents who can produce obedient, well-functioning children.

Parental Value Systems

Maybe you are focused on becoming a super parent and are reading everything you come across, listening to experts and ready to evolve. Or maybe you are just looking for good ways to set boundaries, and act in integrity because you notice that your children have a hard time listening to what you want. Maybe you are tired of being strict and long to be able to act in a way that helps your child in finding their own voice. Questions about the values that drive us often only become apparent when it comes to parenting.

At a dinner party when Tom and Emma are six years old, their parents start talking about what kind of parenting they think is best.

"Our job as parents is to make sure our children succeed in life," Tom's father David claims.

"But is success really that important? Isn't the most important thing that the children feel our love? That they are accepted as they are?" asks Emma's mother Sofia while offering David more food.

"But don't you know that "permissive" parenting has long been proven to be harmful. And it's worse now than ever, with all the screens and technology that children are exposed to. And it's worse now than ever with all the screens and technology that children are exposed to. Children benefit from clear boundaries and a chance to perform when it counts," says David, putting down his cutlery.

Sofia puts her hand on David's hand (knowing that he can easily become very involved when this topic comes up).

"But there's a difference between just letting everything go and pushing children to achieve things from a young age," Sofia replies. "To me it is worrying that even seven-year-olds are reported to have performance anxiety."

"I think my child is most happy when he feels that he can succeed at something. He gets so angry when he loses, and that's good because then he tries a little harder next time."

"Yes, Emma can also explode if she loses when we play football," laughs Robert."

"Of course, it can be like that, but I want my children to feel accepted, regardless of whether they perform or not. I also want them to be involved in making decisions about things that affect them."

The parents don't agree on an answer to their dilemma. Perhaps because there are advantages as well as disadvantages from both outcome-focused and relationship-focused parenting. Perhaps because there are pros and cons to both. Perhaps because there is no perfect parenting manual.

Parents who encourage their children to focus on achievements, at best teach self-discipline and how to work towards a goal. They might also teach them other skills like study techniques and organization skills that will serve them well throughout their lives.

They might be present for their children, driving them to training sessions, and cheering them on in times of adversity. On the downside, a single-minded focus on results in all aspects of life can drive both parents and children to high levels of stress.

The child may feel that they need to perform to be enough, to be accepted and loved, and constantly feel bad if they don't manage to reach what they think is expected of them.

One common blind spot in only placing focus on individual success, is that parents fail to show the child the value of cooperation, group norms and belonging. If we are to believe the genetic research, it seems to be mostly genetic if a child develops into for example a highly competitive, individualistic personality or not. Still, we want to support our kids in having the joy of making friendships.

There are some obvious benefits to a parenting style focused on developing a close, equal relationship with the child. Most of all it is fun and nurturing for everybody. Hopefully a child who develops a respectful, reciprocal relationship with their parents also learns to love and respect themselves. Maybe they can relax more, because they can trust that there is unconditional love for them, even when they are not at their best or make mistakes.

And just like parenting that focuses entirely on results and performance, there are drawbacks of more egalitarian parenting. One blind spot is that parents can become so focused on supporting their child's exploration of life that they fail to set important boundaries.

Emma's early childhood was largely characterized by her parents wanting to affirm her in everything. They helped her dance in the street, sing in the subway, and pick any flowers that she saw and liked. It was a good time, but when seven-year-old Emma repeatedly pulled apples from their neighbor's apple trees, breaking several of the trees' branches, only to then throw the apples into the ditch, they realized they needed to deal with her behavior. When they brought it up, she was at first very upset, accustomed as she was to boldly embrace everything life had to offer and being supported in it.

Emma's father appealed to her, telling her that the neighbors were concerned about their trees and that if she wanted an apple, she should ask them first. She responded by hissing back that she wasn't going to do that at all. Emma's mother tried to say that the neighbors would be sad if the trees broke and that they would not like Emma if she hurt their trees. She responded by shaking her head and walking away. The next day, to her parents' frustration, she did the same thing.

Her parents went through despair, shame, resignation and anger. Both preferred requests to demands and found it difficult to set limits. At the same time, they were ashamed of Emma's insensitivity. Eventually, they realized that in their eagerness to be supportive, they had been too lenient and had ended up blaming Emma, when in fact, it was they themselves who couldn't bear to be seen as obstructionists. A clear 'no' early on would have been more helpful for Emma. The realization that she might get into trouble unless she learned to take in the needs of others was a wakeup call for them all.

While every child is unique and the importance of parenting is sometimes overstated, there are things children learn from adults that affect them later in life. For example, if the child does not learn to respect the boundaries of others, they might encounter problems later in forming relationships. Paradoxically, because the child does not realize where the boundaries of others are, he or she may find it difficult to form deep relationships with others, even though it was exactly these kinds of relationships the parents wanted them to experience by centralizing their needs. Children who always receive support from others without being asked to contribute, may be less able to develop truly reciprocal relationships. Their inability to understand that others have boundaries may end up with them being rejected by other children their own age.

Regardless of how much a child's development depends on how parents manage their role as caregivers, time with growing children gives parents a second chance to mature emotionally. Marshall Rosenberg divided emotional maturity into three phases. He called them, emotional slavery, the obstinate phase, and emotional freedom, and said that we need to go through the first two to get to the third. Perhaps Rosenberg's naming of the first two phases is a bit unfortunate, as it makes them seem bad or undesirable. At the same time, they are phases we need to go through in order to discover the position where we can stand up for our own needs as well as for the needs of others.

Rosenberg described the third phase like this: "Emotional liberation involves stating clearly what we need in a way that communicates we are equally concerned that the needs of others be fulfilled."[62]

As parents to young children, we must face the fact that some of our needs will not be met for long periods of time in order to make room for the needs of our children. Young children are not emotionally capable in the way we, hopefully, are. But there is a tipping point when even the most capable parent needs the support of others, and we are reminded of the beauty of the expression that it takes a village to raise a child.

The question of who has the right to make decisions is an issue that often comes up among parents who are focused on equal parenting. With humankind's painful experience of hierarchies, it is easy to see a why a decision-making order with the parent at the top might be seen by many as something bad. It is not difficult to understand how the allergy to "power over" is reinforced given the amount of violence that children have endured over generations.

But there is a difference between the parent deciding *because* they are the parent, and cooperation that considers the fact that the parent has more knowledge and experience and can therefore often make more informed decisions. Saying no is sometimes the best support we can give our children. Parenting relies on adult approval and disapproval helping the child understand boundaries and the needs of others. Before interdependence is installed, feelings of shame can help the child calibrate their behavior. It is not about shaming or blaming, but about using the emerging awareness of shame as a seed for reciprocity and care.

Parenting in Relation to Shame

1. Learn to manage your shame constructively

Take time to reflect on how you experience shame and how you act when you experience shame. Learn new behaviors if you do not find the old ones constructive.

2. Reflect on your self-image

Do you have enough self-distance to put up with "dumb mom" or "mean dad," so that you can set a firm boundary even when your child doesn't like it or when others do not think you are a great parent?

3. Be a role model - do your own shame exploration

Seeing adults deal with strong emotions in a connecting way instead of shaming, is a gift for children. What do you need to manage uncomfortable emotions while staying connected to yourself and others? Asking for support is also being a role model.

4. Beware of trying to be "the perfect parent"

How much inner space do you need to create in daring to admit to your own mistakes? Do you need to be heard first in what you see as the cause of your actions before you can hear someone else? Can you say you are sorry?

5. Set limits before you get angry

Do you sometimes wait too long to say no? Do you wait so long that you lose warmth for the child? What do you need to remember to reestablish connection once you have set limits on the behavior? Can you show that it is possible to accept the person without appreciating the behavior?

6. Acknowledge your needs for belonging, acceptance and dignity

What do you do when you feel rejected? How do you deal with being treated in a way you don't find respectful? What can you ask others to do to experience acceptance, belonging and dignity in your role as a parent? What can you do on your own?

7. Reflect on secondary shame

Who are you ashamed of in your environment? Are you ashamed of something the child says, does or does not do? Is the child's behavior a blow to your self-image? How does it manifest itself? Are you acting in the way you want?

8. (Teenage) parent - time to realize that your child has matured?

Maybe it's time to move some boundaries and make more decisions together? To be liked, do you pretend to be different from what you are? Do you remember what it was like as a teenager when adults seemed hypocritical and tried to fit in?

9. Listening goes a long way

What do you need to do to let go of the idea of always being the fixer and instead just be there? Listening means you are present, not that you must take responsibility for changing anything.

10. Accept children's feelings, instead of diminishing or reinforcing them

Can you accept that your child might be feeling shy or ashamed? What do you yourself need in order to allow children to feel what they feel without diminishing or magnifying the feelings? Do you see the difference between shaming and accepting the feeling of shame that occurs in the child?

Parenting with Developmental Goggles

"Human development is a journey, not a destination. Let us embrace each chapter, knowing that within its pages lie the lessons, growth, and resilience that shape our magnificent evolution."

UNKNOWN

It is a privilege to wrestle with the challenges of parenting, a chance to grow. Understanding human development helps parents to adapt their actions to support their child in the ways best needed. Parents benefit from clarity in these two areas:

- Understanding children's developmental stages and what they need from adults during these stages.
- Understanding your own developmental level as a parent.

As has been mentioned earlier, be careful in the belief that one strategy works for all children or all parents. The most effective parenting is not static, but needs to be adapted to the situation. At a certain developmental level, clear rules are the best support, but at others, more mutual interaction are more supportive. Parents need to adapt to the child's age, developmental level, social context, and the current situation, but also to their own maturity.

Developmental theories are often linked to children's physical development and, increasingly, to knowledge on how the brain develops. Researcher Terri O'Fallon has created a model of how our consciousness develops and how it does not limit itself to the early years of a person's life. She believes that our development continues into adulthood. At the heart of the Stages Model, as O'Fallon has named her model, are three questions to help us understand from which level of development someone is mostly acting at:

1. Is the individual's focus on the individual or the collective?
2. Is their learning style receptive, active, reciprocal, or interpenetrating?
3. Is their focus on concrete objects, more subtle or abstract objects, or on very subtle things, such as awareness itself?

One way to understand development is to categorize it into horizontal and vertical growth. When we grow horizontally, we add knowledge or skills at the same level of complexity. Vertical development implies an increased ability to gain perspective and awareness. O'Fallons Stages model describes how we gain an increase in complexity, depth, inclusiveness, and/or perspective as we develop in both directions. Horizontal learning allows you to do quantitatively more similar things, while vertical development adds qualitatively different new capacities.

Although research and theories on adult development have been questioned for various reasons, many of us probably agree that we continue to develop to some degree, not only horizontally but also vertically, even after a certain physical age. We can deepen the abilities we have but we can also gain new insights and clarity.

Though increasing development usually means a positive gain in capacity for any individual, one's developmental stage does not capture everything that is important about parenting (or any other context). For example, someone at an earlier developmental level can still have a greater capacity to listen to, respond to, and care for a child, compared with someone at a later developmental level.

Some people seem to reach a stage of development from which they operate and relate at for most of their adult lives. But when our lives and environments require it, development is a life-enriching driving force.

The Stages Roadmap

PP	TIER	Question 1: Is the object of awareness Concrete, Subtle, or MetAware?	Question 2: Is the experience Individual or Collective? SOCIAL PREFERENCE	Question 3: Is the experience Receptive, Active, Reciprocal, or Interpenetrative? LEARNING STYLE	STAGE NAME
1	Concrete		Individual	Receptive	Impulsive
1,5	Concrete		Individual	Active	Egocentric
2	Concrete		Collective	Reciprocal	Rule Oriented
2,5	Concrete		Collective	Interpenetrative	Conformist
3	Subtle		Individual	Receptive	Expert
3,5	Subtle		Individual	Active	Achiever
4	Subtle		Collective	Reciprocal	Pluralist
4,5	Subtle		Collective	Interpenetrative	Strategist
5	MetAware		Individual	Receptive	Construct Aware
5,5	MetAware		Individual	Active	Transpersonal
6	MetAware		Collective	Reciprocal	Universal
6,5	MetAware		Collective	Interpenetrative	Illumined

In the 1980s, Robert Kegan and Lisa Lahey, two researcherat Harvard, began to study patterns of continued development in adults. "We discovered the possibility of life after adolescence!

Despite the popular - and, at the time, scientific - view that our minds, like our bodies, don't get 'taller' after adolescence, we found that some of our adult subjects were able to develop whole patterns of increasingly complex and agile ways of perceiving the world."[63]

Models help us understand how human development takes place. However, a model is a model, and development is not always as linear as the model might make it seem. Sometimes we can even retreat back to earlier stages because of trauma, or because we don't have the necessary support from our environment.

Don Beck, one of the authors of the book *Spiral Dynamics*, said that "Development is messy, not symmetrical, with multiple mixtures rather than pure types. These are mosaics, meshes and blends."[64]

It is of value for caregivers to consider their own stage of development in order to understand where they have their pitfalls. Like Emma's football coach in chapter eight, we might value inclusion and that everyone is given a voice, and then not see that the child is struggling in a totally different area. While the early stages of development in a person's life often can be linked to age, it is valuable to look beyond that exact connection. For example, a caregiver may be operating from the same level as their teenager. We sometimes assume that others see the world the way as us, so it is useful to consider whether our current stage of development is leading us to have unrealistic expectations or overlooking something in our parenting.

Children may well understand that there are things that adults can do that children cannot. But at a certain age, the words "you can't smoke because it's dangerous," loses their effect, especially if you continue to smoke.

If we assume that parenting works best if it is adapted to the child's developmental level, because what is beneficial for children at one developmental level can get in the way at the next, it is good to understand how children develop. Below are some thoughts on what can be important when we take advantage of the clarity in the first stages of Terri O'Fallon's developmental model.[65] The different stages are referred to by number, and sometimes also by name, unlike other developmental models where, for example, colors have been used, such as in the model of Spiral Dynamics.

1.0 Impulsive

The newborns major challenge is to form an attachment to its environment with very few tools. The mother's voice, which it has already learned to recognize in the womb, sounds slightly different, but can still be soothing. Impressions of light that lack clear contours, gradually become possible for the child to categorize. Soon they can regulate their visual acuity to catch the faces of the people they are most attached to.

It is easy to romanticize the infant. We forget that although they live in the moment and seem to be one with everything, they are working towards being able to separate themselves from their environment because it gives them a range of survival benefits.

The first task for adults is to create a loving and committed environment that is safe enough for the receptive, impulse-driven infant. Children benefit from an environment that helps them develop their senses and learn what is needed for their next step in life. Another task during the first period of young life is to provide the child with closeness and at the same time limit stress on their immature nervous system. Avoiding excessive stimulation makes it easier for babies to sort out their impressions. One way is to unwind regularly in an adults arms and cry if they need it.

Even if the child does not understand the meaning of words, use language to help them build language concepts. Eventually play peek-a-boo and other games that train the child's ability to visualize. Encourage the first sounds and physical challenges of crawling, standing and eventually taking their first steps. Play music, read simple stories and let the bonding process take its course. If parents take care of themselves, it is probably easier to be there for the infant when they need it the most.

1.5 Self-centered

Somewhere between twelve and eighteen months of age is the most common time for an individual to move on from the first receptive phase. The child moves from passive reception to active engagement. Exploration is still done on their own, or possibly side by side with someone. The central drive now is to discover their own power and to interact with what is directly in front of them. The challenge for adults is to provide a safe place for children to explore in and learn. The child needs enough space to move around in, but at the same time knows that there is a familiar embrace to come back to

"Listen, they play for me," said Tom, and his mother laughed.

Tom was three and sitting in his stroller during a walk outside a music school. The sounds of an orchestra could be heard clearly through the window they passed. Sofia was about to tell her son that the music was not played for him, but then held herself back when she realized it was true in her son's universe.

Tom's expression is an example of what innocent self-centeredness can look like. He is at the center of his attention, and this is neither morally bad nor good. It is a developmental phase that gives him the best chance of surviving and finding his way in life. In time, he will begin to take in the experiences and needs of others, understand rules, and become interested in playmates.

When adults around the child are overly restrictive, the child is inhibited. If adults show no limitations at all, there is a risk that the child will hurt themselves, others or objects. Children learn both from being told 'yes' and 'no.' The restrictions are internalized and give them a growing ability to do more on their own.

A challenge for you as a caregiver of children at this stage is to restrict the child without disrupting their attachment to you. One way is to let the child leave your side, but to welcome them back as soon as they want to return. Sing, laugh, dance and communicate, no matter how much the child talks. Take responsibility for your emotions by linking them to your own needs and values and help your child to express theirs. Create safe structures and teach them concepts such as *mine* and *yours*. Support your child in participating in social situations, for example by showing them how they can express *gratitude* and *regret*. A simple "thank you" and "sorry" will take them far at this stage.

Let your child express their power, for example by wrestling. Teach them about consent by asking them to stop wrestling as soon as the one they are wrestling with says no. Provide support to follow agreements, stick to rules in a relaxed and playful way, and keep the promises you make yourself.

At the end of this phase, be prepared for creative lies (as was explored in chapter 6) and respond to them with interest. Let the child know that you understand that they are presenting alternative truths or confabulating, while showing warmth and maintaining connection. Remember that a child at this stage has not yet developed the capacity to clearly differentiate their imagination from reality.

Continue reading to the child, if they are open to it. Try to find stories that match the child's development and supports them in installing the skills needed to control their own lives.

Remember that this particular child may benefit more from other ways of taking in the world as they prepare for the next stage.

2.0 Rule-driven

At the age of four to six, most people move from a first-person perspective (everything is about me) to a second-person perspective (others and a sense of "we" are important). They may experience life through this perspective until they turn eleven, or later as teenagers, and in rarer cases may function from this level of development for most of their lives. At this stage, reciprocal play with playmates becomes increasingly important, and with this comes the challenge to discover how cooperation and friendship work. Games with more advanced rules and cooperation become fun and meaningful.

Key for caregivers now becomes the ability to renegotiate freedom and agreements, as the child grows in their ability to do things on their own. Even if the child is curiously exploring new areas, the world can still feel scary and sometimes they need to return to the familiar and limited world they know. Showing that we want to be involved in every step of our child's new hobby, to ensure they feel we are there, can be motivating for them. It is different from micromanaging, which can be pacifying and inhibit motivation.

Some of the principles here are to talk to the child in the way you want them to talk to themselves. Continue to connect, listen and let them know where your boundaries are. Allow children to compete if they enjoy that, and to strive for goals in the areas they are interested in. Support them in accepting setbacks and help them celebrate successes.

Support the child to initiate and create reciprocal friendships outside the family. Encourage increased independence and to relate with consent. Continue to be the adult who sometimes makes difficult decisions and who introduces more perspectives. Stay open to dialogueue when the child expresses frustration with your decisions. But use your parental power to protect, and learn to distinguish it from being tempted to use your power to punish or control.

A caregiver who is rule-oriented, and has a strong focus on norms, principles and fitting in, provides security. The downside is that the space that caregiver leaves for the child can become small and suffocating. If adults show no restrictions at all, there is a risk that the child will hurt themselves, others or objects. Children learn from being shown boundaries and learn to understand 'yes' and 'no.'

"I don't want to go to the party."

When Emma turns five, she starts saying no to invitations to parties but also to simple visits at a friend's house. At first, her clear no makes her father proud about her ability to make up her own mind. However, he quickly realizes that she says no to everything and is often disappointed afterwards when she hears about all the fun things other children have had.

As he wants to understand more, he carefully chooses a moment (when they are both relaxed) and asks her if she notices that she sometimes feels disappointed about not having been to a party. To his relief, she nods. Her agreeing makes it easier for him to present his plan. He asks her to think of the disappointment she sometimes feels after she has missed a party because she turned down going to it. "Would she be willing to trust him if he thought it was better to say yes next time?"

After a few months, Mark is pleased to see that the arrangement has worked out better than expected. He likes to see his little girl exuberantly jumping into the car at the end of a party, after leaving in a huff. He had to bite his tongue not to say, "I told you so," or "you see, it was unnecessary to be so angry."

Emma likely experienced uncomfortable feelings even just thinking of arriving for a party, perhaps worrying about how she would be received. Her perception of the nervousness was that it felt 'negative' and a signal to say no, which made her turn down even fun things. She has not yet developed the ability to think abstractly in time which makes it difficult to realize that worry and nervousness can be transformed into joy and excitement.

Emma was allowed too early to make decisions that were difficult for her developmental level. But her father learnt to calibrate it by taking back some of her responsibility for the choices she wanted to make. With support, she could experience nervousness in a different way. It was still exciting to leave home but it didn't lead to a no at all times.

2.5 Conformist

By early adolescence, most individuals have internalized the family's values and understood them enough to start questioning them. They are still rule-oriented, but increasingly able to prioritize what is important in different contexts in which they find themselves. Most often, they become better at clearly understanding why they are choosing one thing over another.

This is a process that started much earlier, when adults around the child were striving to live up to their own values in relation to others, a process that matures over time.

The more a person can sort out rules and anchor their own values, the less likely they are to be attracted to destructive peer pressure. With the right support, the individual explores more of their unique self; questioning and formulating their own thoughts, and by putting more words to feelings, needs, dreams and values. They are shaping their attitude to life, no longer buying into everything they hear others say and becoming more of an individual who stands on their own.

Tom's father David's parenting is based on rules and on living according to certain principles. This has provided security for Tom, who always knew the rules. When Tom starts questioning the family rules in his teenage years, it becomes more difficult for them to work together because Tom is not used to collaboration and now pushes to express his own voice. David tries to limit Tom even more, which at this stage of development is often counterproductive.

David's blind spot is that he can't stand Tom questioning his rules and instead of talking about it, he tries to push even harder or rejects Tom. Until now, Tom has been loyal, but the fact that he now dares to question his parents could actually be seen as a sign of development, rather than as a problem.

David would do well to recognize that being overly principled can lead to Tom becoming negatively affected by peer pressure as he gets older. Although everyone is influenced by groups they belong to, Tom may find it difficult to set boundaries with someone who wants him to do things against his will if he doesn't practice with his parents. Or he might become forceful in trying to enforce his own principles in some situations. He may struggle to find meaning in belonging to a group that does not exactly match the principles he has learned and become rootless.

A parent who is keen for their child to fit in, might be good at supporting their child to make friends. They are aware of the social game and what the child needs to do to belong. The downside is that if the parents' only focus is on acceptance, the child's unique voice may be given little space. Their children either become over-affirmed, with the child's well-being coming from the outside, which might lead to them easily succumbing to peer pressure and praise. Or the children might develop a more oppositional orientation, where they reject the social acceptance they desperately need and behave in a way that embarrasses their parents.

Caregivers might become dismissive of children that do not live up to the morals the caregiver expects. When rigid rules about morality become more important than showing love, parents cause harm to their relationship, even if they think they are doing something for their child's own good. Their children may develop principles, but these principles are often applied without regard to the real well-being of others. To clarify: the child, just like their parents, uses moral principles to humiliate and hurt people instead of letting those principles support them. However, the child can also live a life that actively rejects the parents' principles and even mocks them.

Parents inevitably find themselves, from time to time, in the recurring dilemma between knowing how permissive and how strict they should be. As the child develops, the parent needs to recalibrate their parenting. One way to balance this is to examine what is best for the relationship. What is best for all of us? Both now and in the longer term?

David's parenting is based on rules and principles. This provides security because his son Tom always knows what the rules are. When Tom starts questioning the family rules in his teenage years, it becomes more difficult for them to cooperate.

As described earlier in the book, Emma's parents have instead been struggling with the consequences of giving Emma too much responsibility and autonomy. They have had to constantly calibrate their permissive approach. Emma, in turn, has found it difficult to deal with setbacks and, for example, to take no for an answer from others.

The fact that Tom and Emma react the way they do is of course not only related to their level of development or how their parents have acted. They have a personality, with their own unique gifts and challenges, plus their individual experiences of life. It is valuable for parents to reflect on how their own childhood experiences create rigid parenting patterns that blind them to how they are impacting their children.

3.0 Expert

From fifteen onwards, the level of development varies more than before. One challenge here is that young adults may be unsure of themselves in one area, but very confident in an opinion they hold in another area. Here, claims can also increasingly be backed up by science or expert opinions. As discussed in Chapter 8, young adults often spend a period of time striving to become experts in some area. They have left behind the tendency to follow every rule and act conventionally. In the search for identity and independence, career and professional choices have become important.

If they find what they want to do, and for example, get an education, the identification with that professional role can become strong. To choose the same career at their caregivers is close at hand as they already might now something about that area.

If our children want to follow in our footsteps we can support that as well as gently remind them, as well as ourselves, that this does not have to be a lifelong choice. If our children want to find a lifestyle or career of their own, we can support them in this.

This is also a period where you can have deep and meaningful conversations with your young adult. Some people never develop to these more subtle levels and continue to focus on the concrete perspectives of life, while others, already as young adults, specialize in one area.

It is as in the previous stages, it is helpful for parents to remind themselves of the challenges they faced at their child's present developmental level, and to understand how their own developmental process affects their parenting.

10
COMMUNICATION - A
MUTATIONAL ADVANTAGE

"You've probably never thought about learning words as a path to greater emotional health, but it is entirely consistent with the neuroscience of construction. Words seed concepts, concepts drive predictions, predictions regulate the body budget, and the body budget determines how you feel. Therefore the more fine-grained your vocabulary, the more precisely your predictive brain can calibrate your "budget" to the body's needs." [66]

LISA FELDMAN BARRETT

Our Language - A Mutational Advantage

It is quite extraordinary, that we humans have the ability to communicate in parables, use irony or understand that a story has a message. We can share our subjective experiences with others, and we can talk about different objects with someone, without having the objects in front of us and still be able to compare them to one another.

The ability to use symbols (such as maps or words) allows us to communicate what is going on inside of us, such as in our feelings, dreams, fantasies and needs. Symbolic thinking makes it possible to talk about objects that we have never seen, or that so far only exist in our imagination. We can talk about things that have happened, but also travel in time and plan for a future that sometimes seems as real as something that has already happened.

Every decision a human being makes is linked to our brain, whose overall purpose can be summarized as ensuring our well-being, balancing our energy budget and protecting us and those closest to us. Emotions have been shown to be important for our learning and memory. To remember something, emotions help anchor the memory. For a long time logic and emotions where seen as separate but as we are learning more about the brain we can see that they are both important for helping the individual. With the support of fitting words, decisions are fine-tuned to meet human needs. Our survival has always depended on the collective, on our ability to form relationships, and cooperate.

Emotions researcher Lisa Feldman Barrett argues that this is more than a philosophical reality, and very much a physical one: "Our words allow us to enter each other's affective niches, even at extremely long distances. You can regulate your friend's body budget (and he yours) even if you are an ocean apart—by phone or email or even just by thinking about one another."[67]

The basics of human biology was largely unchanged for some time after our ancestors left East Africa less than a hundred thousand years ago and spread across the globe. Discoveries by Nobel Laureate Svante Pääbo, a Swedish biologist specializing in evolutionary genetics, make it possible to take a long-term view of human communication.[68] Pääbo and his research team at the Max Planck Institute for Evolutionary Anthropology found that, less than 200 000 years ago, a mutation in two of the 715 pairs of FOXP2 genes occurred in Homo sapiens, a discovery for which he received the Nobel Prize in 2022. The mutation gave us an evolutionary kick, accelerating and refining our ability to speak and developing different languages and modes of communication.

According to Pääbo's research, the gene mutated only in the human species (we share the gene with other mammals), allowing us to communicate in complex ways such as in written and symbolic language. It is likely that our capacity for complex thinking and communication has, in turn, further developed the ability to visualize. Those who were able to convince others to support them in creating masterpieces that had not yet seen the light of day moved culture forward.

An amazing human trait is that we can not only communicate with others, but also learn to talk to ourselves. Having created an inner calming or comforting dialogue by thinking or talking to ourselves in a certain way, we can also encourage and maybe even empathize with ourselves. As we try to anticipate how our actions will affect others, we evaluate what could happen if we don't acknowledge what we have done or intend to do.

After a timeless period at the beginning of life, we eventually become aware of time and can use the idea of time passing as a way to deal with challenges. We develop the ability to remind ourselves that a situation will pass, or change. Later, as young adults, we are also able to talk about what has happened to gain perspective, but also about what we hope will happen in the future. Lisa Feldman Barrett describes the importance of giving our children communication skills. "When you teach emotional concepts to children, you are doing more than communicating. You are creating reality for these children – social reality. You're handing them tools to regulate their body budget, to make meaning of their sensations and to act on them, to communicate how they feel, and to influence others more effectively." [69]

The seed of language we are born with, if supported, develops throughout our lives. Just over 200 000 years ago, before the

mutation that Pääbo and his team found evidence for, adult language development is estimated to have been at a level equivalent
to that of a modern child. That's hard to imagine, since everyone in
the present, with a few exceptions, develops past that level of communication. Most contemporary adults are able to relate to things
not only from the first person perspective (themselves/me) but can
also see that same things from a second person perspective (you).
Moreover they can also take a step back and view this from a we-
perspective. Doing so with ease, sometimes lead to underestimating
just how extraordinary this capacity is, and how hard it can be for
a young child.

Our communication skills are not only a personal matter, but
also part of influencing and shaping the world around us. When
children learn to put their inner experiences into words, it is not
just about learning more expressions, but about opening the door
to social relationships as they gain codes to shared "we-spaces." Lisa
Feldman Barrett goes further, arguing that communication is not
just about our language and that concepts affect us far more than
we might think. "Social reality is not just about words – it gets
under your skin. If you perceive the same baked good as a decadent
"cupcake" or a healthful "muffin," research suggests that your body
metabolizes it differently. Likewise, the words and concepts of your
culture help to shape your brain wiring and your physical changes
during emotion."[70]

Individual Language Development

The term 'critical period' is used for the limited period in an organ-
ism's life when different skills need to be stimulated and used to
develop. This applies to humans but also to animals. For example,
say a young bird has an accident and is found by people who, in
their eagerness to protect it, lock it up. Although in this way it is
protected, the fledgling may fail to develop the ability to attract

females if the accident occurs during a certain period of the bird's development. A baby bird that missed out on hearing its own species sing may still make sounds, but if they differ from those of the rest if the species, it may be rejected or ostracized.

Similarly, humans seem to have a critical period for language learning. If a child is exposed to language late or for some reason not at all, he or she will have difficulty developing language fully. For understandable reasons, it is difficult to study in depth what happens when a child's language development is not stimulated. But there are tragic examples of children who have been stunted in their communication development that we can learn from.

Genie was locked up until she was 14 years old.[71] Chelsea was born with a severe hearing impairment. But she was diagnosed as mentally retarded and treated accordingly. Isabelle was in hiding with her deaf mother until the age of six. None of these three individuals developed their language and all lacked common human concepts.[72] What distinguished the children was the extent of their late language development. Isabelle started her language development at the age of six and achieved age-appropriate language mastery after a short time, about one year. Genie's language development began much later, slowing down considerably after about five years, when she reached the level of a two-year-old. Chelsea, who missed the critical period entirely, did not even develop the basic grammatical structures found in Genie's language.

Throughout history, there have been children who, for various reasons, grew up with animals and never heard humans speak. Many of the stories have luckily enough turned out to be tall tales, but there are some that are confirmed.

Another tragic example was a one-year-old girl in Portugal who was locked in a chicken cage by her mentally ill parents. This was in the early 1980s and the girl spent eight of her first nine years with chickens. When the girl was released, she could not speak, and even as an adult she could only learn the most basic words. Her mental age was estimated to be at around two years, and her development was different from that of a child raised in close contact with humans.

We are born with the ability to develop speech, but our language needs a context to develop. As social beings, we mature and grow through our connection with other people. Our language, but also our way of communicating in general, develops through interaction with others. Feedback from the outside is an important part of the development of individuals, and with the individual, the group develops, which can give feedback that allows the individual to grow further.

When asked how to help his children develop into geniuses, Einstein is said to have replied "read to them." According to Mats Myrberg, Professor of Special Education at Stockholm University, nine out of ten words we use are something we have learned from written text. A seven-year-old has a vocabulary of between five and seven thousand words. A seventeen-year-old who has read and/or listened to texts regularly has between 50 000 and 70 000 words, while a seventeen-year-old who has not done so may have as little as 15 000 to 17 000 words.

It is estimated that an adult needs at least 50 000 words to keep up with news broadcasts or to understand instructions, for example. Through genetic research, we now know that reading skills do not develop in the same way in all individuals.[73] We also now know that genetically, some children really enjoy being read to, while others do not like it very much. They develop more from other activities and other types of stimulation. Even a genius like Einstein can be partly mistaken.

Unlike children who have not been supported through the critical language period, such as Isabelle, Chelsea or Genie mentioned earlier, children who have been supported, can usually rapidly expand their vocabulary all the way into adulthood and further.

We cannot expect children to be able to express themselves in the same way as adults. Nor can we expect them to have a deeper capacity for empathic listening. Moreover, this capacity varies between individuals.

How we communicate with children, what expressions we use with them and why, may affect them more than our advice to them. Children learn by interacting with us and how they learn to communicate affects the way they think and relate to others.

Young children can learn several hundred new words in a week with the right stimulation. The words are attractive to learn because they seem to carry magic. Just imagine how amazing it is when a child learns the words 'ice cream' and a yummy chilledsugar bomb appears in front of them. The word apple is perhaps even more magical, as it often delivers immediate results (at least if the child has health-conscious parents).

As children learn to read and write, deciphering symbols such as letters, they gain even more tools to create their own inner images for others to take part in. The movement towards greater complexity in our thinking has taken us from the hunter/gatherer stage to today's focus on technology and information exchange.

This movement, whether we like it or not, presents us with new challenges, calling on us to develop our communication skills. It places new demands on both parents and children in our time, but also provides new opportunities.

There are numerous communication methods aimed at handling conflicts and creating and deepening connection between people. Thanks to our advanced thinking, we can use different methods and constructs to structure our communication. Marshall Rosenberg's process, Nonviolent Communication (NVC), is one of them. And since this approach is an important inspiration for this book, here is a short introduction.

Nonviolent Communication (NVC)

Nonviolent Communication (NVC) is an approach to strengthening interpersonal communication that has proved to be a useful way to manage conflicts, create human connection and cooperation. The approach is based on the human being's unique ability to put words to their inner subtle self and the ability to listen with empathy, even beyond words.

In his book *Nonviolent Communication, a Language of Life*, Marshall Rosenberg presents a way of communicating that starts with a perspective making it easier to take responsibility for what we feel and want. NVC as a form is based on four components - observations, feelings, needs and requests. The four components are used both when we listen to others and when we want to express ourselves in the most communicative way possible. The intention behind this form is connection (not to express oneself in a certain way).

The best use of the form is to help us learn ways of communication that can help us connect to ourselves and others. To help us to be clear in our intention to communicate something, there are also several key differentiations and assumptions about human connection. For example, it is assumed that there are always common human needs behind the motivation of someone's actions or expressions. This assumption, that we can find those common human denominators, even behind hostile communication, can help us remain open to connection with others.

This approach works best when used both in everyday life and in the midst of a conflict. If you start using the NVC approach and components only when there is a conflict or a crisis, it is likely to be counterproductive. Children (of different ages) easily develop an "NVC allergy" and resist us when we use certain words or phrases. Furthermore, if your children learn that expressing your emotions poses a danger, as they will be held responsible for them, your desire to express how you feel can have an effect opposite to what is intended.

Rosenberg encouraged us not only to be clear about what we want to ask of others, but also to be aware of our intention behind the requests. For example, what is the intention behind wanting our children to come home at a certain time? What do we want by expressing dissatisfaction with something a teenager has done? What do we hope to get back when we express disappointment?

Rosenberg explained what can happen when we make demands without being clear about our intentions: "My own children gave me some invaluable lessons on the 'subject of demands.' For some reason, I had gotten the idea that my job as a parent was to make demands. But I learned that I could make any kind of demand and still not get my children to do anything. It was a humbling lesson about power, especially for those of us who think that just because we are parents, teachers or managers, it is our job to change others and make them behave.

The young people let me know that I can't make them do anything. All I could do was make them wish they had done it through punishment. So, eventually they made me realize that every time I was foolish enough to make them wish (through punishment) that they had complied, they had their ways of making me wish I hadn't. My own children let me know that I can't make them do anything. All I could do was make them wish they had done it by punishing them." [74]

In short, diagnoses, labels and demands are language that often contribute to shame and guilt. Our communication and behavior affects what others feel, but we don't have the power to decide how it affects them inside. We can choose our words, but not decide how someone else receives them. It is important to remember that when it comes to young children, the line between the child's mind and the adult's words and actions is very thin.

Words have the power to hurt and manipulate and the more we are aware of this, the better we can choose to listen in a way that benefits both us and our relationship with others. Young children have little awareness that their own words, 'silly mummy,' can hurt and need to be taught this. It is important to remind children how words can hurt others in a similar way to physically hitting someone. But we can't expect children to understand this right away, it may take many reminders before they learn where our boundaries are.

Again, it is perfectly possible to express requests in ways other than shaming or demanding. And because others have the freedom of interpretation, the person we are talking to may still feel guilty, no matter how hard we try not to blame them. That someone feels shame or guilt is not automatically a sign that someone else has blamed or shamed them.

Blaming and Shaming

In what situations do you blame or shame your children?
What are your needs at that moment?
What kind of support, and from whom, do you need it?
Is there a way to stand up both for your needs and the child's?

Blaming and shaming is often unconscious and can be described as "desperate expressions of unmet needs." If we want to change communication patterns, they first need to be made conscious. Although we can feel ashamed without anyone else shaming us, blaming communication has a huge impact on most of us. In addition to words, things like grandfather's body language, a teacher's tone of voice, our friend's unreadable gaze, or a particular story from someone close to us, all also play a big role in how we perceive something.

Because shame and guilt are uncomfortable states, children are more easily controlled when they feel them, and it can therefore be tempting to blame and shame. Something adults rarely reflect on is that continuously communicating in this way can have a negative impact on our connection with children.

The essence of blaming language is to place all responsibility for our feelings on the other person, as in the following examples:

"I get angry because you didn't do what I asked you to do."

"I feel disappointed because you only care about yourself."

"Grandpa feels lonely because you never visit."

When we realize that blaming often affects our connection with the other person negatively, and become aware of our habit of frustratingly linking our feelings to the behavior of others, we can practice connecting what we feel to what we need.

"My anger came from actually being afraid that your little brother would get hurt. How do you feel now?"

The adult can take more responsibility by rephrasing something they have said, for example, that someone "only thinks about themself" and say:

"What I meant was that it is important for me to feel like I belong, even though I am an adult. If you don't want to give me a hug, I wonder if you are willing to tell me why you don't want to?"

We can also, when listening, guess what others need by paying attention to what they feel. When we can link what others feel to what they need, rather than making ourselves ultimately responsible for the feelings of others, our feelings of guilt are alleviated. Knowing that guilt often obscures empathy and intrinsic motivation, we can, for example, help a child take in someone else's reality without blaming:

"For me, it's important to talk about this because Grandpa has said he feels lonely. I guess he has a need for companionship, and it would make a difference for him to have visitors. Shall we go there for a while together?"

To better hear others, we can also listen with the same attitude and connect what others know to what they need:

"Do you feel disappointed when I got so angry because you didn't understand what was expected of you in this situation?"

Or,

"Do you want to choose when you give someone a hug?"

"Are you feeling disappointment because you would have liked more support in this situation?"

As parents, we often save time if we find ways to be heard with empathy by a third person before communicating challenging messages to our children. NVC is not about 'sounding nice,' but about choosing what we say so that we can build trust and connection. In many cases, it is more connecting when adults acknowledge their inability and tell us that they don't know how to express themselves in any other way than to demand. An important part of our communication is about our intention, about why we want to express something. Do we want obedience or connection? Would we rather meet our needs, the needs of others, or put in the extra effort needed to see if everyone's needs can be met? What is more important to us, getting what we want or creating satisfying relationships?

When we realize that we are trying to motivate others with guilt, we can be honest about it and ask for their help in communicating further.

"I need help. I don't want to demand that you to go to Grandpa's house. At the same time, it makes me conflicted because I know that he wants you to come and I know that you don't find it super fun. Do you have any ideas on how we can talk about this?"

"No, I don't."

"My impulse is to blame you as I have so often done, but I don't want to. What is it like for you to hear that I struggle to communicate with you in a way that works for both of us?"

Another example:

"Grandma feels sad because you never call. You make her feel forgotten and unimportant."

Instead of expressing yourself like the person above and risking blocking communication, one trick is to reveal how we think we can contribute to what someone else needs:

"Grandma feels important when someone calls her. I guess it gives her a moment of meaning. Would you be willing to talk to her together with me for five minutes?"

Communication in relationships becomes habitual. Our close ones expect us to express ourselves in the way they have previously experienced us expressing ourselves. If we have been constantly blaming the child up until now, communicating differently once will not erase the effect of all previous communication.

If children have learned that when adults express emotions there is danger, because they will be made responsible for them.

Examples of Language and Attitudes That can Lead to Shame and Guilt

Expressing our feelings without asking the other person for anything: "I feel lonely and abandoned."

Blaming our feelings on what someone else has done: "I feel sad because you..."

Suggesting that someone should do something without asking for it: "No one cares anyway so there is no use asking for support."

Confusing what we feel with what we think others are doing to us: "I feel neglected, overlooked, abandoned, manipulated..."

Interpretations and morally loaded labels or analyses (implying shame or guilt for the listener) instead of expressing our requests to them: "You are so selfish." Or, "She's a stuck-up wimp."

Implying that we know what other people's intentions are or how they feel:

"The way you express yourself means you don't care."

"You don't know what I need because you don't love me."

Expressing what we feel, need and want through sighs, faces and gestures.

Walking in Someone Else's Shoes

An important part of the approach of Nonviolent Communication is about listening to what is going on in others. It includes inviting an empathetic attitude and guessing what someone feels and needs in order to connect.

Most children from about the age of eight can, with the help of others, change their perspective (even if briefly) and see the world through other people's eyes. Only then can the child move beyond their self-centered focus and take the first steps towards empathy. Although young children are warm and some seem to be good listeners, they are unable to focus on what others are feeling for long periods of time. This is not to say that children don't care about how others feel, but their ability to empathize is limited until their brains can handle the challenge of empathic attention to others.

The Swedish researcher Ulla Holm, who earned a doctorate in empathic studies in 1985, used these words to define the concept: "The essence of the concept of empathy is the ability to understand another person's feelings (empathic understanding) and to be guided by that understanding in dealing with the other person."[75]

Marshall Rosenberg summarizes empathy slightly differently: "Empathy is a respectful understanding of what others are experiencing. It means listening to others with our whole selves, with all our senses."[76]

It is easy to think that someone is either compassionate or not. But like many things, empathy develops over the course of a lifetime. Various researchers are investigating everything from the role of the brain in the development of empathy, to how personal trauma or a stressful childhood can hamper it. In addition to biology, cultural and environmental values also influence how much space our development of empathy gets.

Unfortunately, there are people who have a great ability to understand what is going on inside another person and then use it only for their own benefit. Just because someone can make a precise guess about what is going on inside another person does not always mean that they care about others.

Empathy is not a static phenomenon, but researchers are adding pieces to the puzzle of understanding the role of the human brain when it comes to empathy. Professor of Psychology Suzanne Benack studied empathy and divided the development of empathy into four stages, based on the concepts of willingness and capacity, to describe the process.[77]

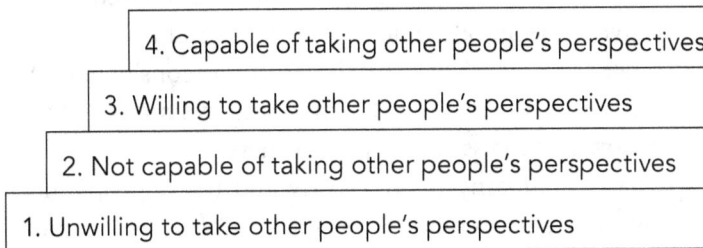

| 4. Capable of taking other people's perspectives |
| 3. Willing to take other people's perspectives |
| 2. Not capable of taking other people's perspectives |
| 1. Unwilling to take other people's perspectives |

According to this way of seeing the development of empathy, on the first level are individuals (children or adults) who are busy strengthening their own self and therefore not willing to take others' perspectives. Rather than taking in more perspectives, the focus is on becoming their own stable individual, creating a core from which to eventually relate to others.

Listening to others is not a central focus at this stage, perhaps especially when they feel pressured or are not fully understood themselves. This stage could be seen as a kind of "healthy narcissism" where the focus outside the individual creates too much stress for them to be empathic.

To try to force someone, regardless of age, to take someone else's perspective is rarely effective. At this egocentric stage it is important to be seen, than to see others. But being seen during this period can hopefully lay the foundation for developing the capacity to see others. An adult still in this phase may struggle with the fact that the brain's autopilot is not set to a supportive level, or that some impulse control is missing.

It may also be the case that a person who is not willing to see the world from other perspectives has been born with physical conditions that make it difficult for empathy to develop. The influence of trauma can also have an impact. Most people can eventually, with the support of others, see the world from other people's perspectives. In order to be able to empathize with others on their own, a certain maturity and interest in changing perspectives is needed. The person may have understood what is considered right and wrong, but now also needs to reflect on why something is considered right or wrong. And even if we see the value of caring, we may need support to know how to express empathy for others.

The capacity for empathy varies greatly and many people need active training to be able to take the perspective of others. As mentioned earlier in this book, it is not until around the age of 25 that many of the intricacies of the human brain have matured. Without that physical maturity, we can't expect full empathy, so perhaps we need to adjust our expectations of teenagers and young adults. Of course, there is more to empathy than just the development of the brain; empathy has to do with things like a person's emotional development and moral maturity, as well as the values of those around them.

Simplified, mirror neurons is a explanation of the strange experience of feeling pain when we see someone else hurt on a biological plane. Perhaps even more remarkable is the fact that we can experience pain, when we hear that someone close to us has cut their hand with a bread knife.

And we don't only react to physical pain; we are also affected by a common emotional field, such as when we see our teenager fumbling for connection with someone we know they are in love with. Their shyness becomes ours.

Mirror neurons led to several survival benefits for us humans because these neurons become engaged when we see someone else doing something we are trying to learn. They allow us to imitate the behavior of others and absorb new knowledge and skills. These amazing neurons are physical pieces of the puzzle that need to be put in place for empathy to develop. Because they allow our brain to 'walk in someone else's shoes', we can empathize with what someone is experiencing. We might guess what someone else is feeling when we meet them by their tone of voice, words, gestures and behaviors, but also by the impulses we receive when the mirror neurons are dancing. Fascinatingly, we can feel ashamed even if we're not the ones 'messing up.' For example, we may feel ashamed if our teenager, or a friend for that matter, falls in front of someone we know it is important for them to make an impression on. We might also feel their pride when they scream with happiness at reaching a goal they have long struggled to achieve. Thanks to our ability to see ourselves in others, it becomes possible to imitate something we see someone else do, but also sense what drove them to act in this way.

Throughout our childhood, we imitate our way to knowledge of various kinds. Our ability to imitate opens the door for us to live for a moment in another world, for example when we hear a story, watch a movie or a play. If an actor plays a sad role, we are affected and easily feel sadness ourselves, even though we know that the expression of sadness is in the actor's script, and thus not real.

Mirror neurons become engaged, albeit to different degrees, when we hear, see, do, or even think about doing a certain action. We are also often affected when someone around us is feeling such strong feelings as shame, fear, despair, anger or stress.

Becoming curious about how others see the world and being willing to take in their perspectives can train our ability to empathize. When we develop empathy, we can eventually take a step beyond humans and seriously care for example about how we affect animals, or even ecosystems. To be able to use empathy when listening, we need to be willing to understand others, but also have the ability to know what to focus on in order to keep empathy alive. This is one of the strengths of the NVC approach where the focus of empathic listening is clearly stated and can be practiced. Simply put, empathic listening is about focusing on what the person feels and needs, regardless of what is expressed. It is about acknowledging that we understand that they have needs that they want met and that they have favorite strategies to meet those needs. We don't have to agree or fix things, but we do want to stay present with them, and maybe find a way forward together.

Emma, at ten, gets angry that she has been forbidden to watch a football match that starts late at night in a place far away from home.

"You can't stop me from going to the game."

If Mari only focuses on what her daughter is saying, she might reply in a way that is not very connecting.

"I hear that you are demanding to go to that football match tomorrow, but it's far too late in the evening."

However, Mari took a deep breath and decided to try to stay connected, and without agreeing to anything, tried to understand why this match was so important to her daughter:

"I guess you want to do something fun? You want me to understand that hanging out with your friends is the best thing you know? Maybe you also want to make your own decisions?"

"Yes, and I'm going! I never get to do anything fun."

"I am so torn when I hear that, because I want you to have fun. And still, this time it's a no, because I want to make sure you are safe. And I do understand if it feels tough to hear my no."

Here, the exact words are less important than for Mari to remember that she wants to connect. The empathy is in the attitude itself and hopefully the choice of words will help it get through. Whatever Emma answers, Mari can try to understand her daughter by hearing what she longs for, dreams about, likes or needs. Mari's guesses are attempts to create an interface for a dialogue rather than to start a wrestling match with words.

In addition, Maria and Emma's father have realized that they have often too been lenient and have not given Emma clarity about where their limits are. Maria is challenged by thinking she is terrible for not letting her daughter go to the game and on maintaining her boundaries in order to create safety. At the same time, she feels proud that she is trying to set a limit while also trying to make connection.

Cradle of Self-criticism

One of the first gifts we receive from a small child is a smile. Delighted, we smile back because that adorable facial expression makes us feel seen and special. The smile, whether due to gas or to the child testing their facial muscles, melts the heart of an adult. After a while, the child notices that their smile creates positivity in those around them. Noticing this empower them and they take their first mini-step towards independence. Eventually, the child may also smile to express joy and a recognition that they have learned something that is important to those around them.

The smiling child is an example of an amazing survival mechanism, where external cues are internalized and promote the individual. Similarly, the six-year-old child has internalized a degree of self-criticism that enables cooperation with others. They internalize likes and dislikes from the environment, which can help them navigate the world. Unfortunately, sometimes an inner voice develops that becomes highly degrading and heavy to bear.

In an attempt to gain more space in life, young people may rebel by skipping school, getting into fights, using chemical substances, or resorting to self-harm. The freedom that comes from temporarily deflecting the fire of the inner critic is liberating.[78] In the excitement, boundaries that were not previously crossed are crossed and risk-taking increases. But the inner critic remains, guided by the original moral map, and can become deafeningly loud when we step outside our moral box.

Whether you believe it or not, it is valuable to think of the inner critic, the brain's autopilot, as a safeguard. It does not give up its mission just because we have managed to silence it for a while. If, as young adults, we've danced on the table, thrown out a few ill-chosen opinions about a friend, had sex with the wrong person or openly professed our love to someone, we can wake up the next day to find a sober inner critic speaking to us. This time with the volume turned up to the max.

Every time we do something that our inner critic claims is not okay, an inner dilemma arises. We grow by doing something new or unfamiliar, but we can experience strong internal stress and start withdrawing again. This becomes even more intense if we become self-critical about being self-critical, because we "should accept ourselves as we are." As long as we judge right-and-wrong thinking as wrong, we are spinning around in a loop of self-criticism where we judge ourselves for being narrow-minded or judgmental. Most people who silence their inner critic's voice discover, regardless of their strategy, that self-criticism is only temporarily silenced.

The first step to discovering the purpose of right-and-wrong thinking is to accept it as a part of our development. The more we pay attention to the voice and create some distance to it, the easier we can study it and see that there are dimensions beyond the autopilot of childhood. Only then can we "meet in the field beyond right and wrong," as Rumi so beautifully invited us to do.

Eventually, we can nuance our approach and see that we all have good and bad sides and that "right" is "wrong" in other contexts. We may even be able to see the projections behind strong judgments, the needs behind self-criticism, and begin to partially shake up old beliefs about life and ourselves. The relief is usually great when we discover a positive driving force behind thought patterns we have hitherto experienced as torture. Whatever the degree of self-criticism, many of us at some point try to silence our inner critic. It rarely has any lasting effect and there is a reason for that. The sorting out of right or wrong, is useful when we need to make quick decisions and we therefore do not want to "throw the baby out with the bath water." We also don't want to judge other that is looking for the discernment of their actions in "right and wrong" as doing something "wrong."

Fortunately, there are effective tools – such as Nonviolent Communication (NVC) – that can help us transform tough inner demands and harsh judgments. One of the core ideas of the NVC-approach is that behind every judgment of ourselves or others are universal human needs. Instead of the impossible task of getting rid of the autopilot, we can use it as a clue to what we need. One big benefit of this is that integrating the needs behind our "should-thinking" usually is less resource-intensive than spending energy on continuously silencing self-criticism. Author Ken Wilber's suggestion to "transcend and include" is valuable advice in this process. Self-criticism such as "no one likes me, I'm hopeless", might be transformed into "I need to be seen" or "I need support to grieve something I don't seem to be able to do on my own."

Self-criticism can have deep meaning when we realize that we can use it to really understand what we need. The inner critic's agitated voice also tends to calm down when we start listening to it with curiosity. In situations where it raises its voice again, it is often valuable to stop and reflect on what we really need.

What an Apology can Achieve

In most cultures, children learn to say "sorry" when they have done something that has hurt someone else or when they've broken something. At best, the words put an end to a conflict and helps young children to play on. An apology at this level does not in itself mean that someone is 'bad' or should be punished but is more like part of a social ritual. "Sorry" is not a magic word that fixes everything in every situation, but it is often enough for young children to let go of something and move on. The word becomes shorthand for "I understand that what I did was not the best for you, and I am sorry for that."

As a child matures, there is value in showing that they can do more than just say the socially correct "I'm sorry" or "excuse me" to rebuild trust. When they make a mistake, break something, hurt someone else, or neglect an agreement, it is valuable to know what they can do to rebuild both connection and trust.

Adults who are ready to 'walk the talk' and apologize for their mistakes become role models, which often has a greater impact than simply asking the child to say they are sorry. Taking the time to listen before apologies or explanations is an important process to understand. Adults need to demonstrate it and not just talk about it.

An apology means very different things depending on where we are on the morality scale. Imagine a seven-year-old child who feels ashamed after doing something that hurt a friend they fear losing friendship with. The words are stuck on their tongue, even a simple apology is difficult to get out, partly perhaps, because it is an admission of inferiority. Saying the words, intended to acknowledge the other person's pain, feels like a threat to the seven-year-old's self-esteem. Overwhelmed, the child looks away, to reduce the influx of impressions on their nervous system as it seems like the only way to deal with the discomfort.

Children (and adults) in such a situation often feel that they have to choose between one of two bad choices, admitting that they are bad or withdrawing. At the same time, they sense that they will be criticized or blamed by adults if they fail to say 'sorry.' Furthermore, they suspect that if they manage to say sorry, the guilt may increase in intensity as they must admit that they have hurt someone else.

At other times, a shame-overwhelmed child snaps at us in a desperate attempt to get rid of the feelings, and tells us that they don't feel like saying sorry at all. Sometimes, all that comes out of the child is a giggle, not because the child finds the situation funny, but because it is the only thing that relieves the pressure of shame. In such a situation, it is often most constructive to wait and to let the worst of the stress subside before continuing the dialogue.

We don't want to avoid dealing with the situation, but we also don't want the child to succumb to self-criticism. It is not about making them avoid regret, but about supporting them to grow and learn from a situation.

It is not only younger individuals who need time to recover from the shock of the shame of having made a mistake that hurt someone else. Sometimes adults need a lot of time to come to a place where they can apologize for their mistakes. The dilemma is that the person who has been hurt and wants to be heard about how the situation affected them, rarely wants to wait.

The Compass of Needs - Analysis and Process Tool

The Compass of Needs is a model for dealing with shame feelings in the present, but also for transforming situations that happened earlier in life.[79] The model creates understanding of others' and our own behaviours, but also helps to transform and integrate the feelings of shame. It makes it possible to put the difficult inner shame process into words, which in itself turns shame feelings into objects we can study and understand better. The Compass of Needs is based on the same assumptions as NVC: that it is possible to understand an action by linking it to the needs that drove it.

At the center of the compass are human needs. Some of the most important needs to examine when it comes to shame tend to be belonging, acceptance and dignity. Each of the four 'compass directions' summarizes strategies we use to avoid feeling shame. In order to escape the uncomfortable shame, we resort to different behaviors such as criticizing ourselves, blaming others, withdrawing or rebelling. All strategies are common, and the intention is to protect the individual. Unfortunately, they all have downsides. Sometimes it damages trust, other times it increases the risk of others feeling rejected, and if we go as far as using physical violence, it can have a profound impact on people's security in relation to us.

The alternative to moving in either direction is a choice the individual can rarely make until at least the age of eleven. Perhaps most people go through life without ever reflecting on why they act the way they do.

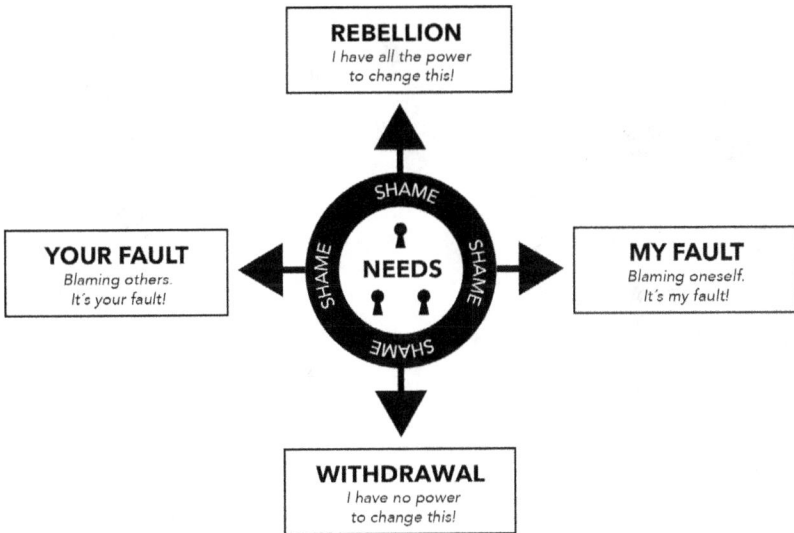

REBELLION
I have all the power to change this!

YOUR FAULT
Blaming others.
It's your fault!

NEEDS

MY FAULT
Blaming oneself.
It's my fault!

SHAME · SHAME · SHAME · SHAME

WITHDRAWAL
I have no power to change this!

Here are some simple steps in using the compass.

Step 1. Note in which compass direction you or someone else is moving in a challenging potentially shameful situation.

Step 2. Remind yourself that behind that strategy there are important needs.

Step 3. Ask yourself if there might be a need for dignity, acceptance or belonging. Be open to whether it is one of those, or another need. Notice any shift inside.

Step 4. Take steps towards meeting that need that became clear, in you, or in the other person.

SOME FINAL WORDS

"There is a meadow beyond right and wrong,
I will meet you there."

RUMI

When I run a training, I sometimes write the above words on a flip-chart. Then I ask the students to discuss in pairs which word is the most important of Rumi's beautiful words. Often this leads to animated discussions about whether there is a right and wrong. Enthusiastic voices argue that there is indeed nothing wrong and the intensity makes it easy to think that they are arguing that they are right. Usually someone ends up saying that the word "beyond" is the most important. Then we can start talking about the difference between the statement that "there is no right or wrong" and that "it is possible to meet beyond right and wrong." This difference is also one of the things I have hoped to show with this book.

At the beginning of my own studies of Nonviolent Communication (NVC), "should patterns" felt like something to be avoided or to be deleted. I used a lot of energy to silence my inner critic as it was "bad to be judgmental," whether it was towards myself or someone else. As I discovered the difference between rebelling and acting out of choice, my relationship with "shoulds" and my inner critic has changed.

Another thing I hope I have been able to describe is the process when the parental voice, with all its "shoulds" moves in and the value of that. And how, through this brain auto-pilot or "inner parent" we become independent. At least I hope it was valuable to understand the importance of the parental voice, with all the "I should" moving in, instead of fighting it. Hopefully, my description of should-patterns has enriched the perspective on our frequently criticized inner limitations. My hope is that by finding greater acceptance for our shoulds or musts, we can use them as a gateway to our needs.

Adult development is less about getting rid of something we have than it is about doing what author Ken Wilber refers to as "transcend and include." I hope that reading this book has made you more curious about yourself as well as about the human developmental process.

That I see shame as a survival advantage that, with the right support, can develop into sensitivity to the needs of others and, by extension, into empathy, I think has not escaped anyone. Integral theory and adult development have become increasingly interesting to me - as seeing us as individuals on a developmental journey helps me lower the demands on myself and others.

When I accept that everyone is where they are in their development, and that they relate from this stage of development, I can more easily access empathy. If I don't assume that others have the capacity to be clear about what they feel and need, but am sensitive to when they may need my help, I can be more helpful in our relationship. When others can show me care, it is great, but if they can't, for whatever reason, I don't need to demonize or blame them. Without the expectation that someone will listen to me or understand me, I can find other ways to connect.

Moreover, if others shame or blame me, I can remind myself that it is their attempt to meet needs. I can communicate or withdraw. I know how to support myself to transform shame into compassion. After many years of working with this I also know how to support others in that process. I can only hope that you avoid turning my suggestions into positive platitudes, claiming acceptance when you are actually frustrated and want others to show up. Because yes, we can be accepting of where someone has their limitations and still express how it affects us, and maybe we can learn some new ways to relate together.

Hopefully I have planted some seeds that can grow and flourish in your human garden.

LITERATURE & REFERENCES

Beck & Cowan (2005), *Spiral Dynamics, Mastering Values, Leadership and Change.* Wiley-Blackwell

Berg, Lasse (2012) *Dawn of the Kalahari : how humans became human.* Real Afrika Books

Bjar & Liberg (2010) Barn utvecklar sitt språk. Studentlitteratur

Bäckström & Rung. (2022) *Sexualitet, samtycke och relationer. En lärobok som gör svåra samtal lättare.* Rebel books

Bradshaw, John (2005) *Healing the Shame That Binds You.* Health Communications

Brown, Brené (2015) *Daring Greatly, How the Courage to Be Vulnerable Transforms the Way We Live, Love, Parent, and Lead.* Penguin Publishing Group

Diamond, Jared (2015) *Why Is Sex Fun? The Evolution of Human Sexuality.* Weidenfeld & Nicolson

Eisler Riane (1998) *The Chalice and The Blade Our History, Our Future.* Harper Collins

Feldman Barrett, Lisa (2018) *How Emotions Are Made. The Secret Life of the Brain. Pan Books*

- (2020) *7 1/2 Lessons About the Brain* Picador

Diamond, Jared (2015) *Why Is Sex Fun? The Evolution of Human Sexuality.* Weidenfeld & Nicolson

Gladwell, Malcolm (2019) *Talking To Strangers, What We Should Know about the People We Don't Know.* Penguin Books Ltd

Hansen, Anders (2019) *Skärmhjärnan. Hur en hjärna i osynk med sin tid kan göra oss stressade, deprimerade och ångestfyllda.* Bonnier Fakta

Hoffman & Larsson (2015) *Cracking the Communication Code. Nonviolent Communication by 42 Key Differentiations.* Friare Liv

Holm, Ulla (2021) *Empati.* Natur&Kultur

Hwang, Philip & Björn Nilsson (2019) *Utvecklingspsykologi.* Natur & Kultur

Juul, Jesper: När barnet ljuger, http://www.family-lab.se/nar_barn_ljuger.asp,). [12/2-18]

Kasthan Inbal, (2004), *Parenting From Your Heart. Sharing the Gifts of Compassion, Connection & Choice.* PuddleDancer Press

Kegan & Lahey (2009) *Immunity to Change. How to overcome it and unlock potential in yourself and your organisation.* Harvard Business Press

Klintman, Mikael (2018) *Gruppens grepp : Hur vi fördomsfulla flockvarelser kan lära oss leva tillsammans*, Thomas Lunderquist, Andreas Olsson. Natur & Kultur.

Klintman, Mikael (2020), *Knowledge resistance.* Manchester University Press

Kohn, Alfie, (2018), *Punishment of Rewards. The Trouble with Gold Stars, Incentive Plans, A's, Praise, and Other Bribes.* HarperOne

- (2018) *Unconditional Parenting.* Atria Books

Levine Timothy, A theory of Human Deception and Deception Detection, Journal of Language and Social Psychology 33, nr 4 (2014) s 378 - 392.

Klüger, Ruth (2001) *Still alive: A holocaust Girlhood Remembered.* Feminist Press

Larsson, Liv (2013), *Anger, Guilt and Shame, Reclaiming Power and Choice.* Friare Liv

- (2013), *A Helping Hand, Mediation with Nonviolent Communication.* Friare Liv

- (2014), *The Power of Gratitude.* Friare Liv

Lindenfors, Patrik (2023) *Äckel : smitta, synd, samhälle.* Ordfront

Martinez, Mario (2016), *The MindBody Code: How to Change the Beliefs that Limit Your Health, Longevity, and Success Paperback.* Sounds true.

Mischel, Walter (2014) *The Marshmallow Test. Understanding Self-control and How to Master It.* Corgi Books

Nagoski, Emily (2017) *Come as You are, The Surprising New Science That Will Transform Your Sex Life.* Simon Schuster

Nathanson, Donald (1994), *Shame and Pride. Affect, sex and the birth of the self.* WW Norton Co

Picoults, Jodi (2008) *19 Minutes. A Novel. Atria/Emily Bestler Books*

Porges & Porges (2023) *Our Polyvagal World. How safety and trauma change us.* WW Norton Co

Rosenberg, Marshall (2015), *Nonviolent Communication: A Language of Life. Life-Changing Tools for Healthy Relationships.* PuddleDancer Press

- (2004), *We can Work it out. Resolving Conflicts Peacefully and Powerfully.* PuddleDancer Press

- (2020) *Life-Enriching Education. Nonviolent Communication Helps Schools Improve Performance, Reduce Conflict, and Enhance Relationships*. PuddleDancer Press

Schore, Allan (2003) *Affect regulation and the Repair of the Self.* W.W Northon&company

Siegal & Payne Bryson (2011) *The Whole-Brain Child: 12 Revolutionary Strategies to Nurture Your Child's Developing Mind. Delacorte Press*

Stålne, Kristian (2017) *Vuxen men inte färdig*. Fabricius resurs.

Wilber, Ken (2000) *Integral Psychology, consciousness, spirit, psychology, therapy.* Shambala Publication.

- (1995) *Sex, Ecology Spirituality, The Spirit of Evolution.* Shambala.

- (2016) *Integral meditation. Mindfulness as a Path to Grow Up, Wake Up, and Show Up in Your Life.* Shambala

Witt, Keith (2014) *Integral Mindfulness: Clueless to Dialed-in. How Integral Mindful Living Makes Everything Better*

- (2007) *The Attuned Family: How to Be a Great Parent to Your Kids and a Great Lover to Your Spouse.* Santa Barbara Graduate Institute

ABOUT THE AUTHOR

For more than 30 years Liv has been teaching, lecturing and writing books. Since 1999 she works with NVC and is a certified trainer for the global organization CNVC (Center for Nonviolent Communication). With her unique knowledge on how shame affect communication and conflict she trains and mediates in conflicts both in Sweden and internationally. One of her mediation contracts is locally between Scandinavian forest companies and the indigenous group, the Same. She coaches and mediates in small and big organization as well as in families.

Larsson has created working models such as The Compass of Needs and The mediation hand, as well as several training programs in mediation, interpersonal communication and coaching. Liv has written 24 books in Swedish including *Anger, guilt and shame, Reclaiming Power and Choice,* and *Mediation with Nonviolent Communication.* Four of her books are written for children. To date, Liv's books have been translated into fifteen different languages. Larsson has translated several of Marshall Rosenberg's books into Swedish, published by Friare Liv, which Liv started in 1992 and now runs together with Kay Rung.

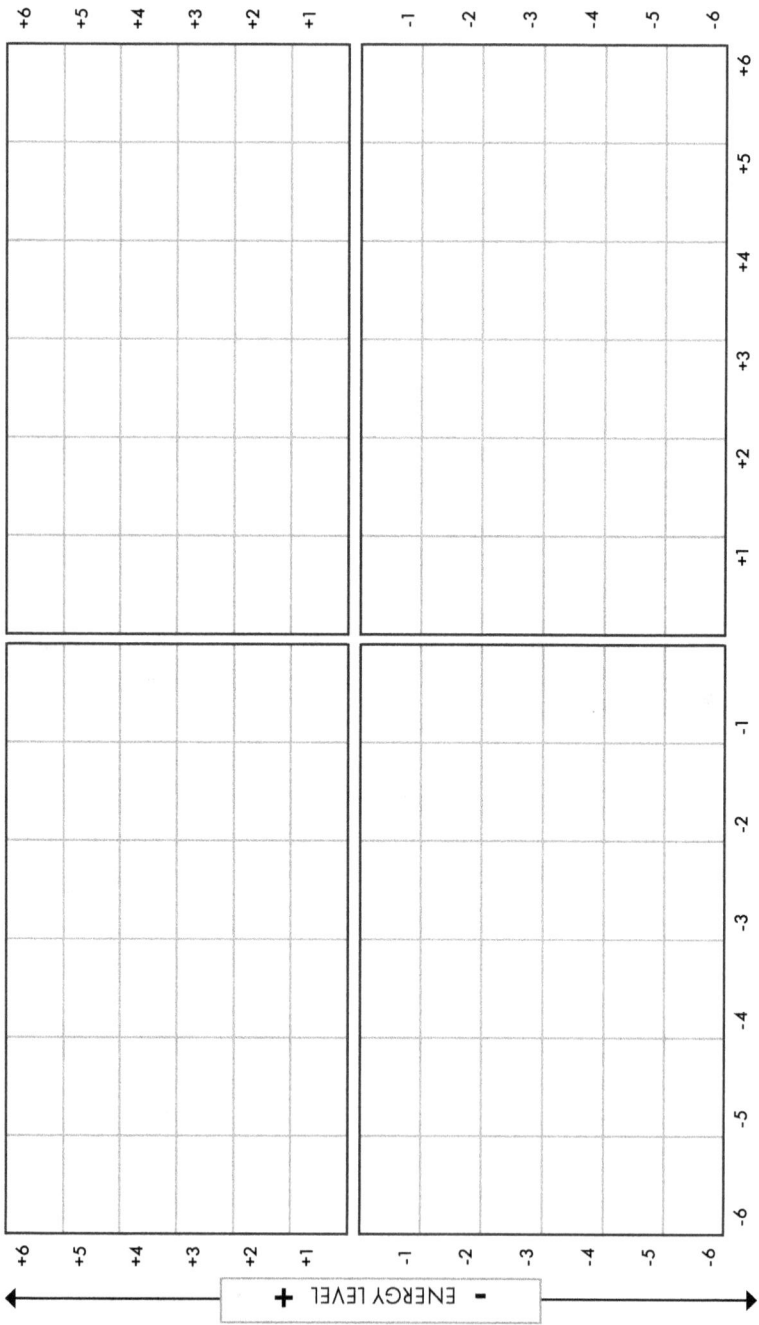

ENERGY LEVEL

+6 +5 +4 +3 +2 +1 −1 −2 −3 −4 −5 −6

VALENCE/LEVEL OF COMFORT − +

+6 +5 +4 +3 +2 +1 −1 −2 −3 −4 −5 −6

THE MAP OF EMOTIONS

This model, "The Map of Emotions", can be downloaded as a pdf to fill it in with your own words:
www.friareliv.com/stuff/mapofemotions.pdf

NOTES

1   Larsson, Liv (2013), *Anger, Guilt and Shame, Reclaiming Power and Choice.* Friare Liv

2   Eisler Riane (1998) T*he Chalice and The Blade Our History, Our Future.* HarperCollins

3   Surveys of what Swedes are ashamed of, from 2007 (United minds) and 2019 (Skanska) show similar figures. In Sweden, we feel very ashamed when we get visitors and think our home isn't clean enough. In other cultures, other things are at the top of the list.

4   Rosenberg, Marshall (2015), *Nonviolent Communication: A Language of Life. Life-Changing Tools for Healthy Relationships.* PuddleDancer Press

5   Ibid.

6   Nathanson, Donald (1994) *Shame and Pride. Affect, sex and the birth of the self.* W.W. Norton&CO.

7   Ensamhet – ett hot mot vår hälsa, Annika Lund. Karolinska Institutet, Först publicerad i tidskriften Medicinsk Vetenskap nummer 1, 2015

8   Feldman Barrett, Lisa (2018) *How Emotions Are Made. The Secret Life of the Brain.* Harper Collins.

9   *The Handbook of Emotions* summarizes various research findings on emotions. One strikingly common thought pattern when it comes to shame is wishing to be swallowed up by the ground beneath our feet. These thoughts are not there when we feel embarrassment.

10 Vidkun Quisling was Norway's Minister of Defense when Norway was occupied by Germany during World War II. He was executed as a traitor in 1945 after collaborating with Hitler's government.

11 Bradshaw, John (2005) Healing the Shame That Binds You. Health Communications.

12 Feldman Barrett, Lisa (2018) *How Emotions Are Made. The Secret Life of the Brain.* Harper Collins.

13 Ibid.

14 Ibid.

15 https://ideas.ted.com try-these-two-smart-techniques-to-help-you-master-your-emotions/

16 Our brains gets sensory input from inside our bodies, including information about our heart rate, breathing, blood pressure, temperature, hormones and metabolism. In a process that Lisa Feldman Barrett calls "body budgeting," your brain makes predictions about what those internal sensations mean in terms of your body's energy needs. With that "meaning" it regulates the body accordingly—by doing things such as speeding up your heart, slowing down breathing, releasing more cortisol, or metabolizing more glucose. At the most basic level, interoception can be defined as the sense that allows us to answer the question, "How do I Feel?" in any given moment.

17 According to Lisa Feldman Barrett and her research team, the classical view of emotions, referring to emotional loops and innate emotional essences, is misleading. She warns against misinterpreting the symbols, metaphors and images scientists have used to explain events in the brain, for example, as real biological events. She questions the value of calling part of our brain a reptile brain or that the brain consists of three different brains and questions whether this is consistent with physical reality.

18 Feldman Barrett, Lisa (2020) *Seven and a Half lesson about the brain.* Picador.

19 Feldman Barrett, Lisa (2018) *How Emotions Are Made. The Secret Life of the Brain.* Harper Collins.

20 Ibid

21 Feldman Barrett, Lewis & Havilland-Jones (2018) *Handbook of emotions.* The Guilford Press

22 Nathanson, Donald L (1994) *Shame and Pride. Affect, sex and the birth of the self.* W.W. Norton&C

23 Brown, Brené (2015) *Daring Greatly, How the Courage to Be Vulnerable Transforms the Way We Live, Love, Parent, and Lead.* Penguin Publishing Group

24 Feldman Barrett, Lewis & Havilland-Jones (2018) *Handbook of emotions.* The Guilford Press

25 Porges & Porges (2023) *Our Polyvagal World. How safety and trauma change us.* WW Norton Co

26 Feldman Barrett, Lisa (2020) *Seven and a Half lesson about the brain.* Picador.

27 Feldman Barrett, Lisa (2018) *How Emotions Are Made. The Secret Life of the Brain.* Harper Collins.

28 Kegan & Lahey (2009) *Immunity to Change. How to overcome it and unlock potential in yourself and your organisation.* Harvard Business Press.

29 Feldman Barrett, Lisa (2020) *7 1/2 Lessons About the Brain,* Picador

30 Rosenberg, Marshall (2015), *Nonviolent Communication: A Language of Life. Life-Changing Tools for Healthy Relationships.* PuddleDancer Press

31 Chapter 10 describes Nonviolent Communication (NVC) which is based on an assumption that behind every "should" there is a human need. Use the "shoulds" as clues to needs, instead of trying to get rid of them.

32 Feldman Barrett, Lisa (2020) *7 1/2 Lessons About the Brain,* Picador

33 If we only resort to tools like NVC when there is a crisis, there is a high risk that it will not work at all. If our communication is tightened only when our needs are not met, children often develop an NVC allergy, i.e. rage when we start using certain words or phrases that they recognize. For the approach to work, it needs to be used both in everyday life, when there is something to celebrate as well as when we are in the middle of a conflict.

34 Plomin Robert (2019) *Blueprint, How DNA makes us who we are.* Penguin

35 Klintman, Mikael (2020) Knowledge resistance. Manchester University Press

36 https://www.forskning.se/2019/12/19/grupptillhorighet-viktigare-an-sanning/ Hämtat 3 september 2023.

37 Jesper Juul: När barnet ljuger, http://www.family-lab.se/nar_barn_ljuger.
    asp,). Hämtat 6 dec 2023.

38 Rosenberg Marshall (2003) *Lifeeriching Eduation, Nonviolent
    Communication in schools for better results, fewer conflicts and deepened
    relationships.* PuddleDancer Press

39 This is "flirting" with an important aspect of NVC - Nonviolent
    Communication, Protective use of Force.

40 Piaget (1896-1980) mapped the development of children up to and through
    the stage he calls 'formal operation.' He focused largely on cognitive
    development, which is only one part of our development and there is much
    to be added on for example emotional development. Later, L Kohlberg
    developed a model of moral development that was partly inspired by
    Piaget's work. Kohlberg in his turned faced some criticism that his model
    was based on an overly masculine view of moral development. Carol
    Gilligan later presented another model of moral development that took
    into account how both women and men can develop in different as well as
    similar ways when it comes to morality.

41 https://kids.frontiersin.org/articles/10.3389/frym.2017.00046#:~:text=Socia
    l%2520exclusion%2520refers%2520to%2520the,even%2520experience%2
    520"painful"%2520feelings

42 Johansson has also conducted experiments focusing on political issues.
    Even though the subjects were "tricked" into justifying a political
    position they did not support, they made post hoc constructions, even
    though important values were at stake. https://www.ted.com/talks/
    petter_johansson_do_you_really_know_why_you_do_what_you_do

43 Truth Default theory. Levine Timothy, A theory of Human Deception and
    Deception Detection, Journal of Language and Social Pshycology 33, nr 4
    (2014) s 378 - 392.

44 Gladwell, Malcolm (2019) *Talking To Strangers, What We Should Know
    about the People We Don't Know.* Penguin Books Ltd

45 Feldman Barrett, Lisa (2018) *How Emotions Are Made. The Secret Life of the
    Brain.* Harper Collins.

46 Luleå 2-3 December 2013. å http://www. valdinararelationer.se/sv/ Vald-i-
    nara-relationer1/Toppmeny/Lar-dig-mer/ Allan-Wade-material

47 Berg, Lasse (2012) *Dawn of the Kalahari : how humans became human*. Real Afrika Books

48 Mischel, Walter (2014) *The Marshmallow Test. Understanding Self-control and How To Master It. Corgi Books*

49 Hansen, Anders (2019) Skärmhjärnan. Hur en hjärna i osynk med sin tid kan göra oss stressade, deprimerade och ångestfyllda. Bonnier Fakta

50 Rosenberg, Marshall (2015), *Nonviolent Communication: A Language of Life. Life-Changing Tools for Healthy Relationships*. PuddleDancer Press

51 Bäckström, Erik & Rung, Nina (2022) Sexualitet, samtycke och relationer. En lärobok som gör svåra samtal lättare. Rebel Books

52 Public Health Agency of Sweden https://www.folkhalsomyndigheten.se/ledaresomlyssnar/fordjupning-for-din-forening/normer/

53 Nathanson, Donald (1994) *Shame and Pride. Affect, sex and the birth of the self.* W.W. Norton&CO

54 Feldman Barrett, Lewis & Havilland-Jones (2018) *Handbook of emotions.* The Guilford Press

55 Bäckström, Erik & Rung, Nina (2022) *Sexualitet, samtycke och relationer. En lärobok som gör svåra samtal lättare.* Rebel Books

56 Martinez, Mario (2016), *The MindBody Code: How to Change the Beliefs that Limit Your Health, Longevity, and Success* Paperback. Sounds true.

57 Nagoski Emily (2021) *Come as You are, The Surprising New Science That Will Transform Your Sex Life.*

58 https://sv.wikipedia.org/wiki/Helen_O%27Connell

59 According to the Washington Post, Trump lied eight times a day the first 100 days of presidency. After the first few days, Trump's lying increased to an average of 23 falsehoods per day, according to the newspaper. During his time as president, he has claimed that half the population of the state of Tennessee cannot afford insurance due to a lack of insurance companies (false) and that the US has the highest tax burden in the world (also not true). He has also repeatedly claimed that his father was born in Germany. Fred Trump was born in New York City, USA. 210404 https://www.washingtonpost.com/politics/2019/04/29/president- trump-has-made-more-than-false-or-misleading-claims/

60 Gibran Khalil (2020) *The Profeth.* Alma Classic

61 Plomin Robert (2019) *Blueprint, How DNA makes us who we are.* Penguin

62 Rosenberg, Marshall (2015), Nonviolent Communication: A Language of Life. Life-Changing Tools for Healthy Relationships. PuddleDancer Press

63 Kegan & Lahey (2009) *Immunity to Change. How to overcome it and unlock potential in yourself and your organisation.* Harvard Business Press. Lahey and Kegan are far from the only researchers to have discovered similar patterns in adult human consciousness but they are some of the most successful in describing and working with them.

64 Beck & Cowan (2005), *Spiral Dynamics, Mastering Values, Leadership and Change.* Wiley-Blackwell.

65 Theoretically, the Stages Model combines several learning and cognitive theories such as Erik Erikson's (psychosocial), Jean Piaget's (cognitive), Lawrence Kohlberg's (moral) and Carol Gilligan's (ethics relationship). Terri O'Fallon consulted Bill Torbert's (action-logic) and Jane Loevinger/ Susanne Cook-Greuter's (ego identity integration), as well as Robert Kegan and Lisa Lahey's theory of leadership development (adult development). Finally, Ken Wilber's integral model also combines these theories with work by Don Beck and Clare Graves in a comprehensive framework. Read more about the Stages model and the later stages at www. stagesinternational.com

66 Feldman Barrett, Lisa (2018) *How Emotions Are Made. The Secret Life of the Brain.* Harper Collins.

67 Ibid·

68 https://erc.europa.eu/news-events/news/ svante-paabo-wins-2022-nobel-prize-physiology-or-medicine

69 Feldman Barrett, Lisa (2018) *How Emotions Are Made. The Secret Life of the Brain.* Harper Collins.

70 Ibid

71 Se https://sv.wikipedia.org/wiki/Vilda_barn för flera källor. Collected 230213.

72 Ibid

73 Plomin Robert (2019) *Blueprint, How DNA makes us who we are.* Penguin

74 (2020) *Life-Enriching Education. Nonviolent Communication Helps Schools Improve Performance, Reduce Conflict, and Enhance Relationships* PuddleDancer Press

75 Holm, Ulla (2021) Empati. Natur&Kultur

76 Rosenberg, Marshall (2015), *Nonviolent Communication: A Language of Life. Life-Changing Tools for Healthy Relationships*. PuddleDancer Press

77 https://eric.ed.gov/?id=EJ373069. Collected 240218.

78 "The inner critic" is a concept used in the Voice Dialogue model created by Hal and Sidra Stone. Simply put, the concept can to create well-needed objectivity around strong self-criticism. Making our inner critic into "a person", can sometimes make it easier to understand and transform. In the NVC approach, the term Inner Educator is often used.

79 The Compass of Needs is created by Liv Larsson and inspired by the work of Donald Nathanson. Larsson has added the aspect of human needs and turned it also into a process tool.

www.ingramcontent.com/pod-product-compliance
Lightning Source LLC
Chambersburg PA
CBHW070611270326
41926CB00013B/2501